I Never Knew That
About

NEW YORK

Christopher Winn

I Never Knew That
About
NEW YORK

ILLUSTRATIONS
BY
Mai Osawa

EBURY
PRESS

9 10

Ebury Press, an imprint of Ebury Publishing,
20 Vauxhall Bridge Road,
London SW1V 2SA

Ebury Press is part of the Penguin Random House group of companies
whose addresses can be found at global.penguinrandomhouse.com

Penguin
Random House
UK

First published by Ebury Press in 2013
This edition published by Ebury Press in 2016

www.penguin.co.uk

A CIP catalogue record for this book is available from the British Library

ISBN 9781785034688

Printed and bound in Great Britain by Clays Ltd,Elcograf S.p.A

MIX
Paper from
responsible sources
FSC
www.fsc.org   FSC® C018179

Penguin Random House is committed to a sustainable future
for our business, our readers and our planet. This book is
made from Forest Stewardship Council® certified paper.

For Joe and Jeanne
New Yorkers through and through

Contents

PREFACE ix

MAP OF NEW YORK x

INTRODUCTION xi

NEW YORK TIMELINE xii

1: NEW YORK HARBOR 1

2: NEW AMSTERDAM & COLONIAL NEW YORK 16

3: LOWER BROADWAY – BOWLING GREEN TO TRINITY CHURCH 33

4: A WALK DOWN WALL STREET 46

5: LOWER BROADWAY – TRINITY CHURCH TO ST PAUL'S CHAPEL. THE
WORLD TRADE CENTER 55

6: LOWER BROADWAY – VESEY TO CHAMBERS. THE CIVIC CENTER 67

7: BROADWAY – CHAMBERS TO CANAL. TRIBECA, CHINATOWN & THE
LOWER EAST SIDE 81

8: BROADWAY – CANAL TO HOUSTON. SOHO & LITTLE ITALY 92

9: BROADWAY – HOUSTON TO UNION SQUARE. THE EAST VILLAGE 103

10: GREENWICH VILLAGE 117

11: BROADWAY – UNION SQUARE TO TIMES SQUARE 130

12: CHELSEA 149

13: GRAMERCY & MIDTOWN SOUTH 159

14: BROADWAY – TIMES SQUARE TO COLUMBUS CIRCLE 172

15: MIDTOWN & THE UPPER EAST SIDE 187

16: THE UPPER WEST SIDE 207

17: CENTRAL PARK 220

18: UPPER BROADWAY – 110TH TO THE HARLEM RIVER 235

GAZETTEER 251

INDEX OF PEOPLE 261

INDEX OF PLACES 267

ACKNOWLEDGEMENTS 272

Preface

New York belongs to the world.

New York is known and recognised and talked about everywhere in the world, and is the most photographed and most filmed city anywhere in the world. The Statue of Liberty, the Empire State Building, Central Park and Times Square are the world's most visited tourist destinations.

New York is also the shop window of America, vibrant, living, glorious proof that determined peoples from every land and every culture, every religion and every background, can join together and achieve spectacular things. In New York you will find Rome and London, Paris and Tokyo, Madrid and Dublin and Shanghai. You will find the world's biggest cathedral, biggest synagogue and biggest financial markets, the world's best theatres and museums and its most iconic skyscrapers.

But there is more to New York than just tall buildings and the most expensive shopping street on earth. New York has its small and hidden places, too, beautiful parks and quiet green spaces, homely villages, chapels, smart squares and fine, unpretentious architecture. And a fascinating history as a trading post, fortress, bustling port and America's first capital.

New York is compressed history. What took London 2,000 years to build, New York achieved in 400 years. New York sprang up on boundless spirit and on dreams. And lots of hard work.

New York has survived fire, pestilence, riots, terrorist attacks, hurricanes, blizzards and floods and each time has bounced back stronger, prouder, more dynamic and more indefatigable.

New York can inspire you or destroy you. It can make you feel alive, or exhaust you and infuriate you. It will never bore you.

Think of *I Never Knew That About New York* as an entertaining friend, one who loves New York and can tell you some of its stories and its secrets, and you will discover that New York is quite simply, as Robert De Niro says, 'the most exciting city in the world'.

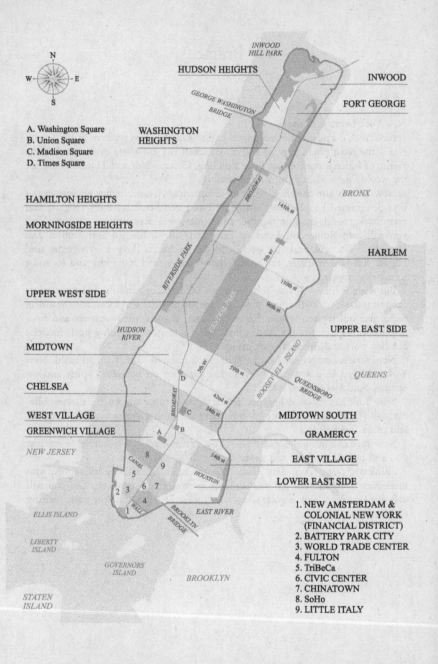

N
W — E
S

HUDSON HEIGHTS
INWOOD HILL PARK
INWOOD
GEORGE WASHINGTON BRIDGE
FORT GEORGE

A. Washington Square
B. Union Square
C. Madison Square
D. Times Square

WASHINGTON HEIGHTS

HAMILTON HEIGHTS

BRONX
BROADWAY
145th st

MORNINGSIDE HEIGHTS

5th av
HARLEM
110th st
96th st

UPPER WEST SIDE
RIVERSIDE PARK
CENTRAL PARK

HUDSON RIVER
UPPER EAST SIDE

MIDTOWN
5th av
59th st
ROOSEVELT ISLAND
QUEENS
QUEENSBORO BRIDGE

CHELSEA
BROADWAY
D
42nd st
34th st

WEST VILLAGE
C
MIDTOWN SOUTH

GREENWICH VILLAGE
A   B
GRAMERCY

NEW JERSEY
8
14th st
EAST VILLAGE
9
5
CANAL
HOUSTON
LOWER EAST SIDE
2 3 6 7
WALL 4
1

ELLIS ISLAND
EAST RIVER
BROOKLYN BRIDGE

LIBERTY ISLAND

GOVERNORS ISLAND
BROOKLYN

STATEN ISLAND

1. NEW AMSTERDAM & COLONIAL NEW YORK (FINANCIAL DISTRICT)
2. BATTERY PARK CITY
3. WORLD TRADE CENTER
4. FULTON
5. TriBeCa
6. CIVIC CENTER
7. CHINATOWN
8. SoHo
9. LITTLE ITALY

Introduction

The focus of *I Never Knew That About New York* is New York Harbor and Manhattan Island, where New York began and which for 270 odd years was exclusively known as New York.

In 1898 five neighbouring cities, or boroughs, consolidated to form the City of Greater New York. They were New York (Manhattan), Brooklyn, Queens, the Bronx and Staten Island. They all have their own unique history and their own vibrant character and each deserves its own book. To try and tell the story of all five boroughs in one book would be to do none of them justice.

In *I Never Knew That About New York* we walk along Broadway, New York's oldest road, its 'Main Street', from south to north, in the footsteps of the city's northward development, and as we go we tour the neighbourhoods that sprang up along the way.

Although each chapter is arranged as a walk it is not necessary to follow the whole walk or indeed to walk at all – each chapter stands alone as an interesting read about this most fascinating city and its history.

If you do decide to follow the walks you will find that each walk starts and finishes at a subway station, and always remains within easy reach of a subway station, so that you may leave or resume the walk at any point.

Finally, to distinguish city from state, the latter is referred to throughout the book as 'The State of New York' or 'New York State'.

New York Timeline

1524 Giovanni da Verrazano becomes the first European to enter New York Harbor

1609 Henry Hudson becomes the first European to sail up the Hudson River

1613 Captain Adriaen Block and the crew of the *Tyger* construct the first European dwellings on Manhattan Island

NEW AMSTERDAM

1624 Birth of New York. Thirty Walloon and Flemish families arrive on the *Nieu Nederland* and establish the first European settlement of New York on Governors Island. Captain Cornelius Mey becomes the first Director of the colony of New Netherland

1625 Dutch under Willem Verhulst establish the first permanent European settlement on Manhattan Island and work begins on Fort Amsterdam

1626 Peter Minuit, 3rd Director of New Netherland, purchases Manhattan Island from the Lenape Indians for trinkets worth $24

1633 First church erected on Pearl Street

1647 Peter Stuyvesant becomes Director-General of New Netherland

1653 New Amsterdam becomes the first legally chartered city in America. Wall is built to protect New Amsterdam against attack from the north

1655 Peach War

COLONIAL NEW YORK

1664 New Amsterdam is handed over to the British and renamed New York

1693 New York's first printing press set up on Pearl Street by William Bradford

1698 First Trinity church dedicated

1700 First Federal Hall built on Wall Street

1720 First shipyard opened on East River

1725 New York's first newspaper, the *New York Gazette*, is printed by William Bradford

1732 New York's first theatre opens on Nassau Street

1733 Bowling Green opens as New York's first park

1735 John Peter Zenger's trial establishes freedom of the press

1754 King's College (later Columbia University) founded

1765 Sons of Liberty formed. Protests in New York against the Stamp Act

1766 Stamp Act repealed. George III statue erected in Bowling Green. St Paul's Chapel completed

1776 Statue of George III toppled. Battle of Harlem Heights. Washington retreats from New York, which becomes British headquarters during Revolution

1783 U.S. wins independence with Treaty of Paris. November 25, Evacuation Day, Washington re-enters New York and the British leave for the last time. December 4, Washington bids farewell to his officers at Fraunces Tavern

NEW YORK

1784 Alexander Hamilton founds Bank of New York

1785 New York named U.S. capital. New York's first Catholic church, St Peter's, opens on Barclay and Church Streets

1789 March 4, First U.S. Congress meets at Federal Hall. April 30, George Washington inaugurated as first U.S. President at Federal Hall. September 25, Bill of Rights adopted at Federal Hall

1790 Capital moves to Philadelphia. Fort George (Fort Amsterdam) demolished

1792 New York Stock Exchange formed

19TH CENTURY NEW YORK

1801 Alexander Hamilton founds *New-York Evening Post*

1804 Aaron Burr kills Alexander Hamilton in duel

1807 Robert Fulton launches first steamboat on Hudson River

1811 Commissioners Grid Plan for Manhattan commenced. Castle Clinton constructed and forts built on Harbor Islands in preparation for war with Britain. City Hall opens

1812 War of 1812

1815 New York's first cathedral, Old St Patrick's Cathedral, opens on Mulberry

1822 Yellow fever outbreak. Many flee to Greenwich Village

1823 New York becomes largest city in U.S.

1824 New York's first tenement opens on Mott Street

1825 Erie Canal opens

1827   Slavery abolished in New York

1834   Henry Brevoort builds house on Fifth Avenue at Ninth Street

1835   Great Fire of New York

1837   Samuel Morse sends first telegraph signal

1842   Croton Aqueduct opens. New York Philharmonic play their first concert at the Apollo Rooms on Broadway

1845   New York Knickerbockers chartered as first baseball team

1846   Present Trinity church dedicated. America's first department store, A.T. Stewart's Marble Palace, opens on Broadway

1847   New York's oldest bar, the Bridge Café, opens on Water Street

1849   Astor Place riots

1851   *New York Times* launched. Brevoort Hotel, first hotel on Fifth Avenue, opens at Eighth Street

1853   New York hosts World's Fair

1857   Haughwout Building, first commercial building in the world to feature passenger elevators, opens on Broadway

1859   Central Park opened to the public. John Jacob Astor III builds house on Fifth Avenue at No. 350

1860   Lincoln gives his famous speech at Cooper Union

1863   New York Draft Riots, largest civil insurrection in American history, against corrupt draft system for Civil War

1866   First Broadway musical premiered at Niblo's Garden

1868   First elevated railroad opens on Greenwich Street

1870   Standard Oil founded by J.D. Rockefeller. Equitable Building, first office block in the world to feature passenger elevators, opens on Broadway

1871   Grand Central Depot opens. Tammany Hall's 'Boss' Tweed imprisoned

1872   Bloomingdale's opens

1879   St Patrick's Cathedral completed

1880   First street-lighting on Broadway. Dakota Building begins construction on Upper West Side. Metropolitan Museum of Art (the Met) opens on Fifth Avenue

1882   W.K. Vanderbilt builds grand mansion at 660 Fifth Avenue

1883   Brooklyn Bridge completed

1886   Statue of Liberty unveiled

1889   New York's first 'skyscraper' the Tower Building completed at 50 Broadway

1892   Ellis Island immigration centre opens. Cathedral of St John the Divine begun

1894   World's first cinema,

Holland Brothers Kinetoscope Parlor, opens at 1155 Broadway

1895 First moving picture to be shown on a screen in front of a paying audience shown at 153 Broadway. Olympia theatre opens on Longacre Square (later Times Square)

1897 World's largest hotel, the Waldorf-Astoria, opens. America's first pizza parlour, Lombardi's, opens in Little Italy

1898 Five boroughs merge to form Greater New York, the world's second largest city

20ᵀᴴ CENTURY NEW YORK

1900 Construction of New York's first subway begins

1902 Flatiron opens on Broadway. The world's largest store, Macy's, opens on Broadway

1903 Lyceum Theater, oldest Broadway theatre still in use, opens

1904 *New York Times* moves to Longacre Square which is renamed Times Square. General Slocum disaster

1907 Plaza Hotel opens

1908 First time ball drop in Times Square

1910 Pennsylvania Station opens

1911 Triangle Shirtwaist factory

fire. New York Public Library opens

1913 Woolworth Building opens on Broadway

1916 New York adopts Zoning Regulations requiring setbacks in tall buildings

1925 *New Yorker* magazine launched

1927 Holland Tunnel opens. America's first cappucino served in Greenwich Village. *The Jazz Singer*, the first 'talkie', premieres at the Warners' Theater on Broadway

1928 The first talking cartoon, Disney's *Steamboat Willie*, premières at the Colony Theater on Broadway

1929 Stock Market Crash

1930 Chrysler Building completed as tallest building in the world

1931 Empire State Building opens as tallest building in the world

1939 Rockefeller Center completed. New York hosts World Fair

1946 United Nations Headquarters opens

1959 Lincoln Centre construction begins. Guggenheim Museum opens

1963 Pennsylvania Station demolished

1964 Verrazano Narrows Bridge opens. The Beatles play Shea Stadium

1967 Singer Building becomes
      tallest building ever to be
      demolished. *Hair* opens at
      Public Theater
1969 Stonewall riots
1973 World Trade Center
      completed

2001 Terrorist attacks on the
      World Trade Center
2012 Hurricane Sandy hits New
      York
2013 One World Trade Center
      (Freedom Tower) completed
      to a height of 1,776 ft (541 m)

CHAPTER I

NEW YORK HARBOR

New York skyline from Staten Island Ferry

NEW YORK exists because of its harbour – although it is not officially called a harbour but rather Upper New York Bay. Five miles (8 km) long from Staten Island in the south to the southern tip of Manhattan in the north and four miles (6.4 km) wide from Brooklyn in the east to New Jersey in the west, the Upper Bay forms one of the largest natural harbours in the world.

Without doubt, the best way to approach New York is by boat. This is how the first explorers came and how, over the last four centuries, millions of immigrants came too. Even today, visitors choose to arrive in passenger ships and cruise liners, while sightseers and commuters continually criss-cross the bay in every kind of maritime craft.

Skyline

Your first view of modern New York from the water is unforgettable. From the rough, windswept waves of the Atlantic Ocean you pass through a narrow channel between two islands into the calmer waters of the Upper Bay. Then on past the welcoming embrace of the Statue of Liberty, the ornate green domes of the Ellis Island immigration centre, and finally the grim brown walls of Castle Williams on Governors Island.

And there it is – New York, the most spectacular urban landscape in the world, a forest of shining glass and steel, copper and gold, spires and turrets, tower upon tower stacked one upon another, reaching for the sky, marching in ragged rows down to the sea. Some of the towers appear to be dipping their toes into the water, while others gaze out brazenly across the bay, proclaiming their power and importance. It seems impossible that the flimsy, low-lying island of Manhattan doesn't topple over or sink under its own weight.

route to the Orient, and four years later he was eaten by cannibals on Guadeloupe, but he did find immortality as THE FIRST EUROPEAN KNOWN TO HAVE SET EYES UPON NEW YORK HARBOR, while his name lives on in the bridge that today spans the narrow channel at the harbour entrance where he anchored his ship.

Verrazano

The First European to see New York Harbor

It was a very much less frenetic scene that greeted the Italian navigator GIOVANNI DA VERRAZANO nearly five hundred years ago, when he anchored his ship, *La Dauphine*, in the narrow channel at the entrance to the bay, just off what is now Staten Island, on 17 April 1524. 'A very agreeable site located between two hills between which flowed to the sea a very great river' is how Verrazano described it.

He had been hired by the French to find a quick way through the American continent to the lucrative trade routes of the East, and it was in pursuit of this goal that Verrazano took a tentative small boat through the narrow channel and into the bay. Finding himself on 'a most pleasant lake', the Italian concluded that this was not the short cut he was looking for, and when 'a contrary flaw of wind blew up' he quickly returned to his ship and weighed anchor to continue the search along the coast.

Verrazano never did find his fast

Verrazano Narrows Bridge

Longest in the World

The VERRAZANO NARROWS BRIDGE opened on 21 November 1964 and links two of Greater New York's five boroughs, Brooklyn and Staten Island. It has a central span of 4,260 ft (1,298 m) and when it was built was THE LONGEST SUSPENSION BRIDGE IN THE WORLD, until overtaken by the Humber Bridge in England in 1981. It is now the eighth longest suspension bridge in the world and still THE LONGEST SUSPENSION BRIDGE IN AMERICA.

Since every vessel that enters New York Harbor has to pass underneath it, the Verrazano Narrows Bridge has an impressive height clearance of 228 ft (69 m) at high water. Even this is only just sufficient for one regular visitor, the QUEEN MARY 2, flagship of the Cunard Line and THE LARGEST OCEAN LINER EVER BUILT. When she passes under the bridge there is sometimes only 10 feet (3 m) to spare – despite the fact that her funnel was made flatter than usual just so that she could make it into New York Harbor – her passage

under the bridge can provide some heart-stopping moments for both spectators and passengers.

The Verrazano Narrows Bridge starred in a famous scene from the 1977 film *Saturday Night Fever* where the film's lead character Tony Manero (John Travolta) and his buddies show off by clambering along the edge of the bridge among the suspension cables. The scene builds to a tragic climax when one of the boys, Bobby C, played by Barry Miller, falls off the bridge to his death.

The Verrazano Narrows Bridge is also the starting point for the annual NEW YORK CITY MARATHON, held on the first Sunday in November.

The name Verrazano applies only to the bridge and not to the channel that flows underneath it, which is simply called The Narrows.

Hudson

An Englishman in New York

In early September 1609, the English navigator HENRY HUDSON entered the upper bay in his little ship the *Halve Maen* (Half Moon) and proceeded to explore along Verrazano's 'very great river'. Like Verrazano, Hudson was seeking a short route through America to the Orient, only in his case he was working for the Dutch rather than the French. Hudson had been told of this great river in a letter from his friend John Smith, the man rescued by the Indian princess Pocahontas, and leader of the Jamestown colony in Virginia. Smith had heard talk from the Indians of a river north of Virginia that led from the Atlantic Ocean to the Pacific, and Hudson decided to survey it for himself.

They sailed up the river for about 100 miles (160 km), almost to where Albany now stands, at which point the water grew too shallow for the *Half Moon*. Hudson realised that while this was a noble river it was not a way through to the East and so he turned around and headed back to the coast. Hudson's crew-mate, Robert Ivet, writes in his journal that on 2 October the *Half Moon* anchored just above the mouth of the river, between high cliffs (now called the New Jersey Palisades) and the island 'that is called Mannahata' – thus making THE VERY FIRST WRITTEN RECORD OF MANHATTAN.

While they may not have found the fabled North-West Passage, Hudson and his crew had nonetheless discovered an outstanding natural harbour, described by Robert Ivet as 'a very good Harbour for all winds', and a new territory full of such promise that Hudson was moved to declare, 'Never have I beheld such a rich and pleasant land.'

When word got back to the Netherlands of Hudson's discoveries, Dutch merchants by the score were inspired to come and explore this bountiful new land for themselves. The treasure that attracted them above all else was beaver fur, and beavers were to be found in abundance along the Hudson. Their pelts were much sought after by the fashionable Dutch middle classes, who used the fur to trim their hats and coats, and BEAVER PELTS became NEW YORK'S VERY FIRST MAJOR EXPORT. So important was the beaver to the founding of New York that a beaver appears on the city seal, and since 1975 the beaver has been the official New York State Mammal.

The great river up which Hudson sailed soon became known as Hudson's River and then simply the Hudson River. The early Dutch settlers referred to the stretch of the Hudson bordering Manhattan as the North River, a name by which it is sometimes still known, but in 1909, during the tercentenary celebrations of Hudson's arrival, it became accepted to refer to the whole river as the Hudson.

Captain Block

One of the first Dutch merchants to follow Hudson was CAPTAIN ADRIAEN BLOCK, who made a profitable voyage to Manhattan in 1610, returning home to the Netherlands with a rich cargo of beaver pelts. In 1613 he made another trip and moored his ship the *Tyger* in the Upper Bay off Lower Manhattan. The *Tyger* was accidentally gutted by fire and Block and his crew were forced to spend the winter on Manhattan – the four makeshift huts they constructed for shelter on the southern tip of the island were the VERY FIRST EUROPEAN DWELLINGS ON MANHATTAN.

New Netherland

In 1621 the Dutch West India Company was founded to promote and administer Dutch trading activities in the Americas, and the company arranged to send a group of settlers, consisting mainly of Walloons and Flemish, to establish a permanent trading base in New Netherland. In the summer of 1624 the 30 or so families arrived on two ships and settled on the flat wooded island off the southern tip of Manhattan that controlled access to the Hudson and East rivers, now called Governors Island, but then known by the native Indians as Pagganck. CORNELIUS MEY, the captain of the lead ship, the *Nieuw Nederland* (New Netherland), became THE FIRST DIRECTOR OF THE COLONY OF NEW NETHERLAND.

Governors Island

Birthplace of New York

GOVERNORS ISLAND covers 172 acres (70 ha) and lies half a mile (800 m) off the southern tip of Manhattan in the north-east corner of New York Harbor.

The colony established by the Dutch on Governors Island in 1624 was THE FIRST PERMANENT EUROPEAN SETTLEMENT IN WHAT WOULD BECOME NEW YORK, and the island is officially recognised as the BIRTHPLACE OF NEW YORK. In 1625, under a new director, WILLEM VERHULST, the settlers moved on to Manhattan Island and founded New Amsterdam.

When the British took over New Amsterdam and renamed it New York, Pagganck, which was by now called Nut Island, was set aside for the 'benefit and accommodation of His Majesty's Governors' and became known as the Governor's Island, although it was not officially named as such until 1784.

The oldest surviving building on the island, and one of the few 18th-century houses remaining in New York, is the Georgian-style GOVERNOR'S HOUSE, erected in 1708 for LORD CORNBURY and called 'The Smiling Garden of the Sovereigns of the Province'.

Through the Ages

In 1710 thousands of refugees fleeing from the devastation wrought by the French in the Palatinate region of what is now Germany arrived in New York and were held in quarantine for a few days on Governors Island. Among them was a 13-year-old boy who would go on to play a major role in the history of New York. His name was JOHN PETER ZENGER (*see* page 6).

Troops were first stationed on Governors Island in 1755, British regiments

JOHN PETER ZENGER (1697–1746) was apprenticed to New York's first and only printer William Bradford before branching out to form his own printing business. In 1733 he was approached by opponents of the corrupt royal governor William Cosby to publish a newspaper in which they could air their views on Cosby, and so Zenger began printing the *New-York Weekly Journal*, in which articles critical of the governor appeared. It wasn't long before he was arrested for publishing seditious libel and thrown into jail, where he languished for ten months. When he was finally brought to trial Zenger was cleared of the charges, despite Cosby attempting to rig the proceedings. Zenger's defence lawyer was ANDREW HAMILTON from Philadelphia, the most famous lawyer in America, who argued that, while Zenger did not deny publishing the seditious articles, he could not be found guilty of libel if the facts in the articles were true.

This landmark judgement for the first time established THE TRUTH AS A DEFENCE AGAINST LIBEL, a cornerstone of the freedom of the press in America. It was often quoted in the debates that culminated in the American Bill of Rights in 1789.

consisting of American colonists, Swiss and Germans soldiers expert in forest warfare, and British volunteers, all recruited for service in the American colonies. They became known as ROYAL AMERICANS and established THE FIRST INFANTRY SCHOOL IN AMERICA on the island.

Two Forts

After the Revolution, Governors Island became the property of New York State, who handed it over to the federal government in 1800 for military use. The island's defences were strengthened with the building of FORT JAY, a star-shaped fort completed in 1808 on high ground in the middle of the island and

named after the 2nd Governor of New York, John Jay. Later came CASTLE WILLIAMS, a semi-circular red sandstone fort completed in 1811 in anticipation of the 1812 war with Britain. In the end, however, no shot was fired in anger from anywhere on Governors Island.

Morse and More

In October 1842 SAMUEL MORSE laid out a telegraph wire along the bottom of the sea between Governors Island and the Battery on Manhattan to find out if he could transmit signals along the wire underwater. He succeeded in transmitting three signals before a vessel that had been anchored between the islands lifted its anchor and brought the wire up with it – no one on board knew what it was and so they cut it.

In the 1890s material from the excavations of the Brooklyn–Battery Tunnel under the East River and the Lexington Avenue subway was used as landfill to enlarge Governors Island by 103 acres (42 ha), to its present size of 172 acres (70 ha).

Flying High

On 29 September 1909, WILBUR WRIGHT took off from the parade ground on Governors Island in AMERICA'S FIRST MILITARY PLANE, THE FLYER, and twice circled the Statue of Liberty at a height of 150 ft (46 m) before returning. As well as being THE FIRST EVER FLIGHT IN A MILITARY PLANE, this was THE FIRST FLIGHT EVER OVER WATER IN AMERICA, and as a safety precaution a red canoe was strapped to the underside of Wright's plane. On 4 October Wright made a 20-mile (32 km) round flight from Governors Island up the Hudson River to Grant's Tomb and back as part of the celebrations marking 300 years since Henry Hudson's first navigation of the river.

The following year aviator GLENN CURTISS landed on Governors Island after flying down the Hudson from Albany, winning a $10,000 prize from Joseph Pulitzer, publisher of the *New York World*.

Wright and Curtiss are the first two names found on the Governors Island EARLY BIRD AVIATION MONUMENT unveiled in 1954 to celebrate the achievements of the first aviators. The bronze propeller on the monument was cast from one of the wooden propellers on Wright's *Flyer*.

Ironically, the Aviation Monument can be found just outside the vast LIGGETT HALL BARRACKS, which was built by the U.S. Army in 1929 supposedly to thwart an attempt by the City of New York to build a municipal airport on Governors Island. Liggett Hall, which almost covers the island from east to west, was at the time THE LONGEST BUILDING IN THE WORLD and THE FIRST BUILDING IN THE WORLD LARGE ENOUGH TO HOUSE AN ENTIRE REGIMENT.

Early Bird Aviation Monument

Coast Guard

In 1966 Governors Island, by then THE OLDEST CONTINUOUSLY OPERATED MILITARY POST IN THE UNITED STATES, was handed over by the army to the U.S. Coast Guard, at which point it became THE LARGEST COAST GUARD STATION IN THE WORLD.

In 1988 President Reagan travelled to Governors Island for a summit on disarmament with Soviet leader Mikhail Gorbachev. This was held in the ADMIRAL'S HOUSE, constructed in 1843 as home for the island's commanding officer.

The U.S. Coast Guard left Governors Island in 1997, and today the island is open to the public from May to September and hosts a variety of concerts and cultural events. Access to the island is by ferry from the historic Battery Maritime Building on Lower Manhattan (*see* page 27).

Statue of Liberty

The STATUE OF LIBERTY was the first glimpse of America seen by the millions of immigrants who arrived in New York from Europe in the late 19th and early 20th centuries saw. They wrote home with stories of this breathtakingly beautiful lady floating above the harbour who, with her gaze fixed towards the sea, her right arm raised in greeting and her torch a guiding beacon, was there to welcome them into New York and to a new life. And so her fame grew until she became emblematic of New York, a potent symbol of liberty and democracy and a new world.

Even today the sight of the Statue of Liberty can bring a lump to the throat and lift the most jaundiced of souls, whether glimpsed from a boat in the bay or from the top of a New York skyscraper.

The idea for the statue originated at a dinner party in France in 1865 when the French statesman EDOUARD DE LABOULAYE, now known as the 'Father of the Statue of Liberty', proposed the creation of a monument to celebrate the friendship between France and America. Also at the dinner party was a young French sculptor called AUGUSTE

BARTHOLDI, who followed up on Laboulaye's suggestion by adapting an idea he had been working on for a vast statue, based on the Colossus of Rhodes, to mark the entrance to the new Suez Canal. Bartholdi travelled to New York and settled on Bedloe's Island, the smallest of the three 'oyster' islands in the Upper Bay, as the site for the statue. Here, it would be visible to every vessel that entered the harbour.

The Statue of Liberty was constructed in Paris over nine years. In 1876 the torch, the first portion of the statue to be finished, was sent over from Paris to the Centennial Exposition in Philadelphia and then moved to Madison Square in New York to try and drum up enthusiasm for the project. In 1885 the completed statue was packed into 214 crates and sent across from Paris in the French ship *Isère*, to await completion of the pedestal.

The Pedestal

It had been decided that while France would construct and pay for the statue, America would build and pay for the pedestal. Raising the funds for the pedestal proved difficult at first until Joseph Pulitzer promised to put the name of every contributor, however small, in his newspaper, the *New York World*.

The pedestal was designed by RICHARD MORRIS HUNT, founder of the American Institute of Architects, and for added strength the base was set within the walls of Fort Wood, a star-shaped fort built on Bedloe's Island by the army in 1811. The pedestal's foundations required 24,000 tons of concrete,

THE LARGEST MASS OF CONCRETE EVER POURED AT THAT TIME.

Dedication

Once the pedestal was complete, it took just four months to erect the Statue of Liberty, which was dedicated on 28 October 1886 by President Grover Cleveland. For the finale, Bartholdi perched on top of the torch and pulled a cord to release the large French flag that had been covering the front of the statue, revealing the statue's face to New Yorkers for the first time and unleashing fireworks, wild celebrations, marching bands and the world's first ticker-tape parade.

Ellis Island

America's Golden Door

ELLIS ISLAND is named after SAMUEL ELLIS, a Welsh New Yorker who acquired the island in 1785. Ceded to the federal government in 1808, it was fortified as a harbour defence and remained a military station until 1890, when the Federal Government assumed control of immigration from the State of New York. On 1 January 1892 Ellis Island opened as AMERICA'S FIRST FEDERAL IMMIGRATION STATION.

First and Last

The FIRST IMMIGRANT REGISTERED THROUGH ELLIS ISLAND, on 1 January 1892, was an Irish girl from County Cork called ANNIE MOORE, who celebrated her 15th birthday on that very day. As

Statue of Liberty

Stats & Facts

The statue's real name is 'Liberty Enlightening the World' – Statue of Liberty is a nickname.

The Statue of Liberty is made of very thin plates of copper sheeting, about the thickness of two pennies, placed over a wrought-iron frame. The frame was designed and built by GUSTAVE EIFFEL, who would later go on to build the Eiffel Tower for the World Fair in Paris in 1889.

She is 151 ft (46 m) tall, THE LARGEST METAL STATUE EVER MADE, while from the bottom of the pedestal to the tip of the torch is 305 ft (93 m).

No one knows for sure who the Statue of Liberty is modelled on. Some think Bartholdi's mother, but the more romantic theory is that Bartholdi was inspired by a woman considered to be one of the most beautiful women in the world at the time, a half-English, half-French actress called ISABELLA BOYER, who Bartholdi had met in Paris. Isabella was a former wife of New Yorker ISAAC SINGER, founder of the Singer Sewing Machine Company.

The seven spikes on Liberty's crown are said to represent the seven seas.

Hidden beneath Liberty's toga, at her feet, are broken chains symbolising freedom from slavery. Slavery had been abolished in the United States in 1865, just 21 years before the dedication of the statue.

In the museum at the base of the pedestal can be found a bronze tablet bearing the text of 'The New Colossus', a poem written in 1883 by a young poet from Greenwich Village, EMMA LAZARUS, to help with the fund-raising. It was presented by friends of the poet in 1903 and includes the famous words, 'Give me your tired, your poor / Your huddled masses yearning to breathe free . . .'

As part of the refurbishment of the statue for her centenary in 1986 the torch was replaced with a new copper torch, covered in gold leaf, and floodlit at night. The original is now displayed in the monument's lobby. Access to the balcony around the torch has been restricted since 1916, after an explosion in nearby New Jersey tore holes in the fabric.

Liberty Island sits in New Jersey waters but is federal property administered by the National Park Service and lies within the territorial jurisdiction of the State of New York.

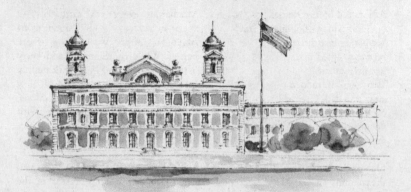

the first immigrant, she was presented with a $10 gold coin by COLONEL WEBER, THE FIRST COMMISSIONER FOR IMMIGRATION. Annie went to stay with her parents on Monroe Street on the Lower East Side, eventually married and had 11 children, and lived in New York for the rest of her life.

The original immigration centre on Ellis Island was made of wood and burned down in 1897. The present building, designed in French Renaissance style, opened in 1900, but with up to half a million immigrants passing through every year it soon proved inadequate, so the island was enlarged with landfill and a further complex of buildings added.

Over 12 million immigrants entered the United States through Ellis Island, America's Golden Door, before it closed in 1954. It was THE GREATEST WAVE OF MIGRATION IN HISTORY and it is estimated that NEARLY HALF OF ALL THE AMERICANS ALIVE TODAY HAVE AN ANCESTOR WHO ARRIVED THROUGH ELLIS ISLAND.

The vast majority of immigrants were processed in less than eight hours and only two per cent of all those who came to Ellis Island seeking to enter America were sent home.

The last immigrant to pass through Ellis Island, in 1954, was a merchant seaman from Norway named ARNE PETERSSEN.

Tourist Trap

Today Ellis Island serves as an immigration museum and is run by the National Parks Service along with the Statue of Liberty.

One of the delights of visiting Ellis Island is that you are allowed to poke around on your own, although an audio guide is available if you want one. Highlights include:

• The Great Hall, through which every immigrant passed, now cavernous and empty but once thronged with anxious men, women and children, seated in rows, and filled with dreams of a new life.

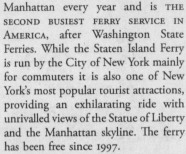

- A beautiful bronze statue of Annie Moore, holding her hat against the sea breeze, sculpted by Jeanne Rynhart.
- Two columns, hidden away in a dark corridor on the second floor, covered in graffiti scrawled by people waiting to be processed. One of the more legible messages on the columns was carved by a Cecchini Guiseppe, who writes in Italian that he arrived at the Battery on 18 May, Saturday, 1901.
- The AMERICAN IMMIGRANT WALL OF HONOUR, inscribed with the names of over 700,000 immigrants who came through the facility, THE LONGEST WALL OF NAMES IN THE WORLD.

Staten Island Ferry

The Best Free Ride in the World

The STATEN ISLAND FERRY carries some 20 million passengers the five miles (8 km) between Staten Island and Lower Manhattan every year and is THE SECOND BUSIEST FERRY SERVICE IN AMERICA, after Washington State Ferries. While the Staten Island Ferry is run by the City of New York mainly for commuters it is also one of New York's most popular tourist attractions, providing an exhilarating ride with unrivalled views of the Statue of Liberty and the Manhattan skyline. The ferry has been free since 1997.

The FIRST ORGANISED STATEN ISLAND FERRY SERVICE, direct ancestor of the present municipal ferry, was begun in about 1810 by a 16-year-old Staten Island boy called CORNELIUS VANDERBILT.

THE FIRST MOTORISED STATEN ISLAND FERRY, a steamboat called NAUTILUS, was introduced in 1817 by the Richmond Turnpike Company, set up by DANIEL TOMPKINS, 4th Governor of New York and Vice President to James Monroe, who wanted to bring in people to Tompkinsville, a village he was developing on Staten Island. In 1838 Cornelius Vanderbilt bought control of Richmond, and later sold it to the Staten Island Railway, run by his brother Jacob. The ferry company then passed through a number of hands until it was taken over by the City of New York in 1901.

CORNELIUS VANDERBILT (1794–1877) was born on Staten Island, the son of a ferryman whose ancestors had emigrated to New Amsterdam from the Dutch village of De Bilt in the 1650s. By the age of 11 he was working on the ferries in New York Harbor, and at the age of 16 he set up his own ferry business running between Staten Island and Manhattan, the direct forerunner of today's Staten Island ferry.

In 1817 Vanderbilt joined forces with Thomas Gibbons, who ran a steamboat service across the harbour from New Jersey to New York, and together they fought to overturn the steamboat monopoly of New York waters granted by the New York State Legislature to Robert 'the Chancellor' Livingston and Robert Fulton, inventor of the first steamboat. In AMERICA'S FIRST SIGNIFICANT ANTI-TRUST CASE the Supreme Court decided for Vanderbilt and Gibbons, ruling that individual states had no power to legislate on commerce between states. Vanderbilt went on to dominate steamboat traffic along the Hudson River between New York and Albany by offering a cheaper and more comfortable service.

After the Civil War, Vanderbilt switched from steamboats to railways, buying up several New York railroads and merging them into one giant corporation. In 1871 he built a depot for his railroads at 42nd Street, where steam trains were obliged to stop and change to horses to travel on into the city. The depot was called Grand Central, and the approach from the north along Fourth Avenue was dug into a sunken tunnel that was eventually covered over, planted with trees and renamed Park Avenue.

When Cornelius Vanderbilt died at his house at 10 Washington Place in 1877, aged 82, he was worth $100 million dollars and the richest man in America.

Well, I never knew this
about
NEW YORK HARBOR

In 1525, one year after Verrazano had sighted the bay, a Portuguese explorer called ESTEVAN GOMEZ, travelling under the Spanish flag, sailed into the Upper Bay while charting America's eastern seaboard, and named the great river he discovered there the Rio de San Antonio. In 1529, thanks to the charts Gomez made and took back home, a Portuguese cartographer called Diego Ribiero was able to produce the FIRST ACCURATE MAP OF AMERICA'S EASTERN SEABOARD. On it, the area around New York is shown as TIERRA DE ESTEVAN GOMEZ. Spain did not press home its claim to the new territory because Gomez informed them that there was no gold to be found there.

The FIRST MAN OF EITHER AFRICAN OR EUROPEAN DESCENT TO LIVE INDEPENDENTLY ON MANHATTAN ISLAND was a half-Portuguese, half-African trader called JAN RODRIGUES, who was put ashore at a temporary Dutch trading post on Lower Manhattan in 1613 by Dutch sea captain Thijs Volckenz Mossel to act as a translator and intermediary with the Native Americans. Rodrigues married a Native American, set up his own trading post as MANHATTAN'S FIRST RESIDENT MERCHANT, and eventually settled in New Amsterdam.

In 1776 New York Harbor became the scene of THE WORLD'S FIRST SUBMARINE ATTACK. The submarine, dubbed the *TURTLE*, was invented by Yale student DAVID BUSHNELL and was designed to destroy British warships anchored in the bay. The idea was that the *Turtle* would be towed into the vicinity of the target and lowered into the water. It would then submerge by admitting water into the hull, approach the target, drill into the hull of the enemy vessel and attach a mine. And so, early on the morning of 7 September 1776, the *Turtle*, piloted by army volunteer Sergeant Ezra Lee, embarked on its first mission, an attempt to place a mine on the hull of HMS *Eagle*, which was anchored in the harbour. Unfortunately for Sergeant Lee, the *Turtle*'s drill failed to bore a hole in the *Eagle*'s hull, the mine floated away free and the submarine was spotted as it bobbed to the surface a few yards from the ship. Lee managed to scramble out and swim away, however, and an hour later the abandoned mine exploded, giving the British fleet a terrible fright and forcing them to move their ships further out into the harbour. The *Turtle* was recovered but her transport ship was eventually sunk near the New Jersey Palisades with the *Turtle* on board, and so the world's first attack submarine was lost at the bottom of the Hudson River.

The BUTTERMILK CHANNEL, which separates Governors Island from Brooklyn, was once so shallow that at low tide farmers from Brooklyn could walk their cattle across to feed on the island. The channel has long since been dredged for use as a shipping lane.

Governors Island once boasted one of the SHORTEST RAILWAYS IN THE WORLD, thought to have been about 1½ miles

(2.4 km) in length. It ran between the island's docks and military warehouses and was scrapped in 1931 leaving no traces remaining.

More Italians entered New York through Ellis Island than any other nationality.

Viewed from the harbour Manhattan Island appears to lie very low in the water, making it extremely vulnerable to flooding in a storm, an impression that proved only too accurate on the night of 29 October 2012. HURRICANE SANDY, coming up from the south, combined with a wintry storm coming down from the north, created a 'perfect storm'. This was added to an unusually high tide swelled by the full moon and resulted in a record storm surge.

Waves in the Upper Bay reached a height of 32.5 ft (9.9 m), THE HIGHEST WAVES EVER RECORDED IN NEW YORK HARBOR, and there was a surge at Battery Park of 13.88 ft (4.2 m), THE HIGHEST SURGE EVER RECORDED AT BATTERY PARK. Hurricane Donna, in 1960, held the previous record surge of 10.02 ft (3 m).

Water poured over the sea defences and huge swathes of Manhattan were plunged into darkness when power stations shorted after being submerged. The subway system suffered the worst damage in its 108-year history as tunnels were flooded, with water reaching the ceiling of the South Ferry subway station at Manhattan's southern tip, and debris left by water littering the tracks. Whole streets in Lower Manhattan lay underwater, all the subway tunnels between Manhattan and Brooklyn were flooded and thousands of trees were felled in the city's parks, which remained closed for days. The New York Stock Exchange was shut for two days because of the weather, for the first time since the Great Blizzard of 1888 which claimed the life of Senator Roscoe Conkling (*see* page 140).

The New York Marathon was cancelled for the first time since it was inaugurated in 1970 and the annual Greenwich Village Halloween Parade was postponed for the first time in its 39-year history, since both the West Village and Chelsea were largely without power.

Just three weeks after the storm, some three million people lined the streets of New York to watch as the Macy's Thanksgiving Day Parade wound its way from Central Park to Herald Square, illustrating once again New York's indefatigable spirit and ability to bounce back after disaster.

CHAPTER 2

New Amsterdam & Colonial New York

Stadt Huys – New York's first City Hall

Very little remains of New Amsterdam, which was founded in 1625, or of Colonial New York as it became in 1664, except for some street names and the old street layout. The modern skyline of Lower Manhattan gives no hint of the alleyways and cobbled thoroughfares that still follow the original plan of the early settlement or of the scintillating history that lurks in the shadows of the skyscrapers. A meander through this part of the city provides a fascinating experience that is quite different from that of any other neighbourhood in New York.

The Battery

Since the dawn of New York in the 17th century the south shoreline of Manhattan Island has been known as THE BATTERY, as this is where the gun batteries of Fort Amsterdam stood in defence of the small Dutch trading post of NEW AMSTERDAM. The Battery was

the single point of entry to New York for the early Dutch settlers, for the first English inhabitants, and for millions of immigrants who came to settle in New York over the next 300 years.

Today, the Battery still bustles with maritime activity, with commuters arriving from Staten Island and New Jersey and tourists coming and going from the harbour islands and pleasure trips around the bay.

Peter Minuit Plaza

Passengers arriving on the Staten Island ferry disembark through the sleek WHITEHALL TERMINAL, opened in 2005, on to the most southerly point of Manhattan, an area now called PETER MINUIT PLAZA.

Here there are bus, taxi and subway connections to the rest of Manhattan, while within the plaza, set amongst trees and tulip beds, is the NEW AMSTERDAM

PLEIN AND PAVILION, opened in 2011 and donated by the Kingdom of the Netherlands to celebrate the founding on this spot of New Amsterdam. The Pavilion is designed to resemble the opening petals of a tulip and the sails of a windmill.

Peter Minuit's surname translates as 'midnight' and at midnight every night a dazzling light show illuminates the New Amsterdam Pavilion in honour of the director who secured Manhattan Island for the Dutch (*see* page 18).

Netherlands Memorial

A short walk up State Street to the north-east corner of Battery Park beside the Custom House brings you to the NETHERLANDS MEMORIAL, a flagstaff pedestal sculpted out of pink granite showing Peter Minuit, in his high collar and buckled shoes, handing over a string of beads to a native dressed in a loin cloth and wearing an Indian head-dress.

Peter Minuit

(1580–1638)

PETER MINUIT, a Walloon, was the 3rd Director of New Amsterdam, in office from 1626 to 1632. He will forever be remembered for purchasing Manhattan Island from the local Lenape Indians for 'trinkets worth $24'.

The much-quoted figure of $24 was arrived at by the discovery in Amsterdam in 1844 of a letter written by Pieter Schagen, a merchant with the Dutch West India Company. Writing in 1626 he states that 'They [the colonists] have bought the island Manhattes from the wild men for the value of sixty guilders'. The New York historian who found the letter, JOHN ROMEYN BRODHEAD, most likely converted the sixty guilders into $24 using the very inexact exchange rate of the day.

It is also likely that the Lenape Indians did not fully comprehend the nature of the transaction. They had no concept of land ownership and probably in their minds were agreeing merely to share the fishing and hunting on Manhattan. So either Peter Minuit pulled off the greatest land deal in history or the Lenape duped him into paying for something they didn't own. Nonetheless the transaction legitimised the Dutch occupation of Manhattan and became a celebrated part of New York's history. And somehow it seems appropriate that New York, the world's most dynamic commercial centre, was founded on a deal.

There is some dispute as to where the actual sale took place. The most likely location was on the north of the island, where the Indians were encamped at the time (*see* page 248), although it's possible that the Indians came to the Dutch settlement and the deal was struck on the site where Peter Minuit Plaza is now.

The memorial was donated by the people of the Netherlands and erected in 1926 to mark the 300th anniversary of Peter Minuit's famous purchase of Manhattan.

Fort Amsterdam

When FORT AMSTERDAM was built on the southern tip of Manhattan to protect the fledgling trading port of New Amsterdam it stood right beside the sea, but over the years landfill and the creation of Battery Park have extended the shoreline out into the bay. The original fort was designed by Inigo Jones in a star shape and was made of wood.

The construction of the fort in 1625 is considered to mark THE FOUNDING OF THE CITY OF NEW YORK. Later, in 1683, the fort was THE FIRST MEETING PLACE FOR THE NEW YORK LEGISLATURE.

In the years that followed, Fort Amsterdam changed hands eight times, and on each occasion was renamed after the ruling sovereign of the current occupiers. During the War of Independence,

when the British ruled New York from the fort, it was called Fort George after George III. It wasn't until after Evacuation Day in 1783, when the British left American soil for the last time, that the fort was finally occupied by the Americans and they chose to demolish it a few years later in 1790.

Custom House

The site of Fort Amsterdam itself is now occupied by the imposing ALEXANDER HAMILTON U.S. CUSTOM HOUSE, known to New Yorkers simply as the Custom House. While the fort was built to protect the tiny trading post of New Amsterdam, the Custom House was built some 300 years later to collect the revenue generated by that trading post, now the mighty flourishing port of New York. Before income tax was introduced in 1913, customs revenue provided by far the largest proportion of the federal government's revenue, and New York provided by far the largest proportion of that customs revenue.

After Fort Amsterdam was demolished

in 1790 it was first replaced by a large brick mansion called GOVERNMENT HOUSE, intended as the home of the new President of the United States, but in that same year the capital was moved to Philadelphia and the house instead became the residence of the first two Governors of the State of New York, GEORGE CLINTON and JOHN JAY.

In 1815 Government House was itself replaced with a row of townhouses, which in due course became offices and were eventually taken down to make way for the Custom House, built in 1907 by one of New York's most distinguished architects, CASS GILBERT, later responsible for the Woolworth Building. Constructed of Maine granite, the Custom House is considered to be THE FINEST BEAUX-ARTS BUILDING IN NEW YORK and a fitting monument to the enterprise and spirit of early 20th-century New York.

Along the front of the building are four white limestone statues by DANIEL CHESTER FRENCH representing the four continents of Asia, Africa, Europe and America, while along the cornice above the entrance are 12 smaller statues depicting the great seafaring nations of history including, somewhat unexpectedly, Belgium. The Belgium statue originally represented Germany, but during the First World War anti-German sentiment demanded that the enemy should not be so glorified and the name Germany was rubbed off the shield and replaced with Belgium. Actually, Belgium is most appropriate since New York was first settled mainly by Walloons from what is now Belgium.

Inside the Custom House is one of New York's great public spaces, a vast rotunda with a dome 85 ft (26 m) high, decorated with murals showing each stage of a vessel's arrival in New York Harbor, from approaching the Ambrose lightship at the entrance to the Narrows, to passing the Statue of Liberty and finally tying up at the pier. They were painted in 1937 by REGINALD MARSH and are redolent of the age of the great ocean liners.

In 1973 the Customs Service moved to the newly built World Trade Center and for the next few years the Custom House lay empty, although it was saved from demolition by being designated a National Historic Landmark. In 1987 the New York Bankruptcy Court moved in, and then in 1994 three floors of the building became home to the New York branch of the SMITHSONIAN NATIONAL MUSEUM OF THE AMERICAN INDIAN.

A WALK AROUND OLD NEW YORK

As you come out of the Custom House, turn right and then right again down Broadway, which soon becomes Whitehall. The third street you come to is Pearl Street. Turn right on Pearl and, across the plaza on your left, beside the entrance to the NEW YORK UNEARTHED URBAN ARCHAEOLOGY MUSEUM (now closed), there is a bust of author HERMAN MELVILLE and a plaque that reads:

On this site, number 6 Pearl Street,
Herman Melville
was born August 1, 1819.

Author of
Moby Dick,
'Bartelby the Scrivener,'
Pierre,
Billy Budd
and many other American classics

Pearl Street

From here we walk back along PEARL
STREET heading east, which will take us
through the heart of old New York. Pearl
Street itself marks the original shoreline
of the East River and gets its name from
the oyster shells (mother of pearl) that
were washed up on the shore here.

In 1656 Peter Stuyvesant, the last Dutch
director, established NEW YORK'S FIRST
MARKET at the junction of Pearl and
Whitehall. Stuyvesant ruled the colony
from a 'great house' that stood near this
spot, and when the British took over New
Amsterdam they named the house and
street Whitehall after the palace from
which Charles II ruled in London.

First Church

As you walk further east along Pearl Street
from Whitehall there is a small plaque set
low in the wall of the two-storey building
on the left that marks the site of THE FIRST
CHURCH BUILT ON MANHATTAN ISLAND.
Put up here in 1633, it was a simple
wooden structure with a Dutch-style
gambrel roof, built for the DUTCH
REFORM CHURCH, NEW YORK'S OLDEST
ESTABLISHED CHURCH. Before this, services

were held in a room above a mill located
on what is now Mill Lane, between Stone
Street and South William Street. The
dominie, or minister, at the time was
EVERARDUS BOGARDUS (1607–47), whose
descendant JAMES BOGARDUS (1800–74)
was a pioneer of New York's cast-iron
architecture.

Fraunces Tavern

At the junction of Pearl and Broad
Streets sits one of the oldest buildings
in Manhattan, FRAUNCES TAVERN, which
occupies the corner of the only complete
18th-century block in New York to
survive the Great Fire of 1835 (*see* page
26). The building was constructed in
1719 as a private home for STEPHEN
DELANCEY, a French Huguenot who
became one of Colonial New York's
wealthiest merchants, owner of a granary,
warehouse and retail store under the
name Delancey and Co.

In 1762 Delancey's house was sold at
auction to SAMUEL FRAUNCES, an
innkeeper from the West Indies, who
converted it to a tavern called the
QUEEN'S HEAD, in honour of King
George III's wife, Queen Charlotte.
Fraunces was a terrific chef, particularly
famous for his puddings, and the tavern

thrived. Despite the royal name of his inn, Fraunces was a supporter of independence from Britain and in the years leading up to the American Revolution the Queen's Head quietly hosted regular meetings of American patriots and the Sons of Liberty.

During the Revolution Fraunces is thought to have worked as an American spy and certainly gave aid to American prisoners of war, for which he was later rewarded by Congress. At the outbreak of the conflict the Queen's Head assumed Fraunces' own name, and at its conclusion George Washington held his victory banquet at what was now Fraunces Tavern.

On 4 December 1783, Washington returned to the tavern for a banquet in the Long Room, at which he bade an emotional farewell to his officers in the Continental army. 'With a heart full of love and gratitude I now take leave of you. I most devoutly wish that your latter days may be as prosperous and happy as your former ones have been glorious and honourable.'

Such was Washington's popularity at this time that he was being urged by many to seize control and declare a military regime, but he was determined that the government of the new United States should not be a military dictatorship. Hence he took his leave and resigned as Commander-in-Chief. Six years later he was invited back to New York to become the nation's first President, while Samuel Fraunces was invited to become steward to the first Presidential household. In 1785 Fraunces sold his tavern, and it subsequently served as the offices of the first U.S. Department of Foreign Affairs, under John Jay.

In 1883, on the centenary of Washington's farewell speech, the SONS OF THE REVOLUTION IN NEW YORK was founded in the Long Room at Fraunces Tavern. The first Sons of the Revolution came together in Pennsylvania in 1876 to commemorate and promote the spirit of the American Revolution and now have branches in most major American states. In 1905 the New York Sons of the Revolution bought Fraunces

The Sons of Liberty

In 1765 a group of American patriots banded together to fight for the rights of the American colonists against the British government. They took their name from a speech given in the British parliament by Isaac Barre, an Irish soldier and MP, in which he described Americans who opposed the policies of the British government as 'Sons of Liberty'. Their most memorable undertaking was the Boston Tea Party in 1773, which was the catalyst for the American Revolution. Their motto was 'No taxation without representation'. Notable Sons of Liberty were John Adams, 2nd U.S. President, and Paul Revere, the Boston silversmith who alerted the colonial militia of the approaching British army before the Battle of Lexington in 1775.

Tavern, which by now was much neglected and due to be demolished to make way for a car park. In one of the first major restorations to be carried out in America, Fraunces Tavern was meticulously rebuilt, while the Long Room upstairs was restored to what it would have looked like for Washington's Farewell in December 1783.

In 1907 Fraunces Tavern reopened with a restaurant on the first floor and a museum in the Long Room dedicated to the Revolution and early American history. The museum now occupies four buildings, and amongst the exhibits is a lock OF GEORGE WASHINGTON'S LIGHT BROWN HAIR and A FRAGMENT OF ONE OF HIS TEETH, contained in a tiny locket set under a glass dome.

Stadt Huys

Across Pearl Street from Fraunces Tavern, under the portico of the tall brown building (85 Broad Street, once the headquarters of Goldman Sachs) is the site where New York took its first hesitant footsteps towards independence. In 1653 the Dutch government, distracted by war with England, granted New Amsterdam some limited municipal powers under the authority of the Director-General Peter Stuyvesant, making NEW AMSTERDAM THE FIRST LEGALLY CHARTERED CITY IN AMERICA. The new council was made up of magistrates, aldermen and a sheriff, and Stuyvesant granted them use of a large public tavern on the waterfront, which served as the STADT HUYS, or City Hall. It remained in use as City Hall until 1697, when the city

government moved to where the Federal Hall now is, on Wall Street. The Stadt Huys was demolished some years later.

In 1979 the investment bank Goldman Sachs began to prepare the area for a massive new tower block to serve as its world headquarters, but because this was such a historic site the city authorities demanded that NEW YORK'S FIRST LARGE-SCALE ARCHAEOLOGICAL EXCAVATION be carried out before any construction started. They uncovered the foundations of not only the Stadt Huys but also of the building that stood next door to it, an English tavern called THE LOVELACE. Built in 1670, the inn was named after FRANCIS LOVELACE, who served as THE SECOND ENGLISH GOVERNOR OF NEW YORK between 1668 and 1673. The foundation stones of the Lovelace, which are amongst THE OLDEST EUROPEAN REMAINS ON MANHATTAN, can be viewed through glass plates in the sidewalk opposite Fraunces Tavern, while the outline of the Stadt Huys is marked out next to it in pale stone. Now continue down Pearl Street and climb the steps on the left that lead up to . . .

Stone Street

The great brown tower block of Goldman Sachs' HQ not only obliterated the site of New York's first city hall but also sliced through STONE STREET, so named because it was one of the first streets in New York to be paved, in about 1655. The line of the lost section of Stone Street is picked out by a brown brick pathway that passes through the lobby of 85 Broad Street and, although this is not advertised, it is accessible to the public.

At the beginning of the narrow eastern section of Stone Street there is a fascinating marker set into the sidewalk showing how the road fits into a map of the original street layout of New Amsterdam. Stone Street is now lined with warehouses and stores built in the middle of the 19th century, after the Great Fire of 1835

In 1996, following years of neglect, the area bordered by Stone Street, South William Street and Pearl Street was made an Historic District and slowly restored. Stone Street was repaved and the empty warehouses were transformed into restaurants and bars, creating a delightfully unexpected haven of character amongst the faceless canyons of the Financial District. On fine summer nights the outdoor tables are filled with people enjoying the hospitality of what has become one of New York's most popular and trendy hotspots.

Mill Lane

Walk up Stone Street to MILL LANE, which was the site of a horse mill, built in 1628, where the first Dutch Protestants worshipped in a specially built upstairs room. Four of the millstones from this mill can be seen in the vestibule of the West End Collegiate Dutch Reform Protestant Church at 368 West End Avenue in the Upper West Side (*see* page 218).

Delmonico's

Walk up Mill Lane and cross South William Street to find DELMONICO'S, NEW YORK'S FIRST RESTAURANT, which opened at 56 Beaver Street in 1837, in a grand new building that rose from the ashes of the Great Fire of 1835. It is said that the columns by the entrance are from the ruins of Pompeii.

Delmonico's was actually founded in a small pastry shop in William Street in 1827 by JOHN AND PETER DELMONICO, brothers from Switzerland, and had several homes in the area before settling permanently at 56 Beaver Street. The restaurant is credited with having THE FIRST PRINTED MENU IN NEW YORK, THE FIRST SEPARATE WINE LIST, THE FIRST INDIVIDUAL TABLES and THE FIRST TABLECLOTHS. It is also the birthplace of the DELMONICO STEAK, OYSTERS ROCKEFELLER, LOBSTER NEWBERG, BAKED ALASKA, EGGS BENEDICT and the Hamburg Steak, a forerunner of the Hamburger.

Hanover Square

With Delmonico's behind you, turn right on to William Street and walk to the triangular patch of land at the end called HANOVER SQUARE, named in 1714 in honour of the British Royal House of Hanover. The 'square' has

been a public area since the days of New Amsterdam, when it was a breezy open space by the waterfront.

Printing House Square

A plaque marks the spot where, in 1693, WILLIAM BRADFORD, NEW YORK'S FIRST OFFICIAL PRINTER, set up NEW YORK'S FIRST PRINTING PRESS, at No. 81 Pearl Street. Many of New York's first publications were produced there:

1693 THE FIRST BOOK PRINTED IN NEW YORK, KEITH'S NEW-ENGLAND'S SPIRIT OF PERSECUTION TRANSMITTED TO PENNSILVANIA

1710 THE FIRST AMERICAN BOOK OF COMMON PRAYER

1725 NEW YORK'S FIRST NEWSPAPER, THE NEW YORK GAZETTE

1731 THE FIRST PRINTED MAP OF NEW YORK, THE BRADFORD-LYNE MAP

India House

The Great Fire of 1835, which began near Hanover Square, destroyed every building in the area, but from the ashes rose the beginnings of a thriving commercial and financial centre. A number of banks built themselves fashionable Italianate palazzo-style headquarters in and around the square and one of those survives, at No. 1 Hanover Square, an impressive brownstone mansion built in 1851 for the Hanover Bank. In 1870 AMERICA'S FIRST COMMODITY MARKET, THE NEW YORK COTTON EXCHANGE, was founded in this building.

In 1914 a group of local businessmen got together and formed a club for like-minded entrepreneurs with an interest in international trade. They took out a lease on No. 1 Hanover Square and changed its name to INDIA HOUSE in honour of the Dutch West India Company, founders of the original trading post. The India House Club still functions.

Queen Elizabeth II
September 11th Garden

Hanover Square today is a peaceful haven amongst the noise and commercial bustle of downtown, as well as the site of a memorial garden given to the people of New York by the people of Britain to commemorate the 67 British victims of the attacks on the World Trade Center. The garden was dedicated by the Prince of Wales in 2005 and officially opened by the Queen in 2010. In 2012 the garden was formally dedicated with a new name, QUEEN ELIZABETH II SEPTEMBER 11TH GARDEN, and thus serves as both a memorial garden and a tribute to Queen Elizabeth's Diamond Jubilee.

The garden contains features created with materials from every part of the British Isles, along with plants and flowers such as those you might find in an English country garden. It is a beautiful place, worthy of these lovely, secret streets in old New York.

GANGLAND MACHINE GUN KILLING, when Al Capone's mob gunned down the Brooklyn mobster Frankie Yale, who was hijacking whisky meant for Capone.

Police Museum

Now walk south from Hanover Square down toward the East River on OLD SLIP, once an inlet where ships would be tied up for loading and unloading. Cross Water Street and after Old Slip Park you will come to a small Florentine palazzo, built in 1911 to house the 1st Precinct Police Station and now home to the NEW YORK CITY POLICE MUSEUM. Highlights here include a Hall of Heroes memorial to all officers killed in the line of duty since 1845, an extraordinarily moving multimedia exhibit explaining the NYPD's role during the 9/11 attacks, a history of the NYPD, some old police cars (you can test the sirens), a mock-up of a jail, an amazing display of old mug shots and, my particular favourite, a Tommy gun used in NEW YORK'S FIRST

The Elevated Acre

Go back to Water Street, turn left, and at 55 Water Street, by the pedestrian crossing, go up the escalator on your left and ascend to the Financial District's best kept secret, an emerald green lawn 30 ft (9 m) above the streets from where there are stunning views across the East River to Brooklyn, the Brooklyn Bridge and Governors Island. This is the ELEVATED ACRE, the perfect place for a quiet picnic and a read of the newspaper – or you can watch the helicopters coming and going from the Downtown heliport on the river below. There is a pleasant land-scaped area of trees and shrubs for shade or privacy, while the main lawn can be used as an auditorium for exhibitions and outdoor movie shows. At dusk a 50 ft (15 m) high sculpture called the

---

The Great Fire of 1835

THE GREAT FIRE OF 1835, the worst urban conflagration since the Great Fire of London in 1666, was caused by a gas explosion in a dry goods store near Hanover Square on the night of 16 December. A strong, gusting wind spread the flames west along Stone Street and north towards Wall Street, and by the time the fire had burned itself out after 24 hours, almost all of the old colonial city of New York had been destroyed. While firefighters had been quickly on the scene, the temperature was so cold that wells and cisterns were frozen solid and even the East River was ice-bound. Any water that could be found either froze in the hosepipes or blew back in the faces of the firemen as icicles.

BEACON OF PROGRESS glows softly with changing colours.

Vietnam Veterans Plaza

Return to Water Street, and at Coenties Slip is the VIETNAM VETERANS PLAZA, a riverside space dedicated in 1985 by Mayor Koch in memory of the servicemen and women of New York who fought in the Vietnam War. The centrepiece of the plaza is a wall of translucent green glass engraved with excerpts from speeches, poems, diary entries and letters written home to their families by service personnel on duty in Vietnam. Twelve granite slabs etched with the names of the 1,741 New Yorkers who died in Vietnam makes up a Walk of Honour, while among the Honour Plaques is one to PRIVATE FIRST CLASS DAN BULLOCK, who altered his birth certificate so that he could join the Marine Corps at the age of 14. He was 15 when he died in Vietnam, THE YOUNGEST AMERICAN SERVICEMAN KILLED IN THE VIETNAM WAR.

On the river side of the Vietnam Memorial Plaza turn right on South Street and walk towards the grey-green bulk of the . . .

Battery Maritime Building

The BATTERY MARITIME BUILDING, Manhattan's last surviving early 20th-century ferry structure, stands next to the Staten Island Ferry's new Whitehall terminal, at the bottom of Whitehall Street. The two buildings were originally an identical pair, but the Staten Island terminal burned down in 1991 and has since been replaced. The BMB was built in 1909 at a time when as many as 17 ferry lines plied the East River between Manhattan and Brooklyn. It is made of green-painted wrought iron and is a fine example of *beaux-arts* Structural Expressionism, a style introduced at the Paris Exposition in 1889 for which the Eiffel Tower was created. When it was built, the terminal served the ferry to 39th Street in South Brooklyn. Today it is the ferry terminal for Governors Island.

The two Whitehall ferry buildings stand on the site of NEW YORK'S FIRST PIER, which was a wooden jetty built

on the East River in 1649 on a rocky ledge that the Dutch called SCHREYERS HOOK, named after Schreyers Toren in Amsterdam. 'Schreyers' means those who weep, and 'Toren' was the tower on which they stood to watch their loved ones sail away.

Our Lady of the Rosary

We are now back at Peter Minuit Plaza. Walk through the plaza with the ferry terminal at your back and you will come to a magnificently out-of-place pink-brick Georgian townhouse with matching chapel attached. It is dwarfed but not overshadowed by the soaring glass skyscrapers that tower behind it, although it is quite probably missed by most of the tourists pouring off the Staten Island ferry. This is the James Watson House, at No. 7 State Street, built in 1793 by an unknown architect for a rich merchant, JAMES D. WATSON, an early Speaker of the New York State Assembly, who wanted a home by the waterfront from which he could keep an eye on his ships in the harbour. One of the oldest buildings and first mansions on Manhattan, it is the only survivor of a whole row of grand, late 18th-century townhouses that graced State Street in the days when New York's 'Quality' still lived on Manhattan's southern tip, enjoying the bracing sea views. In 1806 the house was extended with a curved and elaborately porticoed addition designed by John McComb Jr. It is believed that the wooden columns of

the addition are in fact old masts from some of James Watson's ships.

By the beginning of the 19th century the harbour area was becoming steadily busier and more commercial and New York society was moving further north. The James Watson House became a hotel, and then in 1885 it was purchased on behalf of the Mission of Our Lady of the Rosary, an organisation set up in 1883 by Charlotte Grace O'Brien, daughter of the MP for Limerick in Ireland, to look after Irish immigrant girls. Between 1883 and 1908, over 300,000 Irish girls arrived in New York and the Mission gave assistance to all of those who had no family or friends to look after them.

The Mission now occupies the new CHURCH OF OUR LADY OF THE ROSARY next door, which was built in 1964 (in Georgian style to blend in with the James Watson House), and serves as a shrine to America's first native-born saint, Elizabeth Ann Seton. The church stands on the site of the house where she lived from 1801 to 1803.

ELIZABETH ANN SETON (1774–1821) was born on Staten Island in 1774 into a prominent Episcopalian family who attended Trinity Church. In 1794 she married William Seton, a well-to-do shipping merchant, with whom she had five children. Some years after they were married, William became ill and the Setons travelled to Italy in the hope that he might recover, but he died there in 1803 leaving Elizabeth to bring up their five children, on her own and penniless. Grateful for the care and succour given to her by Catholics in Italy, Elizabeth returned to New York and converted to Catholicism, much to the dismay of her Episcopalian relatives.

No longer made welcome by friends and family in New York, where anti-Catholic sentiment was rife, Elizabeth moved to Baltimore. Here, in 1810, with the support of a rich Catholic convert Samuel Sutherland, she founded THE FIRST FREE SCHOOL IN AMERICA, ST JOSEPH'S ACADEMY AND FREE SCHOOL. A year later she founded THE FIRST RELIGIOUS ORDER IN AMERICA, THE SISTERS OF CHARITY OF ST JOSEPH, dedicated to caring for the children of the poor.

Mother Seton, as she became known, died of tuberculosis in 1821 at the age of 46. She was canonised by Pope John Paul VI in 1975.

From the Elizabeth Ann Seton Shrine go left across State Street into . . .

Battery Park

In 1790, the rubble produced when Fort George was demolished was used as landfill for the creation of BATTERY PARK. Today the park is a breezy, well-maintained open space of 25 acres (10 ha) filled with trees and flowerbeds, fountains, monuments and memorials. From the Promenade, which recalls the days when 17th- and 18th-century New Yorkers would parade along State Street in all their finery, there are exceptional, salt-caked views of the Statue of Liberty, Ellis Island and the harbour, extending as far as the Verrazano Narrows Bridge when the weather is clear.

Battery Park is one of the few places in New York where you can find real solitude. Here, where New York began, the fresh air, the lapping of the waves against the granite seawalls and the windy cries of the gulls can, for just a while, tune out the constant crash and chaos of the city.

A happy hour or so can be spent pottering around and studying the different memorials and statues in the park, which are being added to all the time. One that particularly stands out is THE AMERICAN MERCHANT MARINERS MEMORIAL, a most unusual and dramatic sculpture dedicated in 1991 and created by a French Venezuelan artist called Marisol Escobar, who lived in Greenwich Village. It is set 40 ft (12 m) out in the harbour on a stone breakwater extending south from Pier A. Three men are balanced on a tilting deck, one of them lying on his stomach and extending his hand down towards a fourth man in the water who is reaching up. Their hands are barely an inch apart, but as the tide rises the drowning man vanishes beneath the waves, only to appear again when the tide drops, to play out the agonising scene once more, day after day. It is movingly realistic, with the drowning man appearing to bob up and down in the water as the waves break over him. The sculpture was based on a photograph of a real event from the Second World War, found in a German magazine by a captured U.S. merchant seaman called George Duffy in 1942. The photograph was of sailors from a torpedoed American oil tanker called the *Muskogee* and was taken by a German journalist from the very submarine that had launched the torpedoes. None of the American sailors were rescued, and the realisation that you are looking at a tableau of men about to die is heart-rending.

Castle Clinton

The circular brownstone fortress of CASTLE CLINTON, now comfortably surrounded by trees in the southwest corner of Battery Park, was constructed in 1811 to defend New York from the British during the build-up to the War of 1812. It was then known as the Southwest Battery and was

designed by John McComb Jr., architect of New York City Hall.

The fortress originally stood on a man-made island some 300 yards (275 m) off shore, connected to the Battery by a timber causeway and drawbridge. In the end the British didn't attack New York and the fort was never used for military purposes. In 1815 it was renamed Castle Clinton in honour of New York mayor DeWitt Clinton and handed over to the city.

Over the next years the fort served many purposes. First it was converted into a place of entertainment known as Castle Garden. The inside courtyard was decorated with flowers and shrubs and a fountain, the top of the perimeter wall was turned into a promenade, and huge crowds flocked to the arena to watch concerts, firework displays, scientific demonstrations, hot air balloons and magic shows. Later the courtyard was roofed over in order to accommodate classical concerts and opera, with the fort becoming for a time New York's leading performance venue.

Eventually the channel separating the fort and the Battery was filled in and the building was used as THE WORLD'S FIRST IMMIGRANT LANDING DEPOT, opening its doors on 3 August 1855. Between 1855 and 1890 some eight million immigrants came in through the fort, mostly Irish families escaping the Great Famine and Germans escaping unrest. When the federal government took charge of immigration in 1889, the fort was closed in favour of a brand new immigration centre being constructed on Ellis Island.

In 1896 the fort reopened as the home of the NEW YORK CITY AQUARIUM, which remained there for 47 years until 1941, the fort's longest tenant. The fort was then designated a National Monument and turned over to the National Park Service to run. They stripped the building of its adornments until it was restored close to its original state and brought back the name Castle Clinton. It now serves as a ticketing office for boats to the Statue of Liberty and Ellis Island.

Well, I never knew this about

NEW AMSTERDAM & COLONIAL NEW YORK

On the west side of State Street, across from the Custom House, sits a small, delightfully eccentric *beaux-arts* building of brick and stone. This is the BOWLING GREEN CONTROL STATION, built in 1905 to 'control' entry to the Bowling Green subway station of the Interborough Rapid Transit Company (IRT), New York's first subway. It is one of only two such street-level station houses left in Manhattan, the other being on 72nd Street. These sturdy control houses were only built for the most important stations and where there was plenty of road space above ground, with most subway entry points having to make do with less substantial steel and glass structures to shelter them from the rain.

Goldman Sachs moved out of 85 Broad Street in 2009 into a new 740 ft (225 m)

tower block in Battery Park City near the World Financial Center.

At the corner of Stone Street and Mill Lane stood the home of ASSER LEVY, THE FIRST JEWISH CITIZEN IN NEW YORK, THE FIRST JEW TO SERVE IN THE NEW YORK MILITIA and THE FIRST JEW TO OWN A HOUSE IN NEW YORK – possibly in all of America. Asser Levy arrived from Amsterdam in 1654 and fought the

Director-General, Peter Stuyvesant, for the rights of Jews to trade, practise their religion and bear arms. Stuyvesant's objections to Jewish citizenship were overruled by the Dutch West India Company, who valued the Jews' commercial expertise, and Asser Levy went on to become one of the wealthiest men in New York, as a trader and as THE FIRST KOSHER BUTCHER IN THE NEW WORLD.

SHEARITH ISRAEL, founded by Asser Levy and his fellow Jewish settlers in 1654, not long after they arrived in New York, is THE OLDEST JEWISH CONGREGATION IN AMERICA. They met in the same room above the mill, on what is now Mill Street, where the early Dutch Reform Church congregation had worshipped 30 years earlier. The mill was eventually demolished and Shearith Israel built AMERICA'S FIRST SYNAGOGUE on the site (now 22 South William Street) in 1730. Today they meet in a splendid neo-classical synagogue on Central Park West on the Upper West Side.

Prince William, of the House of Hanover, third son of George III, resided in Hanover Square for a while during the Revolution when New York was in the hands of the British. He was serving as a midshipman in the Royal Navy and was sent to New York to boost morale. He later acceded to the throne as WILLIAM IV, THE ONLY BRITISH MONARCH EVER TO HAVE LIVED IN AMERICA.

Perhaps the most talked-about event at Castle Garden occurred on 11 September 1850 when the Swedish Nightingale, JENNY LIND, performed before a sell-out crowd of 15,000 on the first night of her American tour. The tour was arranged by the great showman P.T. Barnum, who so successfully built up expectations for a woman he had never heard sing that tickets for the first night had to be auctioned – with the very first ticket going for the astronomical sum of $225.

CHAPTER 3

LOWER BROADWAY – BOWLING GREEN TO TRINITY CHURCH

Old Standard Oil Building

'Broadway is the main artery of New York life – the hardened artery'
WALTER WINCHELL, AUTHOR OF 'ON BROADWAY', THE FIRST GOSSIP COLUMN

BROADWAY, New York's most famous street, was originally an Indian trail called the WECKQUASGEEK, which followed the line of a natural ridge diagonally across the lower part of Manhattan. The Dutch named it Heere Straat, or High Street, due to its elevated position, and it became an important trade route to the north of the island and to the colony of New Netherland beyond. Eventually the road was widened to take larger wagons and was referred to as the Brede Weg, or Broad Way.

North of Union Square the road was known as the Bloomingdale Road, and led to the village of that name which occupied part of what is now the Upper West Side. As New York expanded northwards the whole trail the length of Manhattan took on the name Broadway, which served, and still serves, as New York's MAIN STREET. Today Broadway runs all the way to the state capital Albany.

New York's history is one of constant northward expansion, with Broadway as the tree trunk from which new neighbourhoods branched out east and west. A walk up Broadway from south to north is a walk along New York's timeline and gives an insight into each step the city has taken on its journey from trading port to modern world-class metropolis.

Bowling Green

Broadway begins at BOWLING GREEN, a pleasant, shady bower of trees, with flower beds, lawns, a round pond and a fountain. Bowling Green began life as a parade ground for Fort Amsterdam. Then it was a cattle market, and in 1677 became the site of NEW YORK'S FIRST PUBLIC WELL.

In 1733, the Common Council leased the 'Piece of Land . . . fronting to the Fort' to three Broadway residents for a rent of one peppercorn a year in order for it to be 'Inclosed to make a Bowling Green there . . . for the Beauty and Ornament of the Said Street' and the 'Recreation and Delight of the Inhabitants of this City'. Bowling

Green is hence THE OLDEST PUBLIC PARK IN NEW YORK.

Peppercorn Rent

A Peppercorn Rent is a nominal payment that allows for the creation of a legal contract. In this case the Common Council didn't want to profit from allowing the land to be made use of, but did want to retain legal ownership.

In November 1765 the newly formed SONS OF LIBERTY marched on Bowling Green, tore down the wooden fence surrounding it, lit a bonfire and set fire to an effigy of the English Governor, CADWALADER COLDEN, who was watching from the ramparts of the fort. They were protesting against the STAMP ACT, which had been introduced earlier that year, and by which all printed materials in the colonies were subjected to a tax, raised to pay for British troops stationed in America. The protests worked and the act was repealed in March 1766. As a sign of gratitude to the king, a gilded lead statue of GEORGE III, seated on horseback with a laurel wreath on his head, was erected in the middle of the park in 1770. The following year an iron fence was put up around the green to prevent it from becoming a 'receptacle for all the filth and dirt of the neighbourhood'.

Toppling the King

Come the Revolution and the good feeling towards George III had dissipated. On the evening of 9 July 1776, fired up by hearing the DECLARATION OF INDEPENDENCE read out in New York for the first time, in the park where City Hall now stands, a crowd of New Yorkers, along with soldiers from the Continental Army and members of the Sons of Liberty, ran down Broadway to Bowling Green, attached ropes to the statue of George III and toppled the hated symbol of oppression from its marble pedestal. The statue was then broken up and sent to Connecticut where the lead was melted down to make musket balls for the Continental Army. Not all of the statue was lost, however, and some small pieces that survived can be seen at the New York Historical Society.

As well as destroying the statue, the rioters somehow managed to saw off all the decorative crowns that capped the posts of the iron fence surrounding the park. The fence itself survived and still protects Bowling Green to this day, although you can see the damage to the stunted posts where the crowns were hacked off. This 18th-century fence, which dates from 1771, is one of THE OLDEST SURVIVING STRUCTURES IN MANHATTAN and a gloriously tangible symbol of the Revolution.

Evacuation Day

North of Bowling Green, just outside the fence, on a small triangle of cobblestones in the middle of Broadway, stands a flagpole commemorating EVACUATION DAY, 25 November 1783, when the British Redcoats departed in a longboat and the British flag was lowered for ever over New York, the last official British outpost on American soil. As a final gesture, the British raised a Union Jack over Bowling Green, then cut the halyard and greased the flagpole to prevent anyone climbing it, so that when George Washington arrived there would still be a British flag flying above the city. Their plan was thwarted, however, when a young sailor called JOHN VAN ARSDALE managed to climb the flagpole, using iron nails as cleats, and replaced the Union Jack with the Stars and Stripes, moments before Washington and his troops rode triumphantly down Broadway to take possession of their new capital.

And so it could be said that the American Revolution started and ended at Bowling Green – with the toppling of King George's statue in 1776 and the raising of the Stars and Stripes seven years later in 1783.

Charging Bull

Just in front of the Evacuation Day flagpole, poised as if about to stampede up Broadway, is one of New York's best-loved sights, CHARGING BULL, a 7,000 lb (3,175 kg) bronze sculpture that has become an icon of Wall Street. The bull first appeared over Christmas 1989, when in the middle of the night between police patrols the sculptor, Sicilian ARTURO DI MODICA, placed it on the street in front of the New York Stock Exchange as a gift to the people of New York. Next morning the new attraction drew admiring crowds, while Di Modica stood nearby handing out flyers, but a few days later the police impounded the bull for obstructing the traffic. Such was the outcry that *Charging Bull* was re-installed at Bowling Green, where it remains on permanent loan to the Department of Parks and Recreation. It is said that rubbing certain parts of the bull's anatomy can bring good luck.

Canyon of Heroes

As you stand on the steps of the Custom House, looking north over Bowling Green, Broadway recedes dramatically into the distance between a wall of soaring skyscrapers like some enormous alpine chasm. This stretch of Broadway running from the Battery to City Hall Park is known as the CANYON OF HEROES, where sporting champions, political and military leaders, and pioneers of air and space travel are acclaimed with New York's legendary ticker-tape parades. Perhaps the most memorable parade, certainly one of the biggest, was held on 13 August 1969 to honour the first men on the moon, Apollo 11 astronauts Neil Armstrong

and Buzz Aldrin, and pilot Michael Collins. It is estimated that some four million people attended.

The first ticker-tape parade was initiated by an office worker during celebrations for the Dedication of the Statue of Liberty on 28 October 1886. A party was held on Broadway for the occasion, during which a worker in one of the brokerage houses along the route opened a window and threw streams of shredded paper from a ticker-tape machine down onto the parade below. Others joined in and soon there was a snowstorm of ticker-tape raining down on Broadway, and so was born the New York ticker-tape parade.

Today the Mayor of New York gets to decide who is honoured with a ticker-tape parade, while all the past parades are commemorated with inscribed metal plaques set into the roadway along Lower Broadway.

Bowling Green West

No. 1 Broadway

NO. 1 BROADWAY might also be called No. 1 New York, for this site stands at the gateway to the city, the start of New York's 'Main Street'.

In 1760 CAPTAIN ARCHIBALD KENNEDY, a prosperous British naval officer, built himself the finest house in Colonial New York at No. 1 Broadway. It was a luxurious Palladian mansion with 'wide halls and spacious rooms', a state drawing room 50 ft (15 m) long and a dining room 'vast and rich'. At that time Broadway was the most fashionable street in town and No. 1 was the prime position – Battery Park had not yet been filled in and the house looked on to the harbour with a garden running down to the water. Kennedy and his wife Anne entertained there royally the 'beauty and fashion of the colony'.

Military HQ

In 1775, with revolution in the air, Kennedy moved his family out, leaving the house vacant, and it was briefly occupied by General George Washington, who recognised the value of its strategic position. After Washington was forced to retreat from New York, the house served as the headquarters of the British commander SIR HENRY CLINTON for the duration of the British occupation of New York.

At the conclusion of the Revolution, when the Americans reoccupied New York, Washington came back to take up residence in the Kennedy Mansion once more, and it was from there that he left for his farewell dinner at Fraunces Tavern in 1783.

Washington Hotel

During the early 19th century Lower Broadway developed from a residential neighbourhood into a commercial one, and the gentry began to move out and build their grand homes further north. The Kennedy Mansion was converted into the WASHINGTON HOTEL, and then in 1884 it was razed to the ground and replaced by the WASHINGTON BUILDING, a commercial office block built for CYRUS

W. FIELD, creator of the Atlantic Telegraph Company, the firm that laid the first transatlantic telegraph cable in 1858.

In 1921 the Washington Building was purchased by the American shipping conglomerate INTERNATIONAL MERCANTILE MARINE COMPANY, which later became UNITED STATES LINES. The façade of the building was remodelled to include a variety of marine symbols with, on the second storey, the shields of all the ports across the world served by the company. United States Lines was THE LAST AMERICAN COMPANY TO OPERATE PASSENGER SHIPS ACROSS THE ATLANTIC and ceased passenger operations in 1969. The grand booking hall at No. 1 Broadway, designed like an 18th-century ballroom, with a mass of columns and chandeliers, is now occupied by Citibank. Entry to the bank from Battery Place is via porticoed doors marked FIRST CLASS and CABIN CLASS. Customers today may choose which door to use.

Steamship Row

By the end of the 19th century all the elegant houses that had lined Broadway to the west of Bowling Green had become offices. Many of the major shipping lines had their headquarters on this stretch of Broadway, and it became known as 'STEAMSHIP ROW'. The WHITE STAR LINE used to occupy Nos. 9–11 and this is where, on 15 April 1912, anxious relatives congregated to await news of the stricken liner *Titanic*.

At No. 25 Broadway is the CUNARD BUILDING, completed in 1921. As befits the offices of the world's biggest and most luxurious shipping line, in the world's busiest and most prestigious port, the Cunard Building is impressive. Bronze doors open on to a grand entrance hall, which acts as a mere appetiser for the spectacular domed and vaulted ticketing hall beyond. Measuring 185 ft (56 m) long and 65 ft (20 m) high, decorated with marble statues, murals and maps, representations of historic ships and ports, sea creatures, dolphins, mermaids and sea horses, this room is undoubtedly one of New York's most marvellous interiors.

Cunard moved out of the building in the 1970s, and in 1977 the ticketing hall was converted into the Bowling Street branch of the U.S. Post Office. What a place to buy stamps!

Old Standard Oil Building

Across BEAVER STREET, whose name recalls the commodity on which New York's prosperity was founded, is the lovely curved façade of the OLD STANDARD OIL BUILDING, at No. 26. In 1895 JOHN D. ROCKEFELLER moved the headquarters of his Standard Oil Company from Cleveland, Ohio, to this brand new landmark building on New York's Broadway. The original ten-storey block was widened and extended upwards to 16 storeys in 1895 while the tower was added in 1921. The tower, which is aligned on the New York grid pattern of uptown rather than on the winding streets of old downtown, is topped by a pyramid modelled on the Tomb of King Mausolos at Halicarnassus in modern-day Turkey, the original Mausoleum. It is crowned with a brazier wrapped in flaming torches, a symbol of the oil industry, which also served as a beacon for ships in the harbour.

Standard Oil, which became known as ESSO, and is now ExxonMobil, moved uptown to Rockefeller Center in 1946 and sold No. 26 Broadway in 1956.

Second Presidential Mansion

No. 39 Broadway stands on the former site of the McCOMB MANSION, which served as THE SECOND PRESIDENTIAL MANSION for the new President, George Washington, between 23 February and 30 August in 1790.

The McComb Mansion was built in 1786 for ALEXANDER McCOMB (or Macomb), a Belfast-born entrepreneur and land speculator, as his townhouse. Located close to the fashionable Trinity Church and with spectacular views of the Hudson from the rear windows, the Mansion House, as McComb called it, vied with the Kennedy Mansion as the finest private house in New York.

(Coincidentally, in 1794 McComb's daughter Jane married Archibald Kennedy's youngest son Robert.)

In 1790, finding that the first presidential mansion in Cherry Street on the East Side had grown too small, President George Washington moved into the McComb Mansion House, along with his household steward Samuel Fraunces, former owner of Fraunces Tavern. After Washington left, the McComb Mansion remained a private house until 1821, when it was converted into a luxury hotel called Bunker's Mansion House.

In 1939 the Daughters of the Revolution placed a plaque marking the former site of the second Presidential mansion on the wall beside the entrance to No. 39 Broadway.

First European Habitation

No. 39 Broadway is also thought to stand where THE VERY FIRST EUROPEAN DWELLINGS ON MANHATTAN WERE PUT UP, the four makeshift wooden huts constructed by Captain Adriaen Block and the crew of the *Tyger* in 1613 (*see* page 5).

New York's First Skyscraper?

No. 50 Broadway is where NEW YORK'S FIRST SKYSCRAPER, THE TOWER BUILDING, was erected in 1888–9 by architect Bradford Gilbert, for John Noble Stearns, a silk importer. Stearns wanted a building with plenty of space and had hoped to buy a couple of adjacent plots on Broadway, but this proved impossible, so

Stearns was confronted with the problem of how to achieve an office with enough room on a very narrow plot. Up until that time buildings had been constructed with exterior walls that supported themselves, requiring those walls to become progressively thicker nearer the bottom to provide the necessary strength. To achieve the amount of office space Stearns needed, his building would have to be tall – so tall that the bottom walls would need to be six feet (1.8 m) thick, leaving a ground floor just eight feet (2.4 m) wide.

Bradford Gilbert's answer was to build an iron skeleton to take the weight of the walls, which allowed him to construct a narrow tower 11 storeys high and 158 ft (48 m) tall. The Tower Building is thought to have been the first building in the world to employ such a metal frame, an innovation that, along with the invention of the elevator, would finally make the building of skyscrapers feasible.

The Tower Building was so tall and

narrow, just 21 ft (6.4 m) wide, and appeared so precarious, that at the first hint of a breeze crowds gathered on Broadway, at a safe distance, and started to place bets on when the whole thing would blow down. In order to prove the durability of his tower, Gilbert climbed an outside ladder to the top of the building during a gale and waved from the window of his office on the top floor. The building's owner John Stearns set out to climb the building with Gilbert, but lost his nerve halfway up and lay down on a scaffolding, unable to move, until the storm had passed.

Gilbert died in 1911 and three years later, in 1914, his pioneering masterpiece was torn down to make way for an even taller building.

There is some dispute over whether the Tower Building can be described as the world's first skyscraper, as others were experimenting with the idea of a skeleton frame at the same time, but Gilbert was the first to actually employ the idea and there can be no doubt that his Tower Building was a major influence in the evolution of tall buildings.

Peach War

NO. 1 EXCHANGE PLAZA, a 1982 office block on the corner of Broadway and Exchange Alley, stands in the middle of what was once an orchard belonging to a Dutch settler called HENDRICK VAN DYCK. In the autumn of 1655, Van Dyck spied a young Indian girl picking a peach from one of his trees, and in a rage he shot and killed her with his rifle. In retaliation, a force of some 500 Indian warriors attacked the colony of New

Amsterdam, which had been left undefended because Director Peter Stuyvesant had taken the garrison to secure the colony of New Sweden on the Delaware River for the Dutch. After ransacking New Amsterdam the Indians moved on to the other Dutch settlements at Hoboken, Staten Island and the Bronx, and some 150 Dutch settlers were killed.

Tallest in the World

No. 66 Broadway was once the address of the tallest skyscraper in the world, the 348 ft (106 m) high MANHATTAN LIFE INSURANCE BUILDING, opened in 1894 and demolished in 1963 to make way for an extension of No. 1 Wall Street.

Trinity Church

The slender Gothic steeple of TRINITY CHURCH soars above Broadway and gazes east down Wall Street, God

keeping an eye on Mammon. The brownstone church is by no means intimidated by the mighty towers of finance that loom all around it – Trinity has been here longer than they and is most probably richer than they are too (*see* below).

The present building is the third church built here, on land that was purchased by New York's Anglican community in 1696. In 1697 Trinity received a royal charter from King William III of England, with the church to pay an annual rent to the Crown of one peppercorn and to be run in accordance with Church of England doctrines. The first church building, a simple rectangular affair, was completed in March 1698.

Property

In 1705 Queen Anne gave Trinity a further grant of more than 200 acres (80 ha) of land west of Broadway. This was known as the Queen's Farm, and it stretched from the present-day Fulton Street right up into Greenwich Village. Although some of this land was later given over to the city, Trinity still owns 26 commercial buildings in Lower Manhattan, a total of nearly six million square feet (557,000 sq m) of commercial office space, which generates rents of millions of dollars every year, making Trinity THE RICHEST PARISH IN THE WORLD – and it still has all the rights to Manhattan's shipwrecks and beached whales.

Some 60 acres (24 ha) of the Queen's Farm had originally belonged to the widow of Everardus Bogardus, dominie of Manhattan's first church, whose heirs in 1671 had happily handed over to the Crown what was then a pretty worthless patch of land. Her descendants eventually realised their mistake and spent much of the next 200 years contesting in court Trinity's right to what is now some of the most valuable land in the world.

Education

In 1709 Trinity founded the CHARITY SCHOOL, whose pupils gathered for lessons in the church tower. Now known as TRINITY SCHOOL, it is THE OLDEST EDUCATIONAL ESTABLISHMENT IN CONTINUOUS USE IN NEW YORK, and the fifth oldest school in the United States.

In 1754 Trinity granted some land north of the church for a new college chartered by King George II to be called KING'S COLLEGE. The first students of what is now COLUMBIA UNIVERSITY met in a small school building near the church.

Fire

In 1776 the church was burned down in a fire that engulfed New York during the Revolution. Once independence had been achieved, a replacement church was begun and in 1784 Trinity's charter was ratified by the New York State Legislature, with the requirement of pledging loyalty to the British Crown removed. In 1787 SAMUEL PROVOST, the Rector of Trinity and chaplain to the Continental Congress, was consecrated as THE FIRST BISHOP OF NEW YORK.

The second Trinity Church was consecrated in 1790 but the structure was unsound and had to be taken down after being weakened by severe snowstorms in 1839.

Present Church

The present Trinity church was completed in 1846. Designed by English-born architect RICHARD UPJOHN, FIRST PRESIDENT OF THE AMERICAN INSTITUTE OF ARCHITECTS, the church is considered one of the finest early examples of Gothic Revival architecture in America, and was one of the very first American churches to have stained-glass windows. The spire, rising to 280 ft (85 m), was THE HIGHEST POINT IN NEW YORK for 44 years until overtaken by the New York World Building in 1890.

The great bronze doors of the church were designed by RICHARD MORRIS HUNT (architect of the Statue of Liberty pedestal) and were installed in 1893. They were donated by WILLIAM WALDORF ASTOR in memory of his father John Jacob Astor III.

Trinity Churchyard

TRINITY CHURCHYARD contains a number of interesting monuments and gravestones. In the section to the north of the church stands the splendid SOLDIER'S MONUMENT, dedicated to the memory of the American patriots who died in British prisons during the Revolution.

Nearby, to the left of the Soldier's Monument, is one of the more unusual gravestones in New York, that of JAMES LEESON, an innkeeper and mason at New York's Jerusalem Lodge, who died in 1794. Carved along the curve of the top of the gravestone are a number of mysterious symbols, which for years went unidentified, until the church newspaper, the *Trinity Record*, came up with an explanation. The symbols were part of a pigpen cipher, or freemason's cipher, a simple code that uses a noughts-and-crosses board to substitute symbols for letters. In this case the message spelt out across the top of James Leeson's gravestone is REMEMBER DEATH.

18th-Century Publicity Stunt?

Another mystery to be found in Trinity churchyard is the grave of CHARLOTTE TEMPLE, a fictional character from one of America's first bestsellers, *Charlotte Temple, A Tale of Truth*, written by SUSANNA ROWSON and published in 1790. The novel is about a young English girl who is seduced by a rakish British army officer and then abandoned, pregnant, in New York. She dies after giving birth. For 200 years the simple brownstone slab bearing Charlotte Temple's name in Trinity churchyard was a place of pilgrimage for fans of the book, who believed that this was the burial place of CHARLOTTE STANLEY, the tragic young New York girl upon whom the story is said to be based. In 2008 the slab was lifted to reveal that there was nothing underneath.

Notable New Yorkers
Buried in Trinity Churchyard

South

ALEXANDER HAMILTON (1755–1804), the first U.S. Treasury Secretary and founder of the Bank of New York.

GEORGE TEMPLETON STRONG (1820–75), lawyer and diarist, whose diary is considered the definitive record of life during the American Civil War.

CAPTAIN JAMES LAWRENCE (1781–1813), American Naval Officer celebrated for his dying words 'Don't give up the ship!', spoken while his frigate USS *Chesapeake* was engaging the British frigate HMS *Shannon* off Boston, Massachusetts.

North

WILLIAM BRADFORD (1660–1752), printer in 1725 of New York's first newspaper, the *New York Gazette*.

FRANCIS LEWIS (1713–1803), the only signatory of the Declaration of Independence to be buried in Manhattan.

ALBERT GALLATIN (1761–1849), fourth and longest-serving U.S. Treasury Secretary, founder and first president of New York University (NYU).

ROBERT FULTON (1765–1815), inventor of the world's first practical steamboat, the *Clermont*, which was launched on the Hudson River in 1807.

Well, I never knew this
about

LOWER BROADWAY –
BOWLING GREEN TO TRINITY CHURCH

There have been more songs written about Broadway than about any other street in the world. Examples are:

'Give My Regards to Broadway' (George M. Cohan)

'Lullaby of Broadway' (music by Harry Warren, lyrics by Al Dubin)

'On Broadway' (Mann/Weil/Leiber/Stoller), sung by the Drifters.

On the south-west lawn of Bowling Green there is a commemorative stone in honour of PETER CAESAR ALBERTI, THE FIRST ITALIAN SETTLER IN NEW YORK. Alberti, a Venetian, landed on this spot from the Dutch ship *King David* on 2 June 1635. He went on to marry a Dutch woman, have seven children, and establish a plantation on Long Island. In 1655, he and his wife were killed in the Indian raid provoked by the Peach War. 2 June is now known amongst New York's Italian community as 'Alberti Day'.

Set in a small flower bed on the lawn to the north of the fountain in Bowling Green is a memorial marker to FRANCIS MAKEMIE, the FATHER OF AMERICAN PRESBYTERIANISM, an Irishman from County Donegal who founded America's first Presbyterian Community at Snow Hill in Maryland in 1683. In 1707

Makemie was arrested at Bowling Green on the orders of the Governor, Lord Cornbury, for 'preaching without a licence'. After spending six weeks in jail, Makemie was acquitted on the basis of the English Toleration Act of 1689, but although found innocent he was forced to pay the court costs, a decision so outrageous that the New York legislature introduced a law prohibiting such a thing from ever happening again. Makemie's acquittal was THE FIRST IMPORTANT VICTORY FOR RELIGIOUS TOLERANCE IN AMERICA and is considered a landmark case.

Among the prominent New Yorkers who died on the *Titanic* were JOHN JACOB ASTOR IV, one of the richest men in the world, BENJAMIN GUGGENHEIM, mining magnate and brother of the founder of New York's Guggenheim Museum, and the co-owner of Macy's, ISIDOR STRAUS and his wife IDA.

Trinity churchyard contains THE OLDEST GRAVESTONE IN NEW YORK, that of RICHARD CHURCHER, who died aged five in 1681, 16 years before Trinity Church received its charter. His gravestone is to be found right at the front of the graveyard to the north of the church, and can be seen through the fence from Broadway.

In the 2004 movie *National Treasure*, starring Nicolas Cage, the 'treasure' was discovered hidden in a secret vault beneath Trinity Church.

When Queen Elizabeth II visited Trinity Church on 9 July 1976, exactly 200 years after the statue of her ancestor King George III had been toppled on Bowling Green, she was presented with 279 peppercorns in back rent.

CHAPTER 4

A WALK DOWN
WALL STREET

New York Stock Exchange

Wall Street

Start point: Trinity Church

WALL STREET takes it name from the wall erected along the northern border of New Amsterdam, on the orders of Dutch director Peter Stuyvesant, in 1653, to protect the city against an invasion from the north by the British. The street also follows the line of the wall, which was a 9 ft (2.7 m) high wooden palisade that ran from the western shoreline, where Trinity churchyard is now, to the eastern shoreline at Pearl Street. The defensive capabilities of the wall were never tested as New Amsterdam was given up without a fight, and the British demolished the wall in 1699. Since the establishment of a permanent home for the New York Stock Exchange at the junction of Wall Street and Broad Street in 1865, the term Wall Street has become synonymous with high finance and is often used to refer to the entire financial district of New York.

No. 1 Wall Street

Across Broadway from Trinity Church is No. 1 WALL STREET, global headquarters of THE WORLD'S LARGEST DEPOSIT BANK, THE BANK OF NEW YORK MELLON CORPORATION. The 50-storey, 654 ft (199 m) high art deco building was completed in 1931 to be the new headquarters of the Irving Trust Company, who moved here from the Woolworth Building. The pointed windows of No. 1 Wall Street mirror the Gothic design of Trinity Church, while the art deco interior is among the most splendid in New York.

In 1988 the Irving Trust Company was taken over by the Bank of New York.

Bank of New York

The BANK OF NEW YORK was founded in 1784, not long after the departure of British troops from New York, by ALEXANDER HAMILTON and a number of prominent New York businessmen, among them ISAAC ROOSEVELT, great-great grandfather of Franklin D. Roosevelt. They all responded to an advertisement in the *New York Packet* for 'Gentlemen of this City to establish a BANK on liberal principles'. Hamilton was chosen to write the bank's constitution, and its first headquarters was established in the mansion home on Pearl Street of shipping merchant WILLIAM WALTON.

In 1789, as THE FIRST U.S. TREASURY SECRETARY, Hamilton was able to negotiate the U.S. GOVERNMENT'S FIRST EVER LOAN. Issued by the Bank of New York, it was for $200,000 and was key to establishing the creditworthiness and economic independence of the new government.

The Bank of New York's stock was THE FIRST CORPORATE STOCK TRADED ON THE NEW YORK STOCK EXCHANGE when the exchange was formed in 1792, and for the first 15 years of its existence the Bank of New York financed virtually all of New York's commercial activity. As the industrial age got underway, the bank raised money for the Erie Canal, railroads and the New York subway system.

In 1988 the bank moved to No. 1 Wall Street and in 2007 it merged with the MELLON FINANCIAL CORPORATION, creating the WORLD'S LARGEST SECURITIES SERVICING PROVIDER.

Now walk east down Wall Street, with your back to Trinity Church, until you reach the junction with Nassau and Broad Streets, and you will find yourself at the very heart of New York's financial district. Across the road, on the corner with Nassau Street stands the . . .

Federal Hall National Memorial

If any place could be said to be the birthplace of the United States as an independent nation then this place is it, for it was here, on the balcony of the original Federal Hall that stood here until 1812, that GEORGE WASHINGTON

was sworn in as THE 1ST PRESIDENT OF THE UNITED STATES, receiving the presidential oath from New York's CHANCELLOR ROBERT R. LIVINGSTON. The date was 30 April 1789 and the event is commemorated by a statue of Washington, positioned on the front steps of the present hall at the actual point where the President would have been standing on the balcony of the old hall. The statue was sculpted by JOHN QUINCY ADAMS WARD and was unveiled in 1883.

The first Federal Hall was built here in 1699 to replace the Stadt Huys on Pearl Street as New York's City Hall. In 1735 the publisher John Peter Zenger was imprisoned and tried in the hall, while in October 1765 the STAMP ACT CONGRESS, attended by delegates from nine of the original 13 states, met there to protest about 'taxation without representation'.

After the Revolution, in 1788, City Hall was enlarged and remodelled by PIERRE L'ENFANT (who would go on to design Washington D.C.) to serve as THE FIRST

CAPITOL OF THE UNITED STATES. It was renamed Federal Hall, and on 4 March 1789 the 1ST U.S. CONGRESS met there to form the new federal government and count the votes that saw George Washington elected as U.S. President. On 25 September 1789, the United States BILL OF RIGHTS was adopted at Federal Hall by the 1st Congress, cementing the freedoms and rights that had been demanded by the Stamp Act Congress in that same hall 24 years before.

In 1790 the federal government transferred to Philadelphia and Federal Hall became City Hall once more. In 1812 the building was pulled down and New York's government moved north up Broadway to a new City Hall on the Commons.

The grand Greek Revival building that stands here today was put up in 1842 as the New York Customs House and was later used as a Sub Treasury, where the country's gold and silver bullion was stored. The bullion was moved to the Federal Reserve in Liberty Street in 1920 and the building is now operated by the

National Parks Services and serves as a tourism centre and museum.

Morgan Bank

Directly across Wall Street on the corner with Broad Street, at No. 23, is the former home of MORGAN'S BANK. JOHN PIERPONT MORGAN (1837–1913) was a businessman, railroad magnate and the dominant banker of his generation. He organised the formation of a number of huge industrial conglomerates such as General Electric, AT&T and the United States Steel Corporation and was so successful at restructuring failing businesses that the process became known as 'Morganization'. In 1907 Morgan was asked by the government to intervene in a banking crisis, which was averted when he contributed money from his own bank to a rescue fund and persuaded other Wall Street bankers to do the same, locking them into the magnificent library at his home on 36th Street, until they agreed to pay up.

The Morgan Bank moved to this corner of Wall Street in 1873, and at the end of the 20th century decided to build a new headquarters on the site. To ensure that there would be enough marble for their new building the bank bought an entire marble quarry in Tennessee. J.P. Morgan himself never got to see his new headquarters, for he died just before the building was completed in 1913. He was succeeded by his son J.P. Morgan Jr.

While all the other banks and financial institutions of Wall Street were throwing up showy skyscrapers to boost their image, the House of Morgan was secure enough in its wealth and reputation to require just four storeys for its new head office, while the name of Morgan was so famous that it was deemed unnecessary to fix a nameplate by the door.

In 1920 an anarchist bomb exploded in the street outside, killing 30 people and spraying the bank with debris. It was assumed that J.P. Morgan Jr. was the target, and as a reminder of the outrage the pockmarks on the wall of

---

The Morgan Library

J.P. Morgan's library, on East 36th Street off Madison Avenue, contains one of the finest collections of rare books and manuscripts in the world and was opened to the public in 1924. It is housed in a palazzo-style building erected in 1902, with an annexe added in 1928. In 1988 the 19th-century brownstone house where J.P. Morgan Jr. lived was incorporated into the library complex via a garden courtyard. Highlights of the collection include a Gutenberg Bible printed in 1455, the world's largest collection of Robert Burns's letters, scraps of paper on which Bob Dylan had scribbled the lyrics to 'Blowin' in the Wind', original drawings by William Blake, and an autographed manuscript of Charles Dickens's *A Christmas Carol*.

the bank have never been repaired. Morgan's Bank eventually merged and vacated No. 23 Wall Street in 2000. The building is now offices.

New York Stock

Exchange

The NEW YORK STOCK EXCHANGE (NYSE) was formed in May 1792 by a small group of traders who met daily in the shade of a buttonwood (sycamore) tree growing outside their offices at No. 68 Wall Street. Later that year they all signed up to what became known as the BUTTONWOOD AGREEMENT, and their tiny, informal organisation grew into THE LARGEST STOCK EXCHANGE IN THE WORLD. Today, a small sycamore tree stands outside the NYSE in memory of the buttonwood tree beneath which the exchange was founded.

One of the first rules the early traders made was that they would only trade with each other, and until 2006 you could still only trade on the NYSE if

you were a member. Membership was limited to 1,366, and in good years seats sometimes changed hands for upwards of $4 million. In 2006 the NYSE became a for-profit, publicly traded company and traders now purchase licences for one year.

For the first years of its existence the stock exchange had no permanent home of its own and would most usually meet at TONTINE'S COFFEE HOUSE on the corner of Wall Street and Water Street. The exchange moved to its present site on Broad Street in 1865, but by the turn of the century business had increased so much that more space was needed, so in 1901 the old exchange building was knocked down and the present, grand neo-classical building opened for business in 1903.

The square in front of the stock exchange has seen many crowd gatherings in times of financial turmoil, most famously during the Great Wall Street Crash of October 1929, which ushered in the Great Depression, when anxious investors massed outside the exchange waiting for news of their stocks and shares.

After 9/11 a huge American flag was draped across the Broad Street Colonnade, and in 2011 the stock exchange was the focus of Occupy Wall Street demonstrations.

No. 40 Wall Street

Continue east on Wall Street until you come to No. 40 on your left. Now the TRUMP TOWER, this was originally the BANK OF MANHATTAN TRUST BUILDING,

morally the tallest because the Chrysler spire was purely ornamental while their Manhattan Building had THE HIGHEST USABLE FLOOR IN THE WORLD, the Observation Deck, which was at least 100 ft (30 m) higher than the Chrysler Building's highest usable floor. It made no difference. No. 40 Wall Street had been the tallest building in the world for less than a month.

Perhaps, then, there was a certain justice when the Chrysler Building itself was overtaken less than a year later by the Empire State Building.

and THE TALLEST BUILDING IN THE WORLD – briefly. It took only 11 months to build, largely because it was involved in a race with the Chrysler Building to be the tallest in the world. When completed in 1930 the Bank of Manhattan Trust Building was 927 ft (283 m) high, 136 ft (41 m) higher than the previous tallest building in the world, the Woolworth Building. More importantly, it was 2 ft (0.6 m) higher than the Chrysler Building, which was about to be topped off at 925 ft (282 m). Walter Chrysler, however, had hatched a dastardly plan, and as soon as the Manhattan bankers were congratulating themselves on owning the tallest building in the world, Chrysler hoisted into place a previously concealed 125 ft (38 m) high stainless steel spire, which gave the Chrysler Building an overall height of 1,046 ft (319 m). Shreve and Lamb, the architects of No. 40 Wall Street, cried foul, claiming that their building was

Nos. 48–95
Wall Street

Continue east on Wall Street. At No. 48 is the MUSEUM OF AMERICAN FINANCE, occupying what was once the banking hall of the Bank of New York Building of 1928. This was the former site of the Bank of New York's first purpose-built head office, constructed in 1797.

No. 52 is where the CITY BANK OF NEW YORK, now Citibank, was founded in 1812. On 20 March 1831 No. 52 became the scene of THE FIRST BANK ROBBERY IN U.S. HISTORY, when a villain called EDWARD SMITH robbed the City Bank of $245,000. He was soon caught and sentenced to five years in Sing Sing prison.

No. 58 is where Alexander Hamilton lived from 1783 to 1790, while working on the Bank of New York.

No. 68 is close to the site of the original buttonwood tree under which the founders of the NYSE gathered, while the Tontine Coffee House, where they later met, stood further down on the corner of Water Street at No. 82.

Diagonally across Water Street at No. 95 is the site of the MERCHANT'S COFFEE HOUSE where, in 1784, the Bank of New York was brought into being, over coffee, by Alexander Hamilton and a group of businessmen.

Not Quite There

Now walk north up Water Street, which was the location of NEW YORK'S SLAVE MARKET until 1762, turn left down narrow Pine Street, cross Pearl Street and on your right is No. 70, the AMERICAN INTERNATIONAL BUILDING (AIB), built by the oil baron Henry Doherty. The AIB building was one of the competitors in the 1930 race to be tallest in the world, and at 952 ft (290 m) high it did beat the Bank of Manhattan Building by 55 ft (17 m) when it was completed in 1932, to become THE TALLEST BUILDING IN LOWER MANHATTAN. The race to be tallest in the world had already been lost by then, first to the Chrysler Building

and then to the Empire State Building.

For 75 years though, the AIB could proudly claim to be THE TALLEST BUILDING IN NEW YORK NOT TO HAVE BEEN THE TALLEST BUILDING IN THE WORLD. Alas, even that consolation was taken away in 2007 by the New York Times Building, which in turn was robbed of the title in 2012 by the Freedom Tower.

Note the 12 ft (3.6 m) high scale model of the building over the entrance, carved in stone and complete with its own scale model of the scale model.

Federal Reserve

Continue west on Pine Street, go right on to William Street, walk north and then turn left on to Liberty Street. The whole block on the right hand side of the street is occupied by the NEW YORK FEDERAL RESERVE BANK, which contains THE LARGEST HOARD OF GOLD IN THE WORLD, held in THE DEEPEST VAULTS IN NEW YORK, 80 ft (24 m) below street level.

Now continue west along Liberty Street and return to Broadway.

Well, I never knew this
about
WALL STREET

ALEXANDER HAMILTON (1755–1804), founder of the Bank of New York, was THE ONLY NEW YORKER TO SIGN THE AMERICAN CONSTITUTION. He co-founded the NATIONAL BANK, the

U.S. MINT and the U.S. COASTGUARD (as the Revenue Marine), and wrote JAY'S TREATY, with which the new U.S. Chief Justice John Jay negotiated favourable trade terms with Britain. In

AARON BURR [1756–1836], meanwhile, despite a distinguished career as a senator for New York and as Vice President to Thomas Jefferson, will always be remembered for murdering Alexander Hamilton. Jefferson dropped him as his Vice President for the election in 1804 and Burr's political career was finished. He returned to practise law in New York and lived out the rest of his long life in obscurity, dying on Staten Island in 1836 aged 80.

1801 he founded the NEW-YORK EVENING POST, which is now AMERICA'S OLDEST CONTINUOUSLY PUBLISHED DAILY NEWSPAPER. For such a distinguished Founding Father, Alexander Hamilton came to a surprisingly sticky end.

As an opponent, both politically and personally, of his fellow New York politician Aaron Burr, Hamilton frustrated Burr's candidacy for the U.S. Presidency in 1800 and for the governorship of New York in 1804. Finally, in July of 1804, Burr could take no more and challenged Hamilton to a duel, after Hamilton had been overheard making some derogatory remarks about Burr at a dinner party, remarks that were later published in the newspapers. Hamilton refused to apologise and they met for a duel in Weehawken, New Jersey, on the morning of 11 July 1804 (duelling was illegal in New York). Hamilton was shot in the stomach and died the next day. He was given a hero's burial, with thousands lining his funeral procession along Broadway to Trinity Church, where he is buried.

ROBERT R. LIVINGSTON (1746–1813), who administered the oath to George Washington in Federal Hall, went on to become THE FIRST U.S. SECRETARY OF FOREIGN AFFAIRS, a position that evolved into Secretary of State. He was later appointed as U.S. MINISTER TO FRANCE during which time he negotiated the LOUISIANA PURCHASE, which more than doubled the size of the United States. The territory gained stretched from the Mississippi to the Rocky Mountains and worked out at roughly 42 cents an acre ($1 a hectare).

On the wall of the Federal Hall in Nassau Street there is a bronze map of Ohio, which commemorates the OHIO COMPANY, a group of Revolutionary Army officers who got together in 1786 to plan and organise the settlement of territory north-west of the Ohio River. In 1787 they met with Congress at Federal Hall to discuss the purchase of the land, and in July that year Congress passed the NORTHWEST ORDNANCE, creating the Northwest Territory, which would become the states of Ohio, Indiana, Illinois, Michigan and Wisconsin.

The highlight of the museum in the Federal Hall National Memorial is the GEORGE WASHINGTON INAUGURAL BIBLE. Printed in London in 1625, the Bible was loaned to Washington for his inauguration by a local New York Masonic Lodge and has since been used at the inaugurations of Presidents Warren G. Harding, Dwight D. Eisenhower, Jimmy Carter and most recently George H. W. Bush, whose inauguration in 1989 took place exactly 200 years after Washington's.

The FIRST RECORDED PLAY IN NEW YORK, as reported in the *New England and Boston Gazette* of 1 January 1733, was a performance of George Farquhar's *The Recruiting Officer* at the 'New Theater' on Nassau Street, on 11 December 1732. The New Theater was a converted warehouse belonging to the acting governor of the colony RIP VAN DAM. There is some suggestion that a rival theatre was set up in a back room of ABRAHAM CORBETT'S TAVERN on Broadway at Beaver Street, near the governor's quarters, by WILLIAM COSBY, who succeeded Van Dam as governor. The two disliked each other intensely.

The Bank of the Manhattan Company, which opened its first office at No. 40 Wall Street in 1799, was founded by Aaron Burr as a rival to Alexander Hamilton's Bank of New York.

In 1946 a U.S. Army Air Force plane crashed into the 58th floor of No. 40 Wall Street, the Bank of Manhattan Trust Building, in thick fog, killing all five people on board. No one in the building, or on the street below, was injured.

CHAPTER 5

Lower Broadway – Trinity Church to St Paul's Chapel. The World Trade Center

The Equitable Building

No. 120 Broadway

THE EQUITABLE BUILDING, which stands at No. 120 Broadway, is a most significant building in the story of modern New York's architectural development, for this was the building that provoked the city's zoning laws, which for 50 years defined the shape of New York's skyscrapers.

When completed in 1915, the Equitable Building was the LARGEST OFFICE BLOCK IN THE WORLD, the HEAVIEST STRUCTURE ON EARTH and boasted MORE ELEVATORS THAN ANY OTHER BUILDING IN THE WORLD. Consisting of two massive blocks connected by a middle wing, and shaped like an 'H' when seen from above, the building can accommodate 12,000 people and provides 1,200,000 sq ft

(111,500 sq m) of floor space, some 30 times the size of the plot on which it stands. It rises straight up to a height of 538 ft (164 m) and casts a seven-acre (2.8 ha) shadow across the city, blotting out the sun completely from the streets below and from the first 20 storeys of the neighbouring buildings.

New Yorkers were mightily worried that if many more buildings like this were put up, then the streets of Manhattan would become dark ravines, cold and sunless, so in 1916 the city adopted a zoning resolution that required all new buildings to incorporate setbacks as they rose in height, allowing sunlight to reach through to street level. The measure had the effect of inspiring some of the world's most admired and distinctive skyscrapers such as the Chrysler Building and the Empire State Building.

Equitable Life Assurance Building

The predecessor of the Equitable Building at No. 120 Broadway was the EQUITABLE LIFE ASSURANCE BUILDING, 130 ft (40 m) high and THE TALLEST OFFICE BLOCK IN THE WORLD when it was built in 1870. It was also THE FIRST OFFICE BUILDING IN THE WORLD TO FEATURE PASSENGER ELEVATORS, one reason why it was sometimes referred to as the 'WORLD'S FIRST SKYSCRAPER'. Tourists flocked there to ride the elevators and take in the view from the roof. Although advertised as fireproof, the Equitable Life Assurance Building burned down in January 1912, in a winter so cold that the water from the

fire trucks froze on to the ruins of the structure, turning it into a giant ice sculpture.

Luck and Joie de Vivre

The bright red cube precariously balanced on the plaza outside the HSBC building at No. 140 Broadway seems to symbolise the roll of the dice, or luck. It was created in 1968 by the Japanese–American artist ISAMU NOGUCHI and certainly brightens up this part of Broadway.

Immediately across Broadway, in ZUCCOTTI PARK, is the equally red, 70 ft (21 m) high abstract expressionist sculpture JOIE DE VIVRE, by MARK DI SUVERO. Zuccotti Park used to be called Liberty Plaza Park, but it was renamed and revamped after the September 11 bombings.

One resident of Zuccotti Park who was unmoved by the death and destruction that rained down around him on that day is DOUBLE CHECK, a bronze stockbroker who was found afterwards still sitting on his park bench checking through his paperwork amidst the dust

and debris. *Double Check*, created by
J. SEWARD JOHNSON JR. and placed here
in 1982, has become a much cherished
emblem of New York's endurance and
spirit.

First Movie Show

It seems fitting that THE FIRST MOVING
PICTURE EVER TO BE SHOWN ON A
SCREEN TO A PAYING AUDIENCE was
shown on Broadway, home of showbiz
in all its many forms. The movie was a
four-minute film of a boxing match
between 'Battling' Charles Barnett and
an Australian boxer called Albert
Griffiths, known as 'Young Griffo',
filmed on the roof of Madison Square
Garden by WOODVILLE LATHAM. The
date of the showing was 20 May 1895,
the place a storefront at No. 153
BROADWAY. Alas, being the site of this
moment in movie history was not
enough to save No. 153 Broadway from
being obliterated, along with all the
other shops in the row, when Singer
Sewing Machines wanted to put up their
new headquarters on this exact spot.

Singer and Steel

The fabulous SINGER BUILDING, 612 ft
(186 m) high and easily THE TALLEST
BUILDING IN THE WORLD when completed
in 1908, was designed by Ernest Flagg as
the headquarters of the Singer
Manufacturing Company, founded in
1851 by Isaac Singer, whose wife was the
model for the Statue of Liberty. The
actual offices were accommodated in the

lower block of 12 storeys while the stunning, 65 ft square (6 sq m) red-brick and
bluestone *beaux-arts* tower, with its
distinctive bulbous top, recognisable
from miles away, served largely as an
enormous advertisement for Singer
Sewing Machines.

On moving its headquarters to the
Rockefeller Center in 1961, Singer sold
the tower to a developer who was
hoping to tempt the New York Stock
Exchange to relocate there, but due to
the shape of the building there was too
little office space and so it was sold to
U.S. Steel, who dismantled the whole
structure and replaced it with the 743 ft
(226 m) high skyscraper we see there
today, One Liberty Plaza.

When the Singer Building was taken down in 1967 it became THE TALLEST BUILDING EVER TO BE LEGITIMATELY DEMOLISHED. With hindsight its disappearance is regarded as one of New York's greatest architectural losses.

Down Time

Embedded in the sidewalk on the northeast corner of Broadway and Maiden Lane is one of Manhattan's most unexpected treats, a large clock with roman numerals set in a brass surround inscribed with the words WILLIAM BARTHMAN SINCE 1884. The clock was put there in 1899 as a novel form of advertisement by WILLIAM BARTHMAN, a German immigrant who set up his jewellery shop at No. 174 Broadway in 1884, when this area was at the heart of New York's jewellery trade.

Known as the 'Downtown Tiffany', Barthman's is the OLDEST JEWELLER IN NEW YORK and was for a long time the only jeweller left in the Financial District. Over the years it has been patronised by Vanderbilts and Guggenheims as well as such luminaries as J.P. Morgan and Lillie Langtry, actress and mistress of Edward VII.

The Barthman Clock can only be accessed from vaults below the pavement, and in 1946 the NYPD estimated that every day 51,000 people stepped over it or trod on it between the hours of 11 a.m. and 2 p.m. But how many of them know it is there?

In 1911 a runaway horse smashed into the Barthman shop window, scattering jewels all across Broadway, but the clock remained undamaged. Ninety years later the shop window was shattered once again, this time by debris from the collapse of the Twin Towers, but still the clock ticked on.

In 2006 William Barthman moved next door to bigger premises at No. 176 Broadway.

Former AT&T Building

The façade of the former AT&T BUILDING, constructed for the American Telephone and Telegraph in 1923 at No. 195 Broadway, boasts MORE CLASSICAL COLUMNS THAN ANY OTHER FAÇADE IN THE WORLD, 198 of them in all, made from Vermont granite. The remarkable lobby is graced with columns too, 50 Doric columns made of marble, with the result that the interior of No. 195 Broadway boasts MORE MARBLE THAN ANY OTHER BUILDING IN NEW YORK.

On 25 January 1915, ALEXANDER GRAHAM BELL, the inventor of the telephone, made the FIRST TRANSCONTINENTAL TELEPHONE CALL from an office on this location, which at that

Time Ball

Before it was AT&T, the site at No. 195 Broadway was occupied by the telegraph company WESTERN UNION, whose headquarters, built in 1875, was crowned with a clock tower 230 ft (70 m) high. It was one of the tallest buildings in New York at the time and from 1877 a Time Ball, prompted by a signal from the National Observatory in Washington D.C., was dropped from the top of the clock tower at exactly noon every day, to serve as a chronometer for the ships in the harbour. Between 1883 and 1912 the Time Ball was also used as the starting point for U.S. Standard Railway Time.

time had the address No. 15 Dey Street – Dey Street runs west off Broadway here. The call was to his assistant, THOMAS WATSON, in San Francisco, and Bell replicated his words from when he made the world's very first telephone call in 1876, 'Mr Watson, come here, I want you,' to which Watson replied, 'It would take me a week now.'

On 7 January 1927, WALTER S. GIFFORD, President of AT&T, placed the WORLD'S FIRST TRANSATLANTIC TELEPHONE CALL from No. 195 Broadway to Sir Evelyn P. Murray, secretary of the General Post Office of Great Britain in London.

On 7 April 1927, Gifford placed the WORLD'S FIRST 'PICTUREPHONE' CALL from No. 195 Broadway to the Secretary of Commerce, Herbert Hoover, who was in Washington. The listeners in New York could see, as well as hear, Hoover in Washington.

St Paul's Chapel

ST PAUL'S CHAPEL comes as quite a surprise. Standing four-square and Georgian amongst the towering neoclassical and art deco office blocks of downtown, it appears almost too perfect to be real. It was built in 1764 as a chapel of ease for parishioners of Trinity who were unable to reach the main church. St Paul's Chapel was modelled

on St Martin-in-the Fields in London –
and indeed, like St Martin, St Paul's was
surrounded by fields when it was built.

The chapel survived the fire of 1776,
which destroyed the original Trinity
Church, partly because it was further
from the heart of the blaze and also
because firefighters positioned themselves on the flat roof wielding buckets
of water to keep the flames at bay.

St Paul's Chapel is now THE OLDEST
BUILDING IN MANHATTAN IN CONTIN-
UOUS USE and THE ONLY SURVIVING
CHURCH FROM NEW YORK'S COLONIAL
DAYS.

Box Pew

The interior of St Paul's Chapel is very
little changed from the April day in 1789
when George Washington attended a
service of thanksgiving here after his inauguration as the 1st President of the United
States. Since Trinity Church was being
rebuilt at the time, Washington continued
to worship at St Paul's Chapel until he
moved to Philadelphia in 1790. Outside
the chapel there is a slightly misleading
sign exhorting you to go in and 'See
George Washington's Pew' – alas, the
splendid box pew inside the chapel is only
a replica of the one Washington sat in,
and you cannot therefore experience the
touch of the very same wood grain that
the 1st President touched.

Wild Turkey

Above the pew hangs THE FIRST KNOWN
COLOUR REPRESENTATION OF THE GREAT
SEAL OF THE UNITED STATES, an original
oil painting done in 1785. The eagle in

the painting more closely resembles a
wild turkey than an eagle, which suggests
that Benjamin Franklin was involved
with the design of this particular seal – he
was a strong advocate for the adoption
of the wild turkey as America's national
bird rather than the eagle.

Across the chapel from Washington's
pew is the GOVERNOR'S PEW, where
GEORGE CLINTON, THE FIRST GOVERNOR
OF THE STATE OF NEW YORK, sat when
he attended the chapel.

Others who have worshipped at St
Paul's Chapel over the years are PRINCE
WILLIAM (later King William IV), who
attended while he was stationed in New
York as a midshipman during the
Revolution, LORD CORNWALLIS, the
British commander who surrendered to
American troops at the Battle of Yorktown
in 1780, and three U.S. Presidents, Grover
Cleveland, Benjamin Harrison and
George W. Bush.

Note the coronet with Prince of
Wales feathers on the canopy of the
pulpit, one of the few royal symbols in
New York to survive the Revolution.

Sanctuary

St Paul's Chapel stands just across the
street from the site of the World Trade

Center, but emerged miraculously unscathed from the collapse of the Twin Towers on 9/11, protected as it was by a giant sycamore tree that had been growing in the churchyard for nearly a century.

In 2005 artist Steve Tobin temporarily moved the stump of 'the tree that saved St Paul's' from the churchyard in order to create a huge bronze sculpture of the roots. The sculpture, called the TRINITY ROOT, was placed beside Trinity Church, while the stump was returned to St Paul's churchyard, where it stands as a defiant memorial to that dreadful day.

In the aftermath of the terrorist attacks, St Paul's Chapel acted as a sanctuary for those seeking shelter from the destruction, and in the following months served as a working centre for the recovery operation, filled day and night with weary firefighters, construction workers, police officers and volunteers. The chapel now houses a permanent display of photographs and exhibits about their remarkable rescue efforts.

A WALK AROUND
THE WORLD TRADE CENTER

Start point: St Paul's Chapel

World Trade Center

Just north of St Paul's Chapel turn left on to Vesey Street and walk to the new World Trade Center site.

September 11 2011

At 8.46 a.m. on the morning of 11 September 2001 the hijacked American Airlines Flight 11, originally bound for Los Angeles out of Boston, flew into the 93rd floor of the North Tower, 1 World Trade Center (WTC). Eighteen minutes later United Flight 175, also bound for Los Angeles out of Boston, hit the South Tower, 2 WTC, between the 77th and 85th floors. At 9.59 a.m. the South Tower collapsed, followed by the North Tower 29 minutes later.

The Marriot Hotel at 3 WTC, was completely destroyed as the Twin Towers fell, and the other three WTC towers were so badly damaged they were later demolished. 7 WTC, located outside the 16-acre (6.5 ha) WTC site, finally came down at 5.20 p.m. that day. Two other buildings, the Deutsche Bank Building on Liberty Street and the Fiterman Hall on West Broadway, also suffered such severe damage that they were eventually pulled down.

Two other planes were hijacked on that day. One was flown into the Pentagon, killing 184 people, while the passengers on United Flight 93 valiantly tried to overpower their hijackers, forcing their plane to crash in a field in Pennsylvania, killing all 40 people on board.

The final death toll may never be known, but between 2,750 and 3,000 people died, either on that day or as a result of the attacks, a heavier loss of life than during the entire Revolutionary War.

National September 11 Memorial and Museum

The WORLD TRADE CENTER site has been substantially rebuilt since the terrorist attacks on 11 September 2001, with five new skyscrapers and the NATIONAL SEPTEMBER 11 MEMORIAL AND MUSEUM, which replaces the Twin Towers.

The whole area is landscaped with trees, including the 'SURVIVOR TREE', a callery pear tree that was rescued from the rubble, revived, and replanted at the memorial site. Within the actual square footprints of the towers are two reflective pools with THE LARGEST MAN-MADE WATERFALLS IN AMERICA cascading down the sides of the parapets. The names of the victims of the terrorist attacks are inscribed on bronze plates attached to the parapet walls. Underground there is a museum dedicated to documenting and explaining the events of that day and its repercussions, with displays, exhibits and photographs.

The tallest and most spectacular of the new World Trade Center towers is ONE WORLD TRADE CENTER, better known as the FREEDOM TOWER, which stands at the north-west corner of the site. The roof of the tower is 1,385 ft (422 m) high, the exact height of the Twin Towers, while the top of the antenna reaches a symbolic 1,776 ft (541 m), making One World Trade Center THE TALLEST BUILDING IN NEW YORK, in place of the Empire State Building.

Battery Park City

Having walked around the site, leave the World Trade Center by the pedestrian bridge over West Street at the north-west corner and walk west along Vesey Street towards the Hudson. You are now in BATTERY PARK CITY, a commercial and residential complex built during the 1980s on 92 acres (37 ha) of landfill, collected largely from the excavations for the original World Trade Center. The neighbourhood was badly affected by the 9/11 attacks and most of the residents were required to leave their homes for some years while toxins and smoke pollutants were removed, but by 2009 the area was fully recovered and is now thriving.

Irish Hunger Memorial

At the end of Vesey Street is the IRISH HUNGER MEMORIAL, dedicated in 2002, which commemorates the Irish Famine of 1845 to 1852. The memorial resembles an Irish hillside and is constructed from materials brought from the west coast of Ireland, including stones from every Irish county and the ruins of an authentic 19th-century Irish cottage. A path ascends to the top of the hill, from where there are splendid views across the Hudson and the harbour.

World Financial Center

Now head to the river, turn left (south) and walk along the waterfront to the WORLD FINANCIAL CENTER, designed by Cesar Pelli and built between 1985 and 1988. There are four office towers that serve as headquarters for a number of the world's leading financial companies, such as Merrill Lynch, Nomura, Commerzbank and American Express.

The towers are grouped about the huge glass atrium of the WINTER GARDEN, a vast public space for concerts and exhibitions, flanked by shops and restaurants and opening out on to a piazza and marina. Sixteen 40 ft (12 m) high Washingtonia palm trees create a spectacular 'palm court' where you can sit on the sweeping white marble staircase and listen to beautiful music while the sun dapples through the trees and sparkles on the water outside. One of New York's great experiences.

All 2,000 panes of glass in the atrium were blown out by the terrorist attacks on 9/11 and had to be replaced, but the Winter Garden was swiftly repaired and reopened to the public in 2002.

Museum of Jewish Heritage

From the World Financial Center continue south along the river walk, enjoying the unobstructed view of the Statue of Liberty, go past South Cove and on to the MUSEUM OF JEWISH HERITAGE, housed in a distinctive hexagonal granite building with a stepped roof. The Museum, which opened in 1997, is designed as a living memorial to the Holocaust and the six sides of the building remember the six million Jews killed during the Holocaust, as well as the six points of the Star of David. The museum inside is organised around three themes on three floors, 'Jewish Life a Century Ago', 'The War Against the Jews' and 'Jewish Renewal'.

Skyscraper Museum

Across Battery Place, adjacent to the Ritz Carlton Hotel, at No. 39, is the SKYSCRAPER MUSEUM, opened in 1997 and THE ONLY MUSEUM OF ITS KIND IN THE WORLD. The museum is devoted to the study of high-rise buildings around the world with particular focus on their role in New York's architectural heritage.

New York's Skyscrapers

NEW YORK HAS MORE SKYSCRAPERS THAN ANY OTHER CITY ON THE EARTH except Hong Kong. Although there is no official definition of a skyscraper, New York possessed at least two buildings, both on Broadway and both now gone, that were

able to stake a reasonable claim to being
THE WORLD'S FIRST SKYSCRAPER, the
Equitable Life Assurance Building at
No. 120 Broadway (*see* page 56) and
the Tower Building at No. 50 Broadway
(*see* page 39).

New York's World Beaters

In 1890 the NEW YORK WORLD
BUILDING on Park Row reached a
height of 308 ft (94 m), to become the
tallest skyscraper in the world. Since
then New York has been able to boast
more of the world's tallest buildings
than any other city.

---

*New York's Matchless Array of Tallest
Non-Religious Buildings in the World:*

MANHATTAN LIFE INSURANCE BUILDING,
66 Broadway. Height 330 ft (100 m).
Tallest skyscraper in the world 1894–1895.
Demolished 1963.

PARK ROW BUILDING, 15 Park Row. Height
390 ft (119 m). Tallest skyscraper in the
world 1899–1901. Now commercial offices
and rental apartments.

In 1901 PHILADELPHIA CITY HALL became the first building in the
world to top the 530 ft (162 m) high spire of Ulm Minster in Germany,
which had, since 1890, been the tallest building in the world. Thereafter
New York's world beaters could genuinely use the title tallest building
in the world. The first to do so was the . . .

SINGER BUILDING, 149 Broadway (Now
1 Liberty Plaza). Height 612 ft (187 m).
Tallest building in the world, 1908–1909.
Demolished 1963.

METROPOLITAN LIFE TOWER, 1 Madison
Avenue. Height 700 ft (213 m). Tallest building
in the world 1909–1913. Now a hotel.

WOOLWORTH BUILDING, 233 Broadway. Height
791 ft (241 m). Tallest building in the world
1913–1930. Offices and luxury apartments.

BANK OF MANHATTAN TRUST BUILDING,
40 Wall Street. Height 927 ft (283 m). Tallest
building in the world 1930. Now the Trump
Building, commercial offices.

CHRYSLER BUILDING, Lexington Avenue. Height
1,050 ft (320 m). Tallest building in the world
1930–1931. When completed was the tallest
structure ever built. Now commercial offices.

EMPIRE STATE BUILDING, 350 Fifth
Avenue. Height 1,250 ft (381 m). Tallest
building in the world 1931–1972 (longest
period of any tallest building). Now
offices and a tourist attraction.

1 WORLD TRADE CENTER. Height 1,368 ft (417 m). Tallest building in
the world 1972–1974. Destroyed by terrorist attack in 2001.

*Well, I never knew this
about*

LOWER BROADWAY — TRINITY CHURCH TO ST PAUL'S CHAPEL. THE WORLD TRADE CENTER

VESEY STREET, which runs off Broadway north of St Paul's Chapel, is named after the FIRST RECTOR OF TRINITY, WILLIAM VESEY.

The Equitable Building at No. 120 Broadway was THE FIRST OFFICE BLOCK IN NEW YORK TO HAVE ITS CORNERSTONE LAID BY THE MAYOR OF NEW YORK.

MAIDEN LANE, which runs east off Broadway near Liberty Plaza, follows the course of a freshwater stream that used to run into the East River. In the 17th century, before the area was built up, Dutch maidens used the stream for washing their laundry, hence the name of the lane. A little way down Maiden Lane, at No. 57, is a plaque commemorating the fact that THOMAS JEFFERSON, 3rd President of the United States, resided here while serving as THE FIRST U.S. SECRETARY OF STATE in 1790. Jefferson rented 'a mean house in Maiden Lane' from Robert Bruce, a grocer, for '100 pounds per year'.

Under the classical portico at the east end of St Paul's Chapel, looking out on to Broadway, there is a large monument to AMERICA'S FIRST HERO, GENERAL RICHARD MONTGOMERY. The monument, which was put up under the orders of Congress on 25 January 1776, was THE FIRST AMERICAN MILITARY MONUMENT EVER ERECTED. In 1775 Montgomery joined the Continental army as a brigadier-general and led an American invasion force into Canada, capturing two forts and the town of Montreal. In December that year he was killed while leading an assault on Quebec, cut down by musket fire with 11 of his men, THE FIRST OFFICER TO DIE IN THE AMERICAN REVOLUTION.

The nearest fire station to the World Trade Center is ENGINE LADDER CO 10 on Liberty Street, on the south side of the site. A plaque on the wall of the station commemorates the five fire-fighters from the company who died on 9/11, while along the Greenwich Street wall is a 55 ft (17 m) long bronze sculpture dedicated to all the 343 fire-fighters who died that day.

The lobby of 3 WORLD FINANCIAL CENTER, the AMERICAN EXPRESS TOWER, is decorated with ONE OF THE LARGEST CYCLES OF MURALS IN THE WORLD, the 318 ft (97 m) HARBORS OF THE WORLD painted by CRAIG McPHERSON over five years from 1987 to 1992. Represented are Venice, Istanbul, Hong Kong, Sydney, Rio de Janeiro and, of course, New York, considered to be the finest natural harbour of them all.

CHAPTER 6

LOWER BROADWAY – VESEY TO CHAMBERS. THE CIVIC CENTER

The Woolworth Building

Cathedral of Commerce

The fantastical, neo-Gothic WOOLWORTH BUILDING at 233 Broadway is the most romantic and beautiful building in New York. It was the masterpiece of CASS GILBERT (who built the U.S. Custom House) for the head offices of store owner F.W. Woolworth. The story goes that Woolworth was once refused a mortgage by the Metropolitan Life Insurance Company and so he told Cass Gilbert that he would pay in cash for Gilbert to build him the tallest building in the world, thus robbing the Metropolitan Life Insurance Company headquarters of that accolade. It cost Woolworth a cool $13.5 million, most of which was for the land.

The lower half of the Woolworth building matches the height of another tallest building, the Park Row Building across the street, while the tower section above reaches a height of 792 ft (241 m), outstripping the Met Life Tower by 92 ft (28 m). The façade is faced with white terracotta, much of it replaced with stone in the 1970s, and adorned with gargoyles, fanciful ornamentation and narrow, precarious-looking stone balconies, the view from which must be both precipitous and exhilarating. There was originally an observation deck on the 58th floor but this was closed in 1945.

The Woolworth Building is reminiscent of the great Gothic churches of Europe, and during the opening ceremony in 1913, S. Parkes Cadman, minister of the Central Congregational Church in Brooklyn, described it as the 'Cathedral of Commerce'. British Prime Minister Arthur Balfour said of the Woolworth Building, 'What shall I say of a city that builds the most beautiful cathedral in the world and calls it an office building?'

Woolworth's offices only occupied a couple of floors, while the rest of the building was rented out to some 1,000 tenants, whose rent presumably helped Woolworth to recoup the cost of the enterprise – although he claimed that the advertising potential of such an eye-catching headquarters meant that the building more than paid for itself.

The magnificent, grandly stepped lobby of the Woolworth Building is not unlike a church crossing, with vaulted ceilings covered in colourful mosaics. Looking down from on high are humorous plaster sculptures of Woolworth himself, counting out nickels and dimes to pay for the work, and Cass Gilbert hugging a model of the building, while Teddy Roosevelt is watching it all through an amused monocle.

Amazingly, the Woolworth Building suffered no structural damage from the collapse of the Twin Towers on September 11, although the building's electricity and telephone systems were knocked out for a few weeks. The terrorist attacks did, however, result in the closure of the magnificent lobby to the public, thus robbing New Yorkers of access to one of the great sights of the city. If you persist, the guards will sometimes allow you to take a quick peek – it's well worth a try.

The Woolworth Building held the title of TALLEST BUILDING IN THE WORLD for 17 years, until overtaken by the Bank of Manhattan Trust Building at No. 40 Wall Street in 1930. It remained the headquarters of Woolworth for nearly 85 years until the company went bankrupt in 1997, when the building was sold to the Witkoff Group.

No. 259 Broadway

The VERY FIRST TIFFANY STORE was opened at No. 259 Broadway on 14 September 1837 by CHARLES LEWIS TIFFANY and TEDDY YOUNG. On the first day of opening, sales at the Tiffany and Young Fancy Good Store, as it was then known, totalled $4.98. In 1841 the store vacated this address and moved further uptown, eventually opening its famous flagship store on Fifth Avenue in 1940. In 2006, Tiffany returned to its Lower Manhattan roots, opening a store at No. 37 Wall Street.

No. 259 Broadway stood above New York's first subway station, the only station on New York's first subway, the Beach Pneumatic Transit, which opened on 26 February 1870. The subway was the brainchild of Alfred Beach, an inventor and editor of *Scientific American* magazine, who had to build his air-driven subway system in secret to avoid the objections of Broadway store owners, such as A.T. Stewart, who opposed the idea. The single-track tunnel ran east from the station beneath No. 259 Broadway, turned south and then ran under the middle of Broadway for 300 ft (91 m) as far as Murray Street. Beach's subway remained open for public demonstration until 1873, when a financial crisis put an end to the project. The tunnel, and the remains of the wooden subway car, were rediscovered in 1912 by engineers constructing the Brooklyn Manhattan Transit subway. No. 259 Broadway no longer exists and the site is now occupied by an eight-storey office block with the address No. 258 Broadway.

A Walk around the Civic Center

Start point: Broadway and Park Row

Park Row

Park Row runs north-east from Broadway towards the Civic Center. In

the late 19th century it was lined with the offices of major newspapers who wanted to be close to City Hall, and was known as 'Newspaper Row'. The *New York Herald* was at the Broadway end, then came the *New York Times*, the *New York Tribune* and the *New York World*.

Park Row Building

Walk up Park Row to No. 15, the Park Row Building, which at 391 ft (119 m) high was the tallest skyscraper in the world when it was completed in 1899, but was overtaken by the long-gone Singer Building on nearby Broadway in 1908. Distinctive features of the Park Row Building are the twin copper-clad domes at the top, which served as observatories, and four life-size sculpted figures projecting above the entrance. The building served as the headquarters of the Interborough Rapid Transit Company and as the first offices of the Associated Press.

Potter Building

At No. 38, on the corner with Beekman Street, stands the glorious red-brick POTTER BUILDING, built in 1886 and famous for its pioneering use of fire-resistant terracotta. The Potter Building replaced the World Building, the first headquarters of the *New York World*, which burned down in 1882. THOMAS EDISON gave THE FIRST PUBLIC DEMONSTRATION OF HIS TINFOIL PHONOGRAPH, the FIRST MACHINE THAT COULD RECORD AND REPRODUCE SOUND, in the offices of the *Scientific American* magazine at the World Building on 7 December 1877.

Next to the Potter Building, at No. 41, is the old NEW YORK TIMES BUILDING, now part of Pace University. The newspaper moved from here to Times Square in 1904. The open space across Spruce Street is known as PRINTING HOUSE SQUARE and is dominated by a statue of BENJAMIN FRANKLIN, seen here in his role as a publisher, brandishing a copy of his *Pennsylvania Gazette*.

Across Park Row, in City Hall Park, there is a statue of another publisher, HORACE GREELEY, founder and editor of the *New York Tribune*, whose offices were on the north side of Printing House Square. The NEW YORK TRIBUNE BUILDING was built in 1875 and was one of the first office blocks to have high-rise elevators.

New York World Building

Next to the Tribune stood the NEW YORK WORLD BUILDING, commissioned in 1883 by JOSEPH PULITZER, who had

bought the *New York World* newspaper earlier in that year. When completed in 1890 the New York World Building was THE TALLEST SKYSCRAPER IN THE WORLD, 308 ft (94 m) high, and THE FIRST BUILDING IN NEW YORK TO SURPASS THE HEIGHT OF THE 284 FT (86 M) HIGH SPIRE OF TRINITY CHURCH. Pulitzer had his office in an enormous dome at the top of the building, from where he could look down on all the other newspapers.

In 1896 he launched the world's FIRST COLOUR SUPPLEMENT, but perhaps his greatest legacy was the PULITZER PRIZE, awarded annually for achievements in journalism, photography and literature. The prizes were established with a bequest from Pulitzer's will to Columbia University, which administers the awards.

Both the World and Tribune Buildings were demolished in 1955 to make way for the extensions of the entrance ramps to the Brooklyn Bridge.

City Hall Park

Lining the west side of Park Row is CITY HALL PARK, originally a pasture for livestock known as THE COMMONS. At one time or another the Commons was home to almshouses, a debtors prison, barracks and a post office, but its main function was as New York's village green. In 1765 New Yorkers gathered here, in THE FIRST MASS PUBLIC DEMONSTRATION AGAINST THE BRITISH, to protest about THE STAMP ACT, before marching off to Bowling Green to burn the governor in effigy. The following year the first of five LIBERTY POLES was raised on the Commons – these were flagstaffs erected as symbols of defiance and there is a replica of one now located on the Broadway side of the park.

On 9 July 1776, the DECLARATION OF INDEPENDENCE was read out on the Commons to George Washington and his troops, after which the crowd marched down to Bowling Green once again, this time to topple the statue of King George III.

In the middle of the park stands a delightful fountain designed in 1871 by Jacob Wrey Mould, who helped to lay out Central Park. This fountain replaced the original CROTON FOUNTAIN, AMERICA'S FIRST DECORATIVE FOUNTAIN, which was erected in 1842 to celebrate the opening of the Croton Aqueduct, bringing fresh water to the city. The Croton Fountain was fed with water from the aqueduct and for the first time in their history New Yorkers had enough water to power a fountain that could propel water 50 ft (15 m) into the air.

Nathan Hale

A little to the north of the Croton Fountain, facing City Hall, is a huge bronze of the young revolutionary hero NATHAN HALE (1755–76), who made a daring attempt to infiltrate behind the enemy British lines in New York, disguised as a Dutch schoolteacher, to gather intelligence about British troop movements. He was captured and, on the morning of 22 September 1776, hanged on a gallows specially erected by the Dove Tavern at 63rd Street and First Avenue. He was 21 years old. His final words, as reported by a British officer who witnessed the hanging, went down in American legend. 'I only regret that I have but one life to give for my country.' The statue, sculpted by Frederick MacMonnies, stands on a pedestal by Stanford White, and is an idealised representation of Hale since there were no portraits of him for the sculptor to work from. It was dedicated by the Sons of the Revolution of New York on the 110th anniversary of Evacuation Day, 25 November 1893.

City Hall

THE NEW CITY HALL was officially opened in 1812, replacing the old hall on Wall Street. It was designed and built by JOSEPH MANGIN, who largely took care of the mildly French Renaissance exterior, and JOHN McCOMB JR., who laid out the handsome interior with its sweeping marble staircase and Rotunda. The exterior was clad with marble, all except for the north side which was brownstone – since the hall was built at the northern extremity of the city, there wasn't anyone important living north of it to be offended. The whole building was refaced with limestone in 1954.

The splendid GOVERNOR'S ROOM inside houses a portrait gallery of prominent early New Yorkers and includes John Trumbull's 1805 portrait of Alexander Hamilton, which appears on the ten-dollar bill.

In 1865 ABRAHAM LINCOLN lay in state beneath the Rotunda, as did ULYSSES S. GRANT, 20 years later in 1885.

DEWITT CLINTON (1769–1828) was the first mayor to move in when the new City Hall was opened. He was the nephew of New York's first and longest-serving State Governor, George Clinton, known as the 'Old Incumbent'. As such, it seems DeWitt was born to run New York, which he did, on and off, as Mayor for 12 years between 1803 and 1815, and as State Governor for eight years during two terms between 1817 and 1828. While in office he championed and oversaw many important projects, including one in particular that would shape New York forever.

Manhattan Street Grid Plan

Officially known as the COMMISSIONERS PLAN OF 1811, the MANHATTAN STREET GRID PLAN was designed to promote the orderly development and growth of New York north of 14th Street. The city was expanding so rapidly, and space on the island was so restricted, that some

sort of method was needed to ensure that best use was made of the land available, and that there was a 'free and abundant circulation of air' to ward off disease.

The Commission was made up of three members, the much respected Founding Father, signer of the Constitution and author of much of it, GOUVERNEUR MORRIS, lawyer JOHN RUTHERFORD and the Surveyor-General of the State of New York, SIMEON DE WITT, DeWitt Clinton's first cousin.

Observing that 'straight-sided and right-angled houses are the most cheap to build', the commissioners came up with a regular grid of straight east–west streets and north–south avenues that more or less ignored the topography of the island.

The twelve numbered avenues, running roughly north–south parallel with the Hudson River, begin with First Avenue in the east and finish with Twelfth Avenue in the west. Fifth Avenue is the dividing line between the east and west streets. The bulge on the lower part of the island east of First Avenue, which would become the East Village, was given four additional avenues lettered A to D, earning the nickname ALPHABET CITY.

The numbered east–west streets are 60 ft (18 m) wide and a fairly regular 200 ft (60 m) apart, meaning that along the avenues there are 20 blocks to a mile. The avenues are 100 ft (30 m) wide, but the distance between them varies slightly, while Lexington and Madison Avenues were inserted at a later date to relieve congestion and create more corner lots on the overcrowded east side.

The idea originally was to dispense with Broadway above 14th Street, because its ancient route cut diagonally across the grid, but such was the outcry that Broadway was permitted to stay, which allowed for the creation of wonderful triangular squares and open spaces wherever it meets the grid.

The actual survey for the grid was performed by JOHN RANDEL JR. and his team, who personally walked out every one of the some 2,000 city blocks between 14th Street and Harlem. They were empowered to enter private property and unsurprisingly were often met with hostility. As much as was possible they allowed existing properties to remain in situ, while those whose properties had to be removed were compensated.

With a number of modifications, the most spectacular being the creation of Central Park in 1853, the plan was implemented more or less as envisioned by the commissioners and has survived for more than 200 years as an essential part of New York's identity.

Erie Canal

DeWitt Clinton also oversaw the creation in 1825 of THE WORLD'S LONGEST CANAL, the ERIE CANAL, known as 'Clinton's Ditch', linking the Hudson River at Albany with the Great Lakes. Almost overnight this secured New York's place as the nation's commercial capital by providing a quick and relatively cheap route for raw materials and goods to travel from the heart of the Midwest to New York.

Tweed Courthouse

North of City Hall is the monumental Victorian neo-classical New York County Courthouse, popularly known as the 'TWEED COURTHOUSE' after Tammany Hall boss William Tweed. Tweed used the building project to embezzle millions of dollars from the budget, which soared from $3 million to $14 million during construction between 1861 and 1871. Some $9 million of that went into Tweed's pocket, more than the U.S. Government spent on buying the whole of Alaska. Such was the scale of the larceny that even hardened New Yorkers were shocked into action, particularly when municipal taxes were raised to pay for it, and Tweed was eventually tried in his own unfinished courthouse in 1871 and sent to jail.

The building remained in use as a courthouse until 1926, then served as offices, and since 2002 has been the headquarters of the Department of Education.

Tammany Hall

TAMMANY HALL was a powerful political organisation founded in 1788 for ordinary working people as a counter to New York's more exclusive clubs for the rich, and it ran New York for much of the 19th century. Formed in New York as the SOCIETY OF ST TAMMANY it took its name from a legendary 17th-century Indian chief called Tamamend, who was believed to have befriended William Penn, and adopted Indian rituals and titles, such as 'braves' for the newest members, and 'Grand Sachem' for the leader. Headquarters was known as 'the wigwam'.

Tammany Hall soon became deeply political in its pursuit of universal male suffrage and laws to protect working men, and was rewarded with federal jobs for supporting the Democratic Presidency of Andrew Jackson in 1828. It bolstered its political base by helping immigrants find jobs and gain citizenship, and was seen as a champion of New York's working poor. Gradually Tammany Hall began to use violence and corruption to get its way, intimidating people to vote for those it supported and putting its own people into positions of influence and power.

Municipal Building

Now walk round to the north side of Tweed Courthouse and cross Chambers Street to the *beaux-arts* Surrogates Court and Hall of Records, which holds the public records of New York going back to 1664.

Boss Tweed

The most notorious of Tammany Hall's leaders was WILLIAM 'BOSS' TWEED, who became Grand Sachem in 1858. Born in Cherry Street on the East Side, in 1823, Tweed learned to play rough as foreman of one of New York's notoriously violent volunteer firefighting companies, who often fought each other to the death for the right to attend a fire. Having survived that, fighting his way to the top of Tammany Hall was easy for Tweed. He got himself elected to the influential New York County Board of Supervisors, from which position he was able to ensure that his cronies were elected to powerful positions in the city government, making up what became known as the 'Tweed Ring'. Contracts for any kind of public work would go only to those who paid the Tweed Ring a percentage, which made the Ring millions of dollars – some estimates reckon that, during the ten years they were operating, the Tweed Ring embezzled up to $200 million.

They finally overstretched themselves with the Tweed Courthouse contract. Up until then they had managed to avoid exposure by paying off journalists and threatening editors with pulling the city's advertising from their newspapers, but in 1869 cartoonist THOMAS NAST began lampooning Tweed in *Harper's Weekly*, and in 1870 the Republican-supporting *New York Times* published a series of exposés about the Ring. Their time was up.

Despite the misdemeanours of 'Boss' Tweed and others like him, Tammany Hall continued to flourish as an influential political machine until Franklin D. Roosevelt stripped them of federal patronage in the 1930s, and by the 1960s the organisation had ceased to exist.

Turn right and walk east to where the enormous bulk of the MUNICIPAL BUILDING looms above the Civic Center, straddling Chambers Street. Standing 580 ft (176 m) high, one of the largest government buildings in the world, and THE FIRST BUILDING IN NEW YORK TO INCORPORATE A SUBWAY STATION IN THE BASEMENT, the Municipal Building was constructed in 1914 to accommodate the added bureaucracy created by the union of the five boroughs. Its monumental design is said to have inspired a number of civic buildings in Moscow, including the main building of Moscow State University.

Turn left (north) along Center Street and walk into Foley Square, which is dominated on the east side by the classical columns of the United States Courthouse, the last work of Cass Gilbert, and the hexagonal New York County Courthouse, built in 1926 to replace the Tweed Courthouse.

Foley Square

FOLEY SQUARE, which sits at the very heart of New York's Civic Center district, was named after THOMAS F. 'BIG TOM' FOLEY (1852–1925), a saloon keeper and prominent Tammany Hall politician.

Collect Pond

The square sits on the site of the COLLECT POND, early New York's principal source of fresh water. The pond was fed by underground springs, covered 50 acres (20 ha), and was so deep, up to 60 ft (18 m) in some places, that there were reported sightings of monsters. In the summer people would come up from the city and sit by the pond to picnic, or they would skate on it in winter, but by the beginning of the 19th century the pond had become so polluted with waste from the nearby slaughterhouses and tanning yards that it was decided to get rid of it. A canal was dug to drain the water into the Hudson River and by 1813 the pond had been filled in. Homes were put up on the reclaimed land and the area became a respectable middle-class neighbourhood clustered around 'Paradise Park'. The canal was later also filled in to create Canal Street.

Five Points

However, the underground springs that had fed the Collect Pond continued to rise, and after a few years the area became boggy and waterlogged, the houses started to sink, and the whole area was soon knee deep in foul-smelling mud. The middle-class inhabitants fled, leaving the place to be inhabited by the poor, mainly Irish immigrants fleeing Ireland's potato famine. The neighbourhood became New York's most notorious slum, known as FIVE POINTS since it was centred around the junction of five streets. By the middle of the 19th century Five Points was ruled by vicious gangs, mainly Irish, as portrayed in the 2002 film *Gangs of New York*, based on the book by Herbert Ashbury.

At the end of the 19th century the Five Points area was finally razed and transformed into the city's Civic Center, but even today the buildings that stand on the site of the Collect Pond require regular pumping out to prevent flooding from the rising spring water.

Croton Aqueduct

The loss of the Collect Pond meant that rapidly expanding New York now had a water supply problem, and to solve this it was decided to bring in water from the CROTON RIVER 40 miles (64 km) north of the city in Westchester County. The river was dammed and gravity brought the water down along a raised iron pipe to the Bronx, where it crossed the Harlem River into the city over the High Bridge Aqueduct at the end of 173rd Street. The water then flowed down the west side of Manhattan into the RECEIVING RESERVOIR, now the site of the Great Lawn in Central Park. From here it was sent to the DISTRIBUTING RESERVOIR, a vast Egyptian-style structure located where the New York Public Library now stands. The opening of the Croton Aqueduct system on 14 October 1842 was celebrated with a triumphant jet of water leaping 50 ft (15 m) into the air from a specially built fountain in City Hall Park.

Today, fresh water is brought to the city from the Catskill Mountains and flows by gravity along three tunnels under the city. It rises again under natural pressure through numerous specially constructed shafts.

Return to Center Street, turn left (south) past the front of the Municipal Building, and make your way across all the traffic islands back to Printing House Square. Walk past the statue of Ben Franklin and continue south on Nassau Street for three blocks. Turn left (east) on to Fulton and continue until you come to the TITANIC MEMORIAL LIGHTHOUSE, brought here in 1976 from its former location on the roof of the now demolished Seamen's Church Institute further down on South Street.

South Street Seaport

Cross Water Street to the SOUTH STREET SEAPORT MUSEUM, founded in 1967 by a group of residents led by Peter and Norma Stanford, who wanted to preserve the area as the historic site of New York's original port. The museum now stands at the heart of 12 square blocks that contain a greater concentration of restored early 19th-century commercial buildings than anywhere else in New York.

Carry on down Fulton and on the right is the beautifully restored SCHERMERHORN ROW, built in 1811 by ship chandler Peter Schermerhorn as warehouses on land reclaimed from the East River. Shops were opened on the ground floor to serve customers using the Fulton Ferry between Manhattan and Brooklyn, and the buildings now house restaurants and galleries as well.

Across South Street is the former site of New York's main wholesale fish market, the FULTON FISH MARKET, which moved to the Bronx in 2005. Along with PIER 17, which extends out on to the water, this area has now been transformed into a shopping mall with restaurants and bars that line the waterfront and affords stunning views of the Brooklyn Bridge, Brooklyn Heights and the harbour.

A splendid place to finish our walk.

Brooklyn Bridge

A very pleasant excursion on a fine day is a walk across New York's grand old lady, the BROOKLYN BRIDGE. There is a walkway running along the middle of the bridge, above the roadway, that affords a uniquely thrilling view of the city and the harbour, as well as allowing you to get a close-up look at a magnificent piece of engineering.

When completed in 1883 the Brooklyn Bridge, with a central span of 1,595 ft (486 m), was the LONGEST SUSPENSION BRIDGE IN THE WORLD, over half as long again as any bridge previously built. It was also the first to be made of steel. The iconic Gothic double arches, 271 ft (83 m) high, were designed as symbolic gateways to the two communities linked by the bridge, New York and Brooklyn, which were separate cities at that time.

The Brooklyn Bridge was the brainchild of German-born engineer John A. Roebling, who conceived of the idea while marooned on the East River in an ice-bound ferry to Brooklyn. He never got to see his masterpiece. Just before construction started in 1869 he died from a tetanus infection picked up after his foot had been crushed between a ferry and a piling while he was conducting a survey for the bridge. Roebling's son Washington took charge of the project, but a year later he too was incapacitated, after suffering the bends while coming up from a caisson on the river bed beneath one of the towers. Washington managed to finish the project by relaying instructions to the building team via his wife, while he watched the proceedings from his house on Columbia Heights through a telescope.

Well, I never knew this about

LOWER BROADWAY — VESEY TO CHAMBERS. THE CIVIC CENTER

One block west of Broadway, on the corner of Barclay and Church Streets, is OLD ST PETER'S CHURCH, built in 1836 and THE OLDEST CATHOLIC BUILDING IN NEW YORK. The first St Peter's, built on this site in 1785, was THE FIRST CATHOLIC CHURCH IN NEW YORK and the parish church of THE FIRST CATHOLIC PARISH IN NEW YORK. In 1800 the parish opened NEW YORK'S FIRST CATHOLIC SCHOOL.

Elizabeth Ann Seton, America's first native-born saint, was received into the Catholic church at St Peter's in 1805.

In 2001 the body of the first officially recorded victim of the terrorist attacks, the Catholic priest FATHER MYCHAL JUDGE, Chaplain to the New York City Fire Department, was brought to St Peter's Church by firefighters and laid before the altar.

The Woolworth Building served as the headquarters of *Mode Magazine* in the TV series *Ugly Betty*.

The first offices of the project to develop the atomic bomb were opened on the 18th floor of No. 270 Broadway in 1942. Because it was located in Manhattan, the project was given the codename the MANHATTAN PROJECT, a name it kept even though the headquarters was moved to Oak Ridge, Tennessee, the following year.

Swaying precariously above Printing House Square at No. 8 Spruce Street is an extraordinary stainless steel and reinforced concrete skyscraper called NEW YORK BY GEHRY, 870 ft (265 m) high and THE TALLEST RESIDENTIAL BUILDING

IN THE WESTERN HEMISPHERE. It was opened in 2011 and designed by Frank Gehry in such a way that it seems to undulate and ripple.

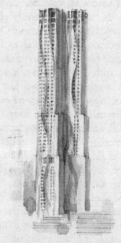

Underneath City Hall, hidden from public view, sits THE MOST BEAUTIFUL SUBWAY STATION IN NEW YORK. City Hall was the starting point for NEW YORK'S FIRST SUBWAY, THE INTERBOROUGH RAPID TRANSIT (IRT), which ran north from City Hall along Lafayette and Lexington to 42nd Street, then west to Longacre (now Times) Square, and finally north again to Harlem. HEINS AND LAFARGE, the architects who designed the early subway stations, intended City Hall to be their 'pièce de résistance'. Not only was this the first station on the line, but the track made a huge loop here to enable the trains to turn round, and this allowed them to give full rein to their imagination. Heins and LaFarge were the original architects of St John the Divine Cathedral, and

City Hall station became the cathedral of the subway. There are vast, vaulted ceilings, arches lined with terracotta tiles by the pioneering Spanish architect Rafael Guastavino, coloured decorative tiles on the walls and warmly glowing chandeliers. On opening day, 27 October 1904, 100,000 people came to have a look and for years afterwards New Yorkers, with no intention of riding the subway, would come down just to sit and gaze. In 1945 the trains were switched from five cars to ten, too long for the City Hall station's curving platforms to accommodate, and the station was closed, its glories becoming but a fading memory to all but a privileged few. Although the southbound No. 6 trains still used the loop to turn round, passengers were made to get off at the station before. Today, however, the guards will let you stay on board as the train makes its turn, and if you look out of the right-hand side of the train you should be able to see for yourself the majestic, secret cathedral of the subway.

Look out for the Tweed Courthouse in the following films: *Gangs of New York*, *Dressed to Kill*, *The Verdict* and *Kramer vs. Kramer*.

Exterior scenes for the classic 1957 film *12 Angry Men*, starring Henry Fonda, were filmed outside the New York County Courthouse, which also features frequently in the television series *Law and Order*.

On the corner of Water Street and Dover Street sits one of the several claimants to the title of NEW YORK'S OLDEST BAR, the BRIDGE CAFÉ, which has been operating here since 1847 in a building dating from 1794. It is definitely NEW YORK'S OLDEST BUSINESS. Mayor Ed Koch used to have a private table here where he would hold court twice a week.

There is a plaque on Pearl Street, where it runs under the approach to the Brooklyn Bridge, marking the site of the FIRST PRESIDENTIAL MANSION, Osgood House, which had the address No. 1 Cherry Street. George Washington lived here during the run-up to his inauguration in 1789 and for the first few months of his term of office as the 1st President of the United States. The house was the forerunner to the White House, and contained the first Presidential Office (now called the Oval Office) and the first public business office (now called the West Wing). The household was run by Samuel Fraunces, who had previously owned Fraunces Tavern. After ten months Osgood House became too small for the rapidly expanding executive office and in February 1790 Washington moved to the larger McComb Mansion on Broadway (*see* page 38).

CHAPTER 7

Broadway – Chambers to Canal. TriBeCa, Chinatown & The Lower East Side

Sun Building – formerly A.T. Stewart's 'Marble Palace'

This section of Broadway is now a rather ordinary stretch of small shops and 19th-century office blocks, interspersed with the odd cast-iron gem, but in the mid 19th century it was for a while home to New York's most fashionable shops, all thanks to an Irish-born entrepreneur called A.T. STEWART.

America's First Department Store

In 1846 A.T. Stewart opened AMERICA'S FIRST PURPOSE-BUILT DEPARTMENT STORE, the A.T. STEWART STORE, at No. 280 Broadway, just north of City Hall

Park, in what is now the SUN BUILDING. Described as 'one of the most influential buildings ever erected in New York City', the A.T. Stewart Store set the architectural style for shops and stores all over America for years to come, and initiated the commercial development of this section of Broadway. Plate glass was imported from France for large display windows on the ground floor and the store was THE FIRST COMMERCIAL BUILDING IN NEW YORK TO ADOPT AN ITALIANATE STYLE OF ARCHITECTURE, soon to be copied throughout the city. It was also THE FIRST COMMERCIAL STRUCTURE IN NEW YORK TO BE CLAD WITH MARBLE, which led to its nickname the 'MARBLE PALACE'.

As well as such architectural innovations Stewart, who had set up his first small store across the street at No. 283 Broadway in 1823, came up with a raft of new marketing ideas such as fixed prices, special sales, fashion shows and changing rooms with full-length mirrors.

By the 1850s, the A.T. Stewart Store was THE LARGEST STORE IN THE WORLD. In 1862 Stewart moved his store further north on Broadway but continued to use 280 Broadway as a warehouse.

In 1917, No. 280 Broadway was bought by the *Sun* newspaper (published 1833 to 1950), from which the building gets its name. Clocks on each corner of the building sport the newspaper's slogan 'The Sun, it shines for all'.

Today the Sun Building houses shops and government offices.

African Burial Ground

In 1991, during excavations for the construction of a federal government building at No. 290 Broadway, workers uncovered 413 sets of human remains, nearly half of them the remains of children, and a large collection of artefacts. They had stumbled upon a vast, forgotten burial ground, THE OLDEST AND BIGGEST AFRICAN CEMETERY IN COLONIAL AMERICA, where some 15,000 free and enslaved Africans were buried in the 17th and 18th centuries. The burial ground covered six and a half acres (2.6 ha) of unproductive swampland situated outside the boundaries of New Amsterdam and Colonial New York, between modern-day Broadway and Lafayette. At that time it was forbidden for Africans to be buried in the cemeteries of Trinity and the other New York churches, and this burial ground was one of the few areas that Africans could call their own.

The remains and artefacts were examined at Howard University, and then in 2003 re-interred at the burial ground underneath grass-covered mounds set beside a black granite monument.

A visitor centre at No. 290 Broadway tells the story of New York's slave trade and the African communities that helped to build New York, including the often overlooked facts that the second explorer to sail into New York Bay was a Portuguese of African descent, Esteban Gomes, while the first settler of Manhattan Island was Jan

Rodrigues, of Hispanic and African descent.

At No. 412 Broadway once stood the APOLLO ROOMS where, on 7 December 1842, AMERICA'S OLDEST SYMPHONY ORCHESTRA, THE NEW YORK PHILHARMONIC, PLAYED THEIR FIRST EVER CONCERT, in front of 600 guests. The first piece of music played was Beethoven's Fifth Symphony and the orchestra was conducted by its founder, URELI CORELLI HILL.

West of Broadway

TRIBECA means 'Triangle Below Canal' and refers to the area south of Canal and north of Chambers between Broadway and the Hudson River. Being immediately north of the colonial city it was one of the first areas to be developed as a residential neighbourhood as the city moved north. By the mid 19th century it had become a commercial district full of warehouses, factories and shops – in the 1960s and 70s these began to be converted into desirable residences that are now much sought after. Today TriBeCa is a neighbourhood of cobbled streets, expensive restaurants, art galleries and million-dollar lofts – one of America's most expensive zip codes.

A WALK AROUND TRIBECA

Start point:
Broadway and Chambers Street

Walk west down Chambers towards the Hudson River. On your right, after

three blocks, is WASHINGTON MARKET PARK, on the site of the old Washington Market, originally established as Bear Market in 1813. By the early 20th century this had grown into NEW YORK'S LARGEST WHOLESALE FOOD MARKET, and its departure to the Bronx in the 1960s sparked the neighbourhood's transformation into a residential area, as artists and crafts people moved into the abandoned food warehouses and lofts.

Continue down Chambers to West Street and turn right. Across the road is the STUYVESANT HIGH SCHOOL, alma mater of jazz musician THELONIOUS MONK, actors JAMES CAGNEY, LUCY LIU and TIM ROBBINS, political advisors DAVID AXELROD and DICK MORRIS, and four Nobel Prize winners.

Harrison Street Houses

Continue north along West Street and take the next turning right into Harrison Street. On your right, once you have gone underneath the Community College building, are the HARRISON STREET HOUSES, a row of beautiful red-brick Federal townhouses with iron railings, white-painted weatherboarding, dormer windows and large back gardens. They were built in 1828 by John McComb Jr. and originally stood on Washington Street, a few blocks north, where they were used as warehouses. Saved from destruction in the early 1970s, they were moved here and immaculately restored as private homes, forming a stylish enclave in the shadow of the towering apartment blocks of Independence Plaza.

Continue along Harrison Street, admiring the handsome 19th-century architecture on both sides, until Hudson, and then turn left (north).

Powell Building

At the next junction, on the north-west corner of Franklin, is the landmark neo-classical POWELL BUILDING (you can see the name in bronze lettering at the sixth-floor level), built in 1892 for chocolate company boss Henry L. Pierce and bought later by confectioner Alexander Powell. The lower floors are now a Nobu restaurant owned by celebrity restaurateur DREW NIEPORENT and actor ROBERT DE NIRO, who also co-own the TriBeCa Grill, one of New York's trendiest eateries, at the far end of the same block down Franklin – De Niro is often spotted eating there.

Carry on along Hudson and take the next right on to North Moore for one block. Across Varick, on the right side, is 8 HOOK AND LADDER, the unmistakable headquarters of the *Ghostbusters*, played by Bill Murray, Dan Aykroyd and Harold Ramis.

Continue on North Moore, zig-zag across West Broadway into White Street, lined with TriBeCa's finest examples of cast-iron architecture, and return to Broadway.

Chinatown

New York's CHINATOWN IS THE LARGEST IN AMERICA and has THE LARGEST CONCENTRATION OF CHINESE PEOPLE IN THE WESTERN HEMISPHERE. The first Chinese to settle in New York were

sailors and traders who entered through the harbour, changed their names and married local women. The FIRST RECORDED CHINESE IMMIGRANT took the name WILLIAM BROWN and married a local Irish woman in 1825.

The FIRST CHINESE GROCERY STORE, WO KEE, opened on Mott Street in 1878 and a small Chinese community built up in the area, which at that time was part of the notorious Five Points slum. More Chinese were prevented from settling by the UNITED STATES' FIRST AND ONLY RACIALLY BASED LEGISLATION, the CHINESE EXCLUSION ACT OF 1882, while the Chinese who were already here ruled and financed their own community through secret organisations called Tongs. The Tongs were formed to protect the Chinese from the infamous gangs of Five Points, but some of them developed into criminal gangs themselves, extorting protection money and fighting each other, with bloody results. When the exclusion act was lifted in the Second World War, Chinatown expanded rapidly and today some 150,000 people live within the two square miles (5 sq km) of Chinatown. The Chinese community still keeps itself to itself and most speak only Mandarin, or their own Chinese dialect, so that even New Yorkers can feel as if they are in a foreign land – which all adds to Chinatown's exotic and colourful atmosphere.

A WALK IN CHINATOWN

Start point: City Hall

From City Hall, walk north through Foley Square and turn right on to Worth. Continue east on Worth to COLUMBUS PARK, Chinatown's only park. This was created in 1897 as part of an attempt by social reformer JACOB RIIS to clean up Five Points, and in particular the infamous MULBERRY BEND, a red-light district plagued with gangs and described by Riis as 'the foul core of New York's slums'.

The person who first brought the terrible conditions of Five Points to the attention of New Yorkers, and stimulated reformers such as Jacob Riis to try and improve the situation, was the English author CHARLES DICKENS, who visited Five Points in 1842 during his feted tour of America. Coming from London he was no stranger to poverty and filth and he gave such a vivid description of Five Points in his 'American Notes' that upper- and middle-class New Yorkers were inspired to come and see these slums for themselves – or to 'go slumming', as they called it.

Walk through Columbus Park to Mulberry and have a look at the infamous 'Mulberry Bend', caused by the

road curving north, originally to avoid the Collect Pond.

Church of the Transfiguration

Now go straight ahead up narrow Mosco Street to Mott Street, THE OLDEST STREET IN CHINATOWN, named after one of the butchers who lived here next to the Collect Pond in the 18th century. On your left is the CHURCH OF THE TRANSFIGURATION, built in 1801 and THE THIRD OLDEST CHURCH BUILDING IN MANHATTAN, after St Paul's Chapel and St Mark's in the Bowery. It was originally Lutheran and then Episcopalian, but in 1853 it was sold to the Roman Catholic church to serve Five Points' huge Irish Catholic immigrant population, which by then had reached some 650,000, making New York THE SECOND LARGEST IRISH CITY AFTER DUBLIN. Reflecting the present ethnic make-up of the area, the church today offers services in Cantonese and Mandarin, as well as English.

Mott Street

Across the street is No. 32 Mott Street, once home to QUONG YUEN SHING & COMPANY GENERAL STORE, opened by Lee Lok in 1891 and THE OLDEST SHOP IN CHINATOWN, which served as somewhere for the early Chinese immigrants to relax and socialise. It closed in 2003, as a result of falling trade after 9/11.

Continue north on Mott Street and at the bend, which mirrors the Mulberry Bend, look up to the roof of the white building on the left of the street at No. 41 to see THE ONLY REMAINING CHINESE PAGODA ROOF IN CHINATOWN.

A little further up Mott Street at No. 65 is one of New York's most historic properties, THE FIRST TENEMENT EVER BUILT IN AMERICA, constructed here in 1824. As New York became more and more crowded the only solution was to build upwards, and this tenement would have been the first building in the neighbourhood much above two storeys. While the ground floor was a shop, each of the six floors above would have contained two, two-bedroom apartments each inhabited by up to 12 people.

Bloody Angle

Retrace your steps down Mott Street, and at the bend turn left into Pell Street, known as Haircut Row for all its barbershops, and then right into DOYERS STREET, named after Hendrik Doyer, an 18th-century Dutch immigrant who owned a distillery and tavern sited where the post office is now. Doyers Street was once THE MOST DANGEROUS PLACE IN AMERICA, thanks to the 'Tong Wars' between the two main rival Chinese gangs, the Hip Sing Tong and the On Leong Tong. Doyers Street is only about 100 yards (90 m) long, but it is one of the few streets in New York with a genuine curve, which makes it the perfect place for an ambush, and in the early years of the 20th century MORE MURDERS WERE COMMITTED ON DOYERS STREET'S 'BLOODY ANGLE' THAN ANYWHERE ELSE IN AMERICA. Beneath the street is a network of tunnels along which Tong members could move around in secret and escape from trouble – or the police – and even today visitors are not encouraged to go down there.

NEW YORK'S FIRST CHINESE THEATRE operated on Doyers Street from 1893 until 1911, and at No. 13 is NEW YORK'S OLDEST DIM SUM PARLOUR, THE NOM WAH TEA PARLOR. The street also boasts a number of clandestine drinking establishments, similar to the old New York speakeasies, that lurk in basements or behind unmarked doors guarded by large, grim-looking bouncers who spend a lot of their time cracking their knuckles. One such place, and you have to know it's there, is the Apothecary or APOTHEKE at No. 9, on the corner. Stride up to the door confidently enough and they will probably let you into the candle-lit lounge filled with medical paraphernalia and the most enormous marble bar you will ever see, where willing practitioners can supply you with the most stimulating concoctions, purely for medicinal purposes, of course.

Oldest Townhouse

Should you make it safely along Doyers Street as far as Bowery, turn left to have a look at the marvellous red-painted EDWARD MOONEY HOUSE, built by butcher Edward Mooney in 1785 and THE OLDEST TOWNHOUSE IN NEW YORK.

At the bottom of Bowery is CHATHAM SQUARE, named after the British Prime Minister William Pitt, the Earl of Chatham. The KIMLAU MEMORIAL ARCH here commemorates members of the armed forces of Chinese origin in the name of LT BENJAMIN KIMLAU, who was shot down behind enemy lines in 1944 during the Second World War. Beside the arch is a statue of LIN ZEXU, a 19th-century Chinese leader who fought against the opium trade.

From Chatham Square you can either return to City Hall along Park Row or take a look around

The Lower East Side

Before the Revolution this part of eastern Manhattan was a farm belonging to James Delancey. As docks grew up along the East River it became an immigrant area, and in the latter half of the 19th century it was the centre of Jewish culture in New York.

A WALK AROUND THE LOWER EAST SIDE

With Bowery at your back, pass behind Lin Zexu and cross Oliver Street into St James Place. One hundred yards (90 m) down on your left is the FIRST SHEARITH ISRAEL CEMETERY, THE OLDEST JEWISH CEMETERY IN AMERICA. It was opened in 1683 to replace an earlier Jewish cemetery, established nearby in 1656, but which has long been lost; hence this oldest surviving cemetery is known as the 'First' cemetery.

Continue down St James Place and turn left into James Street to the small Greek Revival church of ST JAMES, completed in 1837 and THE SECOND OLDEST CATHOLIC BUILDING IN NEW YORK after St Peter's Church. In 1836 the first chapter of the Ancient Order of Hibernians, an Irish fraternity organised in response to anti-immigrant and anti-Catholic attacks on the Irish community, was established in the unfinished church here.

Further down James Street, turn left on to Madison and left again into Oliver Street. The four-storey Victorian townhouse at No. 25 was the home from 1907 to 1923 of Five Points' most eminent son, New York governor ALFRED E. SMITH. In 1928 he entered the presidential race as the Democratic candidate, becoming THE FIRST CATHOLIC EVER TO BE NOMINATED FOR PRESIDENT. He lost to Herbert Hoover, but will be remembered as one of New York's most popular politicians. He lived in the Lower East Side all his life.

Oldest Clothes Shop

Take the next right into Henry Street and walk east. The first junction you come to is Catherine Street where, three blocks south on the corner with Cherry Street, the VERY FIRST BROOKS BROTHERS STORE OPENED in 1818. Brooks Brothers is THE OLDEST CLOTHING RETAILER IN AMERICA.

Cross Catherine and continue east on Henry Street, noting the grand doorways of the tenements at Nos. 39–43 on your left, in particular the voluptuous figures on the corbels of No. 41, such as one might find on a ship's prow. We are close to the waterfront here and no doubt many of the tenants were sailors who would have appreciated such artistry.

St Augustine's

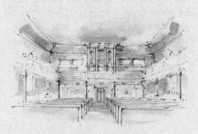

Walk on under the Manhattan Bridge, and after six more blocks you will arrive at ST AUGUSTINE'S CHURCH, a plain brownstone building that holds a fascinating mystery. In 1799 New York passed a gradual emancipation act that required all slaves in the state to have been freed by the end of 1827. St Augustine's was built a year later in 1828, and yet here are NEW YORK'S LAST SURVIVING SLAVE GALLERIES. High up at the back of the church, accessed by a cramped stairway and concealed from the gaze of the congregation, these galleries with their plain wooden benches were where slaves were made to sit, out of sight, during services. Perhaps the good folk of St Augustine's sent their naughty children to sit up there instead.

Seward Park

After visiting St Augustine's, retrace your steps back down Henry Street, turn right on Montgomery and immediately left on to East Broadway, and after a five-minute walk you will come to SEWARD PARK. This was laid out in 1899, and in 1903 was equipped by the city with THE FIRST MUNICIPAL PLAYGROUND IN AMERICA. To the north of the park, on Grand, is the SEWARD PARK HIGH SCHOOL, where Sammy Cahn, Tony Curtis, Estelle Getty from the Golden Girls, Zero Mostel, Jerry Stiller and Walter Matthau all went to school.

Carry on along East Broadway, turn right on to Forsyth Street just before Manhattan Bridge, and then fork right on to Eldridge Street to visit the ELDRIDGE STREET SYNAGOGUE at No. 12, standing flamboyant and magnificent amongst the plain office blocks and tenements.

Eldridge Street Synagogue

Built in 1887, this was THE FIRST MAJOR SYNAGOGUE BUILT BY EASTERN EUROPEAN

JEWS IN AMERICA. At the end of the 19th century, with the succession of the anti-Semite Russian Csar Alexander III, vicious pogroms were conducted against the Jews in countries like Russia, Poland and the Ukraine and many Jews fled to New York, settling in the immigrant-friendly Lower East Side and making New York THE LARGEST JEWISH CITY IN THE WORLD after metropolitan Tel Aviv, which it still is.

The synagogue these Jews built for themselves, both as a place of worship and a place of welcome and help for new immigrants, is a resplendent masterpiece of Moorish Revival architecture, with an enormous rose window of 12 rosettes representing the 12 tribes of Israel, set above five Moorish windows that symbolise the five books of the *Torah*. Inside is a riot of woodwork, carvings, chandeliers, stained glass and brightly coloured frescoes.

For 50 years the synagogue was the centre of Jewish life in the Lower East Side, with a congregation of many thousands, but in the 1930s the neighbourhood changed, the Jewish community moved on, and the synagogue fell into disrepair. In the 1980s the Eldridge Street Project was formed to restore the building to its former state, and today the synagogue is open to be admired once more.

Now continue up Eldridge Street as far as Hester. Songwriter IRA GERSHWIN was born on the corner here, at No. 60.

Turn right on to Hester, go across Allen and then left on to Orchard, named after the orchard of James Delancey, which covered this area in colonial days. Walk north up Orchard, cross Grand and Broome, and stop at No. 97 Orchard Street to pay a visit to . . .

The Tenement Museum

It is estimated that some 7,000 people passed through this tenement between 1863, when it was built, and the 1930s. Typical of the tenement houses that were thrown up throughout the Lower East Side during the 19th-century immigration rush, it contained 22 apartments over five floors, and a basement saloon, but no hot water or flush lavatories, which were only made compulsory by the Tenement House Law in 1901. In 1935 the residents were evicted and the upper storeys sealed because modifications required by new housing laws were too expensive. And so it remained until 1988, when the building was rediscovered, with the apartments still in their original state, and opened up as a museum.

The different floors have been restored to show what apartments were like at different times in the tenement's history, and you can see how the German Jewish Gumpertz family would have lived in the 1870s and the Italian Catholic Baldizzi family in the early 20th century. It is almost impossible to imagine how these families survived in such appalling conditions, but a visit here is a fascinating experience and certainly makes one value every inch of space and glimpse of daylight.

Continue north up Orchard, noting how the street becomes more gentrified with boutiques and restaurants as you move north, and at East Houston turn right to find the most celebrated survivor of the Jewish Lower East Side.

Katz's Delicatessen

This New York institution was founded in 1888 as Iceland Brothers and was taken over by the Katz brothers in 1910. It soon became a focal point for the local Jewish community, and especially for actors from the Jewish theatres along

Second Avenue. During the Second World War the owners sent food out to their sons who were serving in the armed forces overseas, and instituted the company slogan, which is written up everywhere on the walls of the deli, 'Send a Salami To Your Boy In The Army'.

A sign hangs above one of the tables inside the deli saying, 'Where Harry met Sally . . . hope you have what she had!' This was the very table where Meg Ryan and Billy Crystal sat to film that famous scene from the 1989 Rob Reiner movie *When Harry Met Sally*, where Meg Ryan fakes an orgasm, prompting a character played by the director's mother Estelle Reiner to turn and say to a waiter, 'I'll have what she's having.'

Well, I never knew this about

BROADWAY – CHAMBERS TO CANAL. TRIBECA, CHINATOWN & THE LOWER EAST SIDE

It was John B. Bogart, city editor of the *Sun* newspaper that occupied the Sun Building at No. 280 Broadway between 1917 and 1966, who came up with the well-known quote about journalism, 'When a dog bites a man, that's not news, because it happens so often. But if a man bites a dog, that's news.'

The Duane Reade drugstore chain opened its first full-service drugstore on Broadway between Duane and Reade streets in 1960.

In 2002 film producer JANE ROSENTHAL, her husband, the real estate philanthropist CRAIG HATKOFF, and actor ROBERT DE NIRO founded the TRIBECA FILM FESTIVAL as an initiative to revitalise the Tribeca area after the 9/11 terrorist attacks, which took place just to the south of the neighbourhood. The festival was an immediate success and is now held annually in spring, attracting upwards of three million people and raising millions of dollars every year.

A couple of blocks east of St Augustine's Church is CORLEARS HOOK, a piece of land that juts out into the East River and forms the easternmost point of the Lower East Side. An important landmark for sailors, it was named after Jacobus van Corlaer, who settled a plantation there in 1638. By the beginning of the 19th century the shoreline had become busy with shipyards and wharves, attracting brothels and streetwalkers seeking the custom of the sailors, and it wasn't long before the prostitutes who frequented the Hook were being referred to as 'hookers'.

CHAPTER 8

Broadway – Canal to Houston. SoHo & Little Italy

Haughwout Building

Haughwout Building

Even in an area renowned for its rich cast-iron architecture, the HAUGHWOUT BUILDING at No. 488 Broadway stands out. Built in 1857 for E.V. Haughwout's Emporium, it is one of New York's oldest surviving cast-iron structures and most certainly its finest. It was designed by John Gaynor and based on the San Sorvino Library in Venice, while the cast iron was forged at Daniel Badger's foundry on the East River. Because it occupies a corner site there are two magnificent cast-iron façades, with 92 keystone arches carrying 92 large windows designed to take advantage of the light provided by the south-west aspect.

There are two reasons why the Haughwout Building is not just one of the most beautiful buildings in New York but also one of the most significant. In order to carry the weight of the two iron façades it was necessary to incorporate the iron into the actual framework of the building, rather than just hanging it off the brickwork, a step that presaged the iron frame technique that would make possible the first skyscrapers.

Secondly, the Haughwout Building WAS THE FIRST COMMERCIAL BUILDING IN THE WORLD TO HAVE A PASSENGER ELEVATOR, a steam-driven affair with a safety break, invented and produced by ELISHA OTIS, which he had first demonstrated at the New York World's Fair in 1854.

With its pioneering iron framework and its elevators, the Haughwout Building was the first building in New York to possess the two essentials required to build a practical skyscraper.

It also, along with A.T. Stewart's Marble Palace, housed one of the first quality retail outlets to be located on Broadway north of City Hall. While many visitors came to E.V. Haughwout's Emporium simply to ride the elevators, others came from far and wide to purchase the high quality cut glass and porcelain for which the Emporium was famous. President Lincoln's wife, Mary Todd Lincoln, travelled up from Washington to order a new set of china for the White House, and chose a design incorporating the American eagle within a wide mauve border, costing $3,000.

Musical Comedy

Musical comedy was born at No. 514 Broadway in 1879, when Ned Harrigan and Tony Hart put on their MULLIGAN GUARDS BALL, regarded as THE WORLD'S FIRST MUSICAL COMEDY, at WOOD'S THEATER COMIQUE, a converted synagogue that stood on the spot from 1862 until 1881. The musical, which was set on the streets of downtown New York, poked fun at gang violence, political corruption, racial tension and the local militia or 'Mulligan's Guards'. Every race and class in New York was lampooned, and hence the play proved popular with everyone – even local politicians turned up, hoping to be seen as good sports who could take a joke.

St Nicholas Hotel

At Nos. 521 and 523 Broadway two small fragments of what was once the largest and most luxurious hotel in the world stand side by side, their stained marble façades criss-crossed by fire escapes, the paint on their windows peeling, their grand entrances despoiled by modern shop fronts. The ST NICHOLAS HOTEL, THE FIRST BUILDING IN NEW YORK TO COST OVER $1 MILLION, opened on 6 January 1853, stretched for 100 ft (30 m) along Broadway and was faced along its length with pure white marble. It WAS THE FIRST HOTEL IN THE WORLD TO HAVE CENTRAL HEATING, boasted 600 rooms, all with hot and cold running water, and was also THE FIRST HOTEL IN THE WORLD TO FEATURE A

'HONEYMOON SUITE' OR 'BRIDAL CHAMBER'.

In 1867 MARK TWAIN, author of the Great American Novel, *The Adventures of Huckleberry Finn*, met his future wife Olivia Langdon at the St Nicholas Hotel, where she was staying for Christmas with her brother, Twain's friend Charles Langdon. That night they all went to hear Charles Dickens give a reading from *David Copperfield* at Steinway Hall.

Little Singer Building

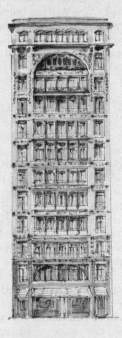

The exquisite LITTLE SINGER BUILDING at No. 561 Broadway was begun in 1903 by Ernest Flagg for the Singer Sewing Machine Company. Five years later, Flagg would go on to build the 47-storey Singer Tower for the same company further down Broadway. The Singer Tower, alas, was demolished in 1967 but happily the 12-storey Little Singer Building, with its ravishing wrought-iron, red-brick and terracotta façade, survived and is now full of very expensive co-operative apartments – in 2012 the penthouse was on the market for $8 million. The building is actually L-shaped and sports a similar façade on Prince Street.

Niblo's Garden

One of Broadway's most celebrated early theatres, NIBLO'S GARDEN, stood at No. 568 Broadway, on the corner of Prince Street. Irish impresario and proprietor of the Bank Coffee House in Pine Street, WILLIAM NIBLO purchased what was then the Columbian Garden in 1823 and proceeded to develop it as a fashionable entertainment centre, with a theatre, saloon, hotel and restaurant, all of which opened in 1829 as Niblo's Garden. The theatre grew by stages and at its height could seat up to 3,200 people, making it the largest theatre on Broadway.

Niblo's Garden hosted many premières. In 1835 P.T. Barnum put on his first show there, featuring an elderly woman called Joice Heth who claimed to be George Washington's nanny and 160 years old. The exhibition was a huge success and marked the start of Barnum's great show-business career.

In 1838 CHARLES KEAN made his debut as Hamlet there, while EDWIN FORREST first appeared as Macbeth at Niblo's Garden in 1839. And it is believed that THE POLKA WAS INTRODUCED TO AMERICA there, in 1844. In 1846 the theatre was destroyed by fire but was rebuilt and reopened in 1849.

The new Niblo's Garden introduced Italian opera to New York in 1850 with a première performance of Verdi's *Macbeth*, starring Angiolina Bosio as Lady Macbeth. In 1851 a nine-year-old ADELINA PATTI made her operatic debut in a charity performance at Niblo's Garden, and in 1855 the tightrope walker CHARLES BLONDIN made his first New York appearance there. Later that same year THE FIRST AMERICAN OPERA, George Bristow's *Rip van Winkle*, was premièred there.

In 1866 Niblo's Garden hosted THE FIRST EVER BROADWAY MUSICAL, a musical extravaganza called THE BLACK CROOK, lasting five hours and featuring rumbustious songs and a hundred scantily clad chorus girls. Fashionable New York was shocked – but flocked to see it.

'It debauched many a pure mind,' wrote Mark Twain, adding that while the special effects were 'gorgeous', the 'actions of the female dancers were scandalous . . . The scenery and legs are everything . . . Girls – nothing but a wilderness of girls – stacked up, pile on pile, away aloft to the dome of the theatre . . . dressed with a meagerness that would make a parasol blush.'

Notwithstanding the traumatised Mr Twain, *The Black Crook* became 19th-century Broadway's most successful production, running for 16 months and earning over $1 million.

In 1872 the theatre burned down again and was rebuilt by A.T. Stewart. On 23 March 1895, Niblo's Garden put on its last performance and a few weeks later was knocked down. The site is now occupied by office blocks.

SoHo

SoHo stands for South of Houston (pronounced Howston) and refers to an area bounded by Lafayette to the east, Canal to the south and West Broadway to the west, although the area west of that, Hudson Square and the South Village, is sometimes referred to as West SoHo.

The area was originally farmland unsuitable for development, but once the Canal created for draining the Collect Pond had been filled in at the beginning of the 19th century, fashionable residences sprang up on the levelled terrain. Shops and grand hotels then began to appear along Broadway, followed by theatres, and the neighbourhood soon became New York's entertainment centre and red-light district, frightening away the wealthy residents.

Over the next 50 years or so warehouses and textile factories moved in, and such were the bustle and noise and heat that SoHo became known as Hell's Hundred Acres. Many of these factories and shops took advantage of the newly invented cast-iron architecture, which was strong and relatively inexpensive. Initially it was used to make decorative façades for old industrial buildings, and then, during the time that SoHo was being built up in the mid-19th century, it became the building material of choice. As development of the city moved north again and left SoHo behind, cast-iron was abandoned and steel took over, and because of this SoHo was left with THE LARGEST COLLECTION OF CAST-IRON ARCHITECTURE IN THE WORLD.

Artists soon moved into the abandoned industrial units of Soho, and the neighbourhood is now one of New York's trendiest areas, full of art galleries, boutiques and, along Broadway, outlets of many of New York's Fifth Avenue stores.

A WALK AROUND SoHo

Start point: Broadway and Canal

Greene Street

Walk west on Broadway for two blocks and turn right on to Greene Street, which runs through the heart of Soho's historic cast-iron district and is lined with galleries and businesses housed in the most glorious and varied examples of cast-iron façades to be found anywhere.

Nos. 8–34 make up THE LONGEST STRETCH OF CAST-IRON BUILDINGS IN THE WORLD.

Nos. 10–14, recognisable by their tenement-style fire escapes, are amongst the earliest cast-iron buildings and date from the 1860s.

The Corinthian columns of Nos. 15–17 date from the 1890s.

Nos. 28–30, with its elaborate mansard roof, is known as the 'QUEEN OF GREENE STREET' and was built in 1873 by Isaac F. Duckworth as a warehouse.

No. 72 is the 'KING OF GREENE STREET', unashamedly French Renaissance and described as the most complex three-dimensional structure in Soho. This was also built by Isaac F. Duckworth, a little before the 'Queen', in 1872, as a warehouse for the Gardner Colby Company's dry goods business.

Subway Map

On the sidewalk outside Nos. 104–110 is NEW YORK'S LARGEST AND MOST UNUSUAL SUBWAY MAP, 90 ft (27 m) long, 12 ft (3.6 m) wide and titled, more or less accurately, 'SUBWAY MAP FLOATING ON A NY SIDEWALK'. It was commissioned by Tony Goldman, the owner of the SoHo Building outside which it is displayed, and executed by Belgian artist FRANÇOISE SCHEIN in 1985. The subway lines are made from ½-inch (1.3 cm) stainless steel bars set into a terrazzo floor, while the 156 stops are made from glass rounds (because of the restricted space only Manhattan is represented). It's hard to tell quite how accurate the map is, and rather confusingly it is orientated with the southern section of the subway facing north. If you study it too closely the brain begins to sizzle slightly and you begin to imagine things, such as imaginary cats staring at you out of imaginary windows.

But hang on a minute. There really are imaginary cats staring at you from imaginary windows, just across the street. In 1975 illusionistic artist RICHARD HAAS transformed the blank side wall of No. 112 Prince Street, home in the early 20th century of an underwear manufacturer, into an amazingly realistic trompe-l'oeil mural of a cast-iron façade facing on to Greene Street. By incorporating existing window openings – and cats – Haas made the mural come alive, and as you gaze up at the wall from Greene Street you are almost tempted to toss the cats a piece of fish. This masterpiece is constantly under threat from people wanting, quite understandably, to develop the corner lot. I hope it survives, for it is a New York treasure.

Federal Houses

Now turn left into Prince Street and walk for five short blocks, enjoying the shops and the architecture. At the junction with Sixth Avenue go straight ahead into Charlton Street to see the most ravishing row of red-brick Federal-style homes dating from 1820. You are now at the heart of the Charlton-King-Vandam Historic District, which boasts THE GREATEST CONCENTRATION OF FEDERAL AND GREEK REVIVAL-STYLE HOUSES IN MANHATTAN.

Playhouse

Having admired the houses, retrace your steps to Sixth Avenue, turn right (south) on Sixth and then right again into Vandam for the SoHo PLAYHOUSE, once the Huron Club, a favourite haunt of Tammany Hall and the Democratic Party. It was transformed into a theatre in the 1920s, and during the 1960s housed a well-known workshop for playwrights run by EDWARD ALBEE, who at the time was writing his famous play *Who's Afraid of Virginia Woolf?*

Mortier House

When you reach the Soho Playhouse you are standing on the site of MORTIER HOUSE, part of the colonial Richmond Hill estate leased from Trinity Church in 1767 by Major Abraham Mortier, paymaster of the British army in New York. George Washington used Mortier House for his staff headquarters while staying in New York in the run-up to the Revolution in 1776.

During his first presidency Washington's Vice President John Adams lived in the house, by now known as Richmond Hill House, and described by Adams' wife Abigail as '. . . the most delicious spot I ever saw. It is a mile and a half from New York. The house stands upon an eminence; at an agreeable distance flows the noble Hudson . . .'

In 1794 Richmond Hill House was purchased by Aaron Burr, who laid out the grid of three streets that would become Charlton, King and Vandam. It was from Richmond Hill House that Burr set out on the morning of 11 July 1804 to row himself across the river for his duel with Alexander Hamilton.

As a result of the backlash following his killing of Hamilton, Burr eventually had to sell the estate at a loss to JOHN JACOB ASTOR (1763–1848) in 1817, a piece of business that set Astor on the road to becoming America's first multi-millionaire and the largest land holder on Manhattan. Astor, who made his first fortune in the fur trade, divided the property into lots and sold off leases to builders, netting himself a tidy sum. He saw long before others that New York would have to expand northwards, and so he sold all his other business interests and invested the money in buying up as much of Manhattan as he could. Consistent with his motto 'Buy and Hold. Let others improve', he rarely built on the land himself but let others do the work while paying him rent for the privilege. When he died at 85, Astor was THE RICHEST MAN IN AMERICA, his

only regret in life being that he wished he had 'bought all of Manhattan'.

Fire Museum

Continue west on Vandam, turn left on to Varick and first right into Spring Street, where you will find the NEW YORK CITY FIRE MUSEUM, located in a 1904 firehouse once the home of the FDNY Engine Company No. 30. Here you can see an extensive collection of firefighting memorabilia, including some magical old fire trucks and displays illustrating the evolution of firefighting from the bucket brigades of New Amsterdam, through the tough volunteer firefighting gangs of the 19th century, to the modern fire-fighting heroes who attended 9/11.

Ear Inn

Carry on west along Spring Street and cross Greenwich to arrive at No. 326 Spring Street, a quite lovely three-storey, pink-brick, Federal-style house that is home to THE SECOND OLDEST WORKING BAR IN NEW YORK, THE EAR INN. The house was built in 1817 for James Brown,

Little Italy

Italians first began to settle in the Five Points district, particularly along Mulberry Street, in the 1850s, and soon developed a close-knit sense of community encouraged by *Il Progresso Italo Americano*, an Italian-language newspaper published and printed in the neighbourhood by Carlo Barsotti, who later ran campaigns to have statues of famous Italians like Verrazano and Columbus erected in the city. The Little Italy that grew up during the late 19th and early 20th centuries began to shrink in the 1960s, encroached upon by Chinatown, and the Little Italy that exists today is really just the northern section of Mulberry Street and one or two blocks either side. Mulberry Street, however, retains a colourful and authentic Italian flavour and is lined with Italian restaurants sporting chequered tablecloths and draped with Italian flags. Little Italy is seen at its best in September during the Feast of San Gennaro celebrations, when Saint Gennaro's shrine and relics are paraded along Mulberry Street to the accompaniment of much music and dancing.

A WALK AROUND LITTLE ITALY

Start point: Broadway and Houston

Nolita

an African–American who was thought to have been an aide to George Washington during the Revolution. It became a brewery and bar some time around 1835, was a speakeasy during Prohibition in the 1920s, and then a drinking establishment known simply as The Green Door. In 1977 new owners moved in who published a musical magazine called *Ear Magazine* in an upstairs room. They decided to name their new bar after the magazine and carefully painted out part of the 'B' on the neon Bar sign outside so that it read Ear – cleverly avoiding a lengthy Landmark Commission review of the new sign.

From the Ear Inn go back to Greenwich, turn left and walk north three blocks to King Street. Turn right into King Street and walk three blocks to Sixth Avenue, noting the delightful Georgian house at No. 20 on your right. Turn right on Sixth Avenue and walk south to Spring Street. Turn left and take Spring Street back through SoHo to Broadway. From here you can either go north to the station at Canal or south to City Hall.

Nolita is an unofficial name for the area south of Houston and 'North of Little Italy'. To explore it, start by walking east along Houston towards the huge red

PUCK BUILDING, famous for its ballrooms and celebrity-studded fashion parties, and for being the setting for Grace's design studio in the TV series *Will and Grace*. AMERICA'S FIRST HUMOROUS MAGAZINE, PUCK, was published here until 1918. As you turn right past the building into Mulberry Street, look up to your right to see the gilded Puck figure on the corner. There is another one over the main entrance in Lafayette.

Walk down Mulberry to the small, three-storey red-brick building on the left at No. 266. It looks a bit like a tenement but in fact houses NEW YORK'S ONLY RUSSIAN CATHOLIC CHAPEL, ST MICHAEL'S, established here in 1936 by Fr. Andrew Rogosh to serve Russian Catholic émigrés fleeing Soviet Russia. The building was put up in 1859 and originally used as a Chancery Office for St Patrick's.

Oldest Manhole Cover

Opposite St Michael's is Jersey Street, a narrow alleyway that runs at the back of the Puck Building. Have a look at the manhole cover at the entrance to the street, which says Croton Aqueduct 1866.

This is a rare remnant from the Croton Aqueduct System and is probably THE OLDEST MANHOLE COVER IN MANHATTAN.

Old St Patrick's Cathedral

A few yards further down Mulberry is NEW YORK'S FIRST CATHEDRAL, OLD ST PATRICK'S CATHEDRAL, completed in 1815 by Joseph Mangin, co-designer of City Hall. When St Patrick's opened it was New York's largest church, and it was the seat of the Roman Catholic Bishop of New York until the new St Patrick's Cathedral opened on Fifth Avenue in 1879. Free concerts are often held in the courtyard in front of the main entrance to the cathedral in Mott Street.

America's First Pizza

Carry on down Mulberry, turn left in Spring Street and walk one block to find LOMBARDI'S, AMERICA'S FIRST PIZZERIA. Gennaro Lombardi opened an Italian grocery store at No. 53 Spring Street in 1897. It quickly became popular with workers from along Broadway, who would buy his thin-crust pizzas, which were cooked in coal-fired ovens and tied up with strings, for their lunch. Lombardi finally acquired a licence to run a full-time pizzeria in 1905 and later introduced the pizza slice, for those who couldn't afford or didn't want a whole pizza. The business remained in the family until it closed in 1984, but was opened again at its present location by a friend of Lombardi's grandson in 1994, and retains the traditional coal-fired method of cooking.

Old Police Headquarters

Retrace your steps to Mulberry, turn left and continue south on Mulberry to Broome Street. Turn right on to Broome Street to see the hugely elegant baroque Old Police Headquarters, which takes up a whole block of Center Street from Broome to Grand. After the Consolidation of the Five Boroughs in 1898 the police department was expanded and required a headquarters with more space than the previous HQ in Mulberry Street. This grand edifice here, which opened in 1909, was designed to 'impress both the officer and the prisoner with the majesty of the law'. In 1973 the police moved again to a new headquarters near City Hall, and in 1987 this building was converted into 55 luxury co-operative apartments.

Walk down Centre Market Place, with the Police Building on your right, then turn left on to Grand and right, back on to Mulberry. Cross Hester and on the right is the rear entrance to THE ROMAN CATHOLIC CHURCH OF THE MOST PRECIOUS BLOOD, the National Shrine Church of San Gennaro, the Patron Saint of Naples. During the Feast of San Gennaro in September, a Mass is held here and then the statue of San Gennaro is taken from its home in the church and paraded around the streets of Little Italy. Now turn right on Canal and return to Broadway.

Well, I never   *knew this about*

BROADWAY — CANAL TO HOUSTON. SOHO & LITTLE ITALY

In the 1830s, JAMES FENIMORE COOPER, author of *The Last of the Mohicans*, lived in a small brick house on Broadway that backed on to Niblo's Garden.

The Astor Building at No. 583 Broadway was built in 1896 on the site of the house where John Jacob Astor died in 1848.

Like many of SoHo's streets, Greene Street is paved with Belgian blocks, a type of quarried stone, resembling cobblestones, but shaped into broadly regular rectangles, like bricks.

German immigrant Heinrich Engelhard Steinweg founded the piano manufacturing company STEINWAY & SONS in a loft at the rear of No. 85 Varick Street in 1853.

The Ear Inn sits just up the road from the ventilation towers marking the entrance to the HOLLAND TUNNEL, THE FIRST MAJOR VENTILATED HIGHWAY TUNNEL IN THE WORLD. The tunnel runs for over 1½ miles (2.4 km) under the Hudson River, linking Manhattan Island and New Jersey, and was THE LONGEST UNDERWATER TUNNEL IN THE WORLD when completed in 1927. The first vehicle to drive through the tunnel was a truck delivering goods to Bloomingdale's.

The baptism scene in the 1972 film *The Godfather* was filmed inside Old St Patrick's Cathedral, as was the ceremony in *The Godfather Part III* (1990) where Michael Corleone, played by Al Pacino, is named a Commander of the Order of St Sebastian.

The Delmonico family of restaurant fame are buried in the vaults beneath Old St Patrick's Cathedral.

The tenement building at No. 247 Mulberry was formerly the home of the RAVENITE SOCIAL CLUB, the most notorious Mafia hangout in Little Italy, and headquarters during the 1970s and 80s of JOHN GOTTI, the 'Dapper Don', capo of the Gambino family. The club was bugged by the FBI at the end of the 1980s to collect evidence against Gotti, and on the night of 11 December 1990 it was raided by the FBI, who arrested Gotti for the murder of previous Gambino capo 'Big Paul' Castellano in 1985. Gotti subsequently died in prison in 2002.

CHAPTER 9

BROADWAY – HOUSTON TO UNION SQUARE. THE EAST VILLAGE

Grace Church

The Cable Building

The impressive CABLE BUILDING, on the corner of Broadway and Houston, was designed in 1893 by Stanford White for the Metropolitan Traction Company, a huge conglomerate that controlled virtually all the cable cars in Manhattan. While the upper floors were given over to offices the basement, which was dug 40 ft (12 m) below the surface to minimise vibration and noise, was filled with massive steam engines, powering giant winding wheels for the steel cables that dragged the cable cars along Broadway from Bowling Green to 36th Street. The cables moved under the street at a constant 30 miles (48 km) per hour, and up to 60 cars at a time could lock on or release as required. In 1901 the line switched to electric power and the Cable Building became redundant after just eight years of service. The engines were removed and the building was given over entirely to offices.

Cousin at Ford's Theater in Washington, in front of Abraham Lincoln, when the President was assassinated by John Wilkes Booth. Laura ran to the presidential box and cradled Lincoln's head in her lap, as he lay mortally wounded.

The Corner House

At No. 670 Broadway once stood The Corner House, built in 1831 for banker Samuel Ward of Prime, Ward & King. He became a recluse after the death of his wife, aged 27, in 1824, and The Corner House was built like a fortress to protect both his privacy and his art collection, THE FIRST MAJOR PRIVATE ART COLLECTION IN AMERICA, which was kept in a special colonnaded extension at the back of the house. His daughter, Julia Ward Howe, wrote the words of 'The Battle Hymn of the Republic':

Previously this was the site of the Gothic-style St Thomas Church, built in 1824 to serve the Episcopal congregation living on what, at that time, was the northern edge of the city. In 1848 John Jacob Astor was brought here from his house on the other side of Houston and laid to rest in the family vault. After the church burned down in 1851 all the Astors were re-interred at the new Trinity Cemetery further north.

> Glory, glory hallelujah!
> Glory, glory hallelujah!
> Glory, glory hallelujah!
> His truth is marching on.

Prelude to a Tragedy

No. 622 Broadway, now a rather attractive cast-iron building was, in the mid 19th century, the site of LAURA KEENE'S VARIETIES THEATER. Laura Keene was a British actress and theatre manager, and THE FIRST FEMALE STAGE DIRECTOR ON BROADWAY. In 1858 Tom Taylor's farce *Our American Cousin* was premièred here, and six years later Laura Keene was playing in *Our American*

The Photograph that made a President

No. 785 Broadway was the address of the last, and most lavish, Broadway studio of MATHEW BRADY, America's most celebrated photographer of the 19th century. In 1844 Brady opened a studio at Broadway and Fulton and became known for his portraits of the prominent people of the time, including

18 of the 19 Presidents alive during his lifetime. His 1850 album 'The Gallery of Illustrious Americans' contained photographs of an elderly Andrew Jackson, 7th President, Senator Daniel Webster, and ornithologist and painter John Audubon.

As he became better known, Brady moved up Broadway, with studios at No. 359 and No. 653 Broadway, before finally arriving at No. 785 in 1860. In February that year he took the photograph for which he is most famous, that of Abraham Lincoln on the day that Lincoln made his famous speech at Cooper Union. Lincoln later declared, 'Brady and the Cooper Institute made me President.'

Iron Palace

Right across the street from No. 785 a nondescript block of flats called Stewart House stands on the site of A. T. Stewart's extraordinary IRON PALACE, opened in 1862 as the successor to his Marble Palace further south on Broadway. The emporium was immense, covering the whole block between East 9th and 10th Streets and was the first building of any size in New York to sport a cast-iron front. There were six storeys and a central courtyard covered by a huge glass dome, while six steam-powered elevators transported customers between floors.

After Stewart's death in 1876 the store slowly began to lose its way and was facing closure when in 1896 it was saved by John Wanamaker, who reopened it as Wanamakers. It became a hugely successful enterprise in its own right until the 1950s, when Fifth Avenue began to emerge as New York's prime shopping street. The Iron Palace burned down in a spectacular conflagration that lasted for two days, in 1956.

Grace Church

The slender spire of GRACE CHURCH acts as a highly visible landmark on Broadway as it stands in the first bend in the road – Broadway was forced to turn north here to avoid the orchards of one Henry Brevoort. By happy chance this left Breevort with a clear patch of land, which he sold in 1843 to Grace Episcopal Church, part of the parish of Trinity, and at that time operating from a modest building at Broadway and Rector Street near Trinity Church.

The clergy and congregation of Grace Church were keen to move north along with the rest of New York Society and wanted a new church building that would announce their arrival from downtown. They specifically wanted Gothic, and to provide it for them they chose an unknown 25-year-old architect called James Renwick Jr. who just happened to be Henry Brevoort's nephew. Renwick's Grace Church, ebulliently Gothic, and the third Trinity Church, designed by Richard Upjohn in rather more staid Gothic style, rose together and both were consecrated in 1846, sparking a rash of Gothic Revival architecture in New York. In 1888 Renwick added the fine marble spire in place of the original wooden steeple.

Grace Church instantly attracted an upmarket congregation drawn from the smart surrounding neighbourhood. Unlike at Trinity Church, the names of the rich folk who attended Grace Church are still written on the pews they rented – the front pew at Grace Church, for instance, we can see was occupied by the Schermerhorn family.

In 1863 showman P.T. Barnum staged the marriage here of his business partner General Tom Thumb (2 ft 9 in or 0.84 m tall), to Lavinia Warren (2 ft 7 in or 0.78 m tall). As the Grace Church website remarks, 'Despite loud professions of distaste for the alleged grotesqueness of the coming spectacle, most of the fashionable world contrived to be there, to jostle each other and even stand on the seats, in order to get a glimpse of it.'

In 1869 the historian The Rev. Matthew Hale Smith wrote, 'For many years Grace

On the Breadline

The leafy churchyard beside Grace Church on Broadway and East 10th Street was once occupied by FLEISCHMANN'S MODEL VIENNESE BAKERY, established here in 1876 by Louis Fleischmann, whose family invented packaged yeast. While the bakery quickly attracted a wealthy clientele, the smell of fresh baking bread also enticed a less salubrious crowd of hungry tramps who gathered outside the shop in the evening hoping for scraps. Fleischmann decided to give the day's leftover bread to the waiting men, and each night from then on, as word got around, more and more people came along to join the very first 'breadline'.

While Fleischmann undoubtedly gave away the unsold bread for altruistic reasons, his generosity did the reputation of the bakery no harm at all, since it proved that bread sold during the day was freshly baked.

has been the centre of fashionable New York. To be married or buried within its walls has ever been considered the height of felicity.'

St Denis Hotel

The office block at No. 799 Broadway was once the smart ST DENIS HOTEL, built by James Renwick Jr., architect of Grace Church opposite, on land owned by his own family. It was opened in 1853 just as this stretch of Broadway was becoming fashionable, and was soon entertaining the New York glitterati.

On 11 May 1877, Alexander Graham Bell demonstrated his telephone here, for the first time in New York, in a second-floor reception room, in front of about 40 people. Clearly they were impressed, for the following year New York's VERY FIRST TELEPHONE DIRECTORY appeared, listing some 200 subscribers. THE VERY FIRST PAID TELEPHONE IN NEW YORK was installed in the office of J. LLOYD HAIGH at 81 John Street in 1877, and was connected to his foundry in Brooklyn, with the wires running across the unfinished Brooklyn Bridge, for which Haigh was one of the contractors.

'Eighteen Miles of Books'

STRAND BOOKSTORE at No. 828 Broadway disputes the title of 'LARGEST SECOND-HAND BOOKSTORE IN THE WORLD' with Powell's Books of Portland, Oregon. Strand's slogan '18 miles of books' is

actually somewhat modest – since they moved here from Fourth Avenue in 1956 they have constantly expanded and now boast 23 miles (37 km) of bookshelves.

Named after the famous Strand thoroughfare in London, Strand Bookstore was founded by Ben Blass in 1927, one of 48 bookshops located on Fourth Avenue between Union Square and Astor Place, on what was then known as 'Book Row'. It is the only one of those 48 bookshops that survives.

The East Village

The EAST VILLAGE emerged from what was an extensive farm or 'bowery' belonging to the last Dutch director Peter Stuyvesant. In the early 19th century wealthy families such as the Astors and the Vanderbilts built themselves houses in the area, but then fashionable New York moved north again and the vacuum was filled with immigrants, mainly Irish and Germans. During the second half of the 19th century the area became known as Klein Deutschland, or Little Germany, while later came immigrants from Poland and the Ukraine. Until the 1960s the area was considered part of the Lower East Side, but then it became popular with artists and writers priced out of Greenwich Village to the west, and began to form its own Bohemian village identity, much of which it retains today.

A WALK AROUND THE EAST VILLAGE

Start point: Union Square

Walk south down Broadway, turn left on to East 8th Street, and cross over Lafayette to give the ASTOR PLACE CUBE a nudge – this 15 ft (4.5 m) steel cube, also known as the Alamo, was created by Tony Rosenthal in 1967 and revolves if pushed.

Astor Place Riots

You are now standing in the middle of ASTOR PLACE, and if you look back you will see a pink 11-storey office building directly across Lafayette. This occupies the former site of the posh ASTOR PLACE OPERA HOUSE, opened in 1847 to cater to the upmarket residents of Greenwich Village and Gramercy.

In 1849 the Opera House invited the renowned English actor WILLIAM MACREADY to perform *Macbeth* there while he was on a tour of America. At the same time, just down the road, the popular American actor EDWIN FORREST was due to perform his *Macbeth* at the Bowery Theater, which drew its audience mainly from the rough Five Points neighbourhood. There was already an unfriendly rivalry between the two

actors, and when this was elevated to 'heroic all-American tough guy actor takes on effete English toff', the stage was set for trouble. During one of Macready's first performances at the Opera House, a crowd from Five Points managed to get into the auditorium and pelt Macready with eggs. He quite understandably threatened to go home to England but was persuaded to have another go by, amongst others, Herman Melville and Washington Irving. On the night of 10 May, as Macready was about the step on stage, the Opera House was stormed by a mob 10,000 strong, armed with bricks and bottles, all shouting for Edwin Forrest. Macready managed to finish his performance and slip out of the theatre in disguise, but by then it was too late. For the first time in New York's history the state militia was called out to quell its own citizens, and when they started shooting into the crowd to restore order, over 100 people were injured with up to 25 killed, many of them innocent bystanders.

The Astor Place Opera House closed the following year, and the outraged audience took their custom to the new Academy of Music, which had opened further north on Irving Place, far, far away from the beastly Bowery mob. The opera house building was eventually demolished and replaced in 1890 by the present office block.

North across East 8th Street, above the entrance to the Astor Place subway station, there is a 1986 reconstruction of one of the elaborate entry kiosks that used to shelter the steps to New York's early subway stations. The design of these kiosks was based on a type of summerhouse found in the gardens of ancient Persia called a 'kiushk' – hence kiosk.

Inside the station itself, which underwent major renovation in 1986, plaques decorated with beavers recall the beaver pelts on which John Jacob Astor's original fortune was founded.

Now cross diagonally over Cooper Square to . . .

Cooper Union

Too poor to go to Columbia College, PETER COOPER (1791–1883) nevertheless became a millionaire by the time he was 40, one of America's first self-made men. Determined to offer others the education he lacked, in 1859 Cooper founded the COOPER UNION FOR THE ADVANCEMENT OF SCIENCE AND ART, NEW YORK'S FIRST FREE, CO-EDUCATIONAL COLLEGE, specialising in architecture, engineering and the practical arts. The centrepiece of the college's huge Foundation Building on Cooper Square is the GREAT HALL, once THE LARGEST LECTURE HALL IN NEW YORK, and big enough to accommodate up to 1,000 people.

On 27 February 1860 Abraham Lincoln, then unheard of in New York, and yet to announce his candidacy for President of the United States, gave an historic address in the Great Hall that came to be known as his 'right makes might' speech, and set him off on the road to the White House. As the *New York Tribune* put it, 'No man ever made such an impression on his first appearance to a New York audience.' If you speak nicely to the chap on the front desk you may be allowed to go downstairs and have a look at the Great Hall, which to all intents and purposes looks much the same now as it did on that momentous night. As you sit there in front of the stage you can almost hear Lincoln's words echoing off the walls. It is a most impressive place.

First Elevator Shaft

Back outside, in Cooper Square, look up at the front of the Foundation Building and you will see on the left side of the roof a round turret a bit like a chimney. This is the top of THE WORLD'S FIRST ELEVATOR SHAFT, put in by Peter Cooper when the building was constructed in 1853. Since the Foundation

Building was taller than any other building in New York, Cooper decided that it should have an elevator and he was confident that a practical elevator would be perfected by the time the building was completed – if it wasn't then he would build one himself. Cooper made his elevator shaft round because he thought that would be the most efficient design and he was amazed when the first elevators turned out to have square shafts. In the end, Elisha Otis, who installed the world's first passenger elevators in the nearby Haughwout Building in 1857, designed a special elevator to fit Cooper's round elevator shaft. There is still an elevator there today, although not the original.

Colonnade Row

Now return to Astor Place and turn left down Lafayette to COLONNADE ROW, all that is left of La Grange Terrace, built by Seth Geer in 1831 and named after Marshall Lafayette's country home in France. There were originally nine houses in the terrace, fronted by 27 Corinthian columns, and amongst the first residents were John Jacob Astor II, future First Lady Julia Gardiner, Cornelius Vanderbilt, Washington Irving and, for a while, Charles Dickens. The 'Quality' eventually moved out as the area deteriorated, and in 1902 five of the houses were taken down to make way for an annexe to Wanamakers department store. The four remaining houses are in a state of some disrepair but give a reasonable idea of how splendid the original terrace must have

looked and, indeed, how fashionable 19th century New York might have looked.

Public Theater

Opposite Colonnade Row is the PUBLIC THEATER, which occupies the former home, built in 1849, of the ASTOR LIBRARY, NEW YORK'S FIRST FREE LIBRARY. This was one of the three collections that were combined to establish the New York Public Library in 1910. When the library building was threatened with demolition in 1965 after all the books had been moved out, theatre producer JOSEPH PAPP, whose Public Theater company had for several years been presenting free Shakespeare in Central Park, persuaded the city to buy the building as a home for his company. The library was converted into six theatres and opened on 17 October 1967 with the première of HAIR, a daring musical production that Papp hoped would broaden the company's repertoire and chime in with the East Village vibe. The following year *Hair* became THE FIRST OFF-BROADWAY MUSICAL TO TRANSFER SUCCESSFULLY TO

BROADWAY and introduced a new genre to the world, the 'rock musical'.

Over the years the Public Theater has gained a reputation for producing new hit shows, the most successful undoubtedly being A CHORUS LINE, which premièred there in May 1975 and subsequently ran on Broadway for over 6,000 performances.

Now continue south down Lafayette and turn left (east) on to East 4th Street. A short way along on the left, standing somewhat incongruously between two scruffy empty plots, is the . . .

Merchant's House Museum

This lovely brick townhouse was built in 1832, and in 1835 became the home of a rich merchant called SEABURY TREDWELL, rumoured to be the last man in New York to wear a pigtail. Tredwell's daughter Gertrude was born in the house and lived there until she died in 1933, aged 92. It turned out that she had kept the house exactly as her father had it, and in 1936 a relative decided to open it up as a museum. All the furniture, fittings, china and glass, clothes and kitchen equipment are from the 19th century and original. The only modifications since Gertrude died are some electrical wiring, some plumbing, and a cast-iron stove in the kitchen. It seems, though, that even these few additions have upset Gertrude, for she is said to haunt the place, and visitors have reported hearing disembodied footsteps or rattling china, and being assailed by blasts of cold air. Whether you believe in ghosts or not, the Merchant's House Museum is certainly an unforgettable experience, a little piece of 19th-century New York preserved in aspic.

Now carry on down East 4th Street and turn left into Cooper Square East. Keeping the park on your left, continue north past the astonishing perforated stainless steel and glass Cooper Union Academic Building at No. 41 Cooper Square. Opened fully in 2011, this extraordinary building, which contains some of Cooper Union's class-rooms, laboratories, art studios and offices, is New York's first LEED certified academic laboratory building. (LEED stands for Leadership in Energy and Environmental Design.)

Turn right on to East 7th Street and walk to . . .

McSorley's Old Ale House

McSORLEY'S OLD ALE HOUSE, established in 1854, is THE FOURTH OLDEST BAR IN NEW YORK. The opening of an Irish bar in this part of town, not long after the closure of the Astor Place Opera House nearby, exemplified the changing nature of the neighbourhood. According to legend, Peter Cooper brought Abraham Lincoln here after Lincoln's famous speech in the Great Hall at the Cooper Union in 1860, and behind the bar there is a faded 'Wanted' poster offering $100,000 reward for 'The Murderer of our beloved President Abraham Lincoln'. The bar staff will swear that the poster is an authentic original from 1865, and it may be true, for another legend says (don't forget this is an Irish bar) that nothing has been taken down from the walls of the bar since founder John McSorley died in 1910. And anyway, after a round of McSorley's Ale (a round here is actually two glasses), who cares? You might even believe that those really are Houdini's handcuffs locked to the bar rail. They only serve McSorley's own ale here, and it comes in two varieties, light or dark.

Distinguished New Yorkers who have partaken of a round of McSorley's Ale here include Teddy Roosevelt, Peter Cooper, Boss Tweed, e.e. cummings and Brendan Behan.

Stuyvesant Street

Now retrace your steps to Cooper Square East, which here becomes Third Avenue, and turn right. Cross St Mark's Place and then turn first right into STUYVESANT STREET to take a look at the GEORGE HECHT VIEWING GARDENS on the left, which mark the former entrance to Peter Stuyvesant's farm or 'bowery'. There is a compass in the middle of the garden which shows that Stuyvesant Street is THE ONLY STREET ON MANHATTAN ISLAND THAT RUNS THE TRUE COMPASS EAST/WEST – the Manhattan grid follows the island's natural 29-degree skew, so that all the other streets run south-east/north-west rather than true east/west. Stuyvesant Street was laid out in the early 1800, by Petrus Stuyvesant, Peter's

great-grandson, before the grid was formed, and was left untouched, in deference to New York's much respected First Family.

Continue along Stuyvesant Street and cross Ninth Street to No. 21, the unusually wide townhouse with the shutters, on the left. This is the HAMILTON FISH HOUSE, built in 1803 by Petrus Stuyvesant as a wedding present for his daughter Elizabeth and her new husband Nicholas Fish, a Revolutionary War officer. Their son HAMILTON FISH (named after Nicholas's friend Alexander Hamilton) was born here in 1808 and grew up to be the 16th Governor of New York and U.S. Secretary of State.

Go to the end of Stuyvesant Street, noting on your left No. 128, the house that forms the end of the terrace where it meets East 10th Street. This was Nicole Kidman's house in the 2005 film *The Interpreter*. Now cross over to . . .

St Mark's in the Bowery

Peter Stuyvesant's farmhouse stood somewhere near here, and this was the site of his private chapel, built in 1660 – making this spot THE OLDEST SITE OF CHRISTIAN WORSHIP IN CONTINUOUS USE IN NEW YORK. When he died on the farm in 1672, Stuyvesant was buried in a vault beneath the chapel. In 1793 his great-grandson Petrus Stuyvesant donated the land on which the chapel stood to Trinity Church on the condition that they

Stewart, the tycoon whose Marble Palace on Broadway was regarded as the first department store. Stewart was fantastically rich and fantastically disliked, and on 7 November 1878 his vault was broken into and his body removed. Nothing more was heard despite the offer of a $25,000 reward. Eventually, after a year, Stewart's widow contacted the body snatchers and offered them $20,000 in cash. Stewart's remains were then handed over in a midnight exchange with three masked men, and the tycoon was finally laid to rest in the new cathedral at Garden City on Long Island whose construction he had funded.

pulled down the old chapel and built a new one. ST MARK'S IN THE BOWERY, designed by John McComb Jr., was consecrated in 1799, making it THE SECOND OLDEST CHURCH IN MANHATTAN, after St Paul's Chapel on Broadway. The steeple was added in 1828 and the cast-iron portico in 1858.

Outside, beneath the east and west yards, are stone vaults where until the middle of the 19th century wealthy members of St Mark's congregation were laid to rest. Notable names buried here include seven generations of Stuyvesants, Nicholas Fish, Abraham Schermerhorn, Elizabeth Beekman, Daniel Tompkins and New York mayor Philip Hone. The inscription on Peter Stuyvesant's grave suggests he was 80 years old when he died – in fact he was 60.

Also buried here, in 1876, was A.T.

Tompkins Square

With the portico of St Mark's behind you, turn left and walk east along East 10th Street for two blocks to Avenue A, the start of Alphabet City. Turn right and then take the first entrance on your left into TOMPKINS SQUARE PARK, named after Daniel Tompkins, the 4th Governor of New York State, (from 1807–17, during which time slavery was abolished in New York) and 6th Vice President of the United States (to James Monroe).

Walk straight to the middle of the park and you will come to the pink marble GENERAL SLOCUM MEMORIAL.

General Slocum

Until the September 11 terrorist attacks, the GENERAL SLOCUM disaster was THE WORST LOSS OF LIFE IN ONE DAY IN NEW YORK'S HISTORY. At 9.30

on the morning of 15 June 1904, the pleasure cruiser *General Slocum* set sail from the East 3rd Street pier, packed with dozens of families from St Mark's Evangelical Lutheran Church, who were out to enjoy their annual picnic excursion. Most of the passengers lived around Tompkins Square, which was then at the centre of the German neighbourhood of Klein Deutschland. As the *General Slocum* steamed up the East River a fire broke out at the stern. There was a brisk wind on the river and by the time the captain had managed to run the ship aground on North Brother Island at Hell Gate, the entrance to Long Island Sound, all three decks of the ship had melted and collapsed. One thousand and twenty-one people died, hundreds of them children. Klein Deutschland never recovered and within ten years most of the German community had left for Yorkville or New York's other boroughs, Queens and Brooklyn.

Leave the park by the way you entered, turn left (south) on Avenue A, then right into St Mark's Place (East 8th Street) and take this street all the way back to Astor Place (four blocks).

Walk of Fame

Just across First Avenue, on the sidewalk outside THEATER 80, is New York's very own WALK OF FAME. In 1971 former actor HOWARD OTWAY opened Theater 80 as a movie house showing films from the Golden Era of Hollywood, the 1930s to 1950s. To celebrate he invited a number of legendary movie stars to a typical Hollywood opening night party and asked them to leave their hand prints and signatures on the sidewalk outside the theatre, as they do outside Grauman's Chinese Theater on Hollywood Boulevard. Others were later added, and amongst those that have survived are the marks of Dom DeLuis, Joan Crawford, Gloria Swanson and Myrna Loy.

Continue west down St Mark's Place to Nos. 19–25. In 1966 Andy Warhol turned this address into a nightclub where he put on a light show called *Exploding Plastic Inevitable*, with music from the Velvet Underground as the house band, and guest turns from the likes of Jimi Hendrix, the Grateful Dead and Jefferson Airplane.

Continue to Astor Place and the end of the walk.

Well, I never **knew this**
about

BROADWAY — HOUSTON TO UNION SQUARE. THE EAST VILLAGE

Nos. 667–677 Broadway is now a modern block of dormitories for New York University, but was once the site of the WINTER GARDEN THEATER, where in 1864, acting brothers Edwin, Julius and John Wilkes Booth appeared together for the one and only time, during a benefit performance of *Julius Caesar* to raise money for a statue of William Shakespeare in Central Park.

Stewart House, the block of flats that replaced the Iron Palace on Broadway, was the home for 25 years of New York-born LEON KLINGHOFFER, the wheelchair-bound businessman who was shot by Palestinian terrorists and thrown overboard from the *Achille Lauro* cruise ship in 1985. Klinghoffer made his name as the inventor of the Roto Broil, a metal oven fitted with a rotisserie and heating element for grilling meat.

In 1997 actors DAVID DUCHOVNY and TEA LEONI were married in the garden of Grace Church.

In the days when cable cars ran along Broadway there was a sharp turn at the corner of Broadway and 14th Street. Since the cable ran at a constant 30 mph (48 kmph), it was incumbent upon the cable car driver to detach from the cable and apply the brake to slow down as they took the corner, but many of the drivers were inattentive, with the result that there were scores of accidents here, some fatal, and the corner became known as 'Deadman's Curve'.

COOPER UNION still attracts students from all over America and tuition remains free. Although Peter Cooper left a generous endowment this is insufficient to cover all the college's costs and the shortfall is made up with donations from alumni as well as rents from the college's real estate holdings. Their most significant property, which pays for a goodly portion of the school's costs, is the land on which the Chrysler Building stands.

New Yorker and founder of Cooper Union PETER COOPER made his first fortune in glue, running a factory by the East River in Kips Bay. A by-product was his own invention of edible GELATINE, to which a few years later a pharmacist added cough syrup to produce JELLO. In 1828 Cooper opened the Canton Iron Works in Baltimore where he built AMERICA'S FIRST STEAM LOCOMOTIVE, THE TOM THUMB. He also invented the fire-resistant iron girders that made possible the cast-iron architecture used to such effect in Soho, and in 1856

In Cooper Square there is a statue of Peter Cooper, sculpted by a Cooper Union graduate, Augustus Saint-Gaudens.

When Peter Stuyvesant arrived back in New Amsterdam from Holland in 1664, he brought with him a pear tree, which he planted on his farm, 'by which my name may be remembered'. It stood and bore fruit on Pear Tree Corner at what is now East 13th Street and Third Avenue for over 200 years, becoming a favourite New York landmark, until in 1867 it was felled when two horse-drawn carriages collided and ploughed into the tree. In 2003 a new pear tree was planted on the same spot by the owner of the shop that stands next to it now, and Pear Tree Corner happily lives again.

introduced the Bessemer process to America. The Cooper Union Foundation Building was one of the first buildings in New York to be constructed using wrought iron girders, which were produced at Cooper's own rolling mill in Trenton, New Jersey. Late in life he started on a political career, standing in the 1876 presidential election as the Greenback candidate, at 85 years of age THE OLDEST PERSON EVER NOMINATED TO STAND FOR PRESIDENT OF THE UNITED STATES.

CHAPTER 10

GREENWICH VILLAGE

Washington Square Arch

GREENWICH VILLAGE, usually referred to as 'the Village', was originally an Indian fishing village called Sapokanican, with a stream running through it known as the Minetta, or 'devil water'. The Dutch transformed it into a tobacco plantation, which under the English evolved into a country village. It was known as Grinwich from as early as 1713, named no doubt by someone who had sailed to New York from Greenwich in England. The village became a refuge during outbreaks of cholera and yellow fever in the city to the south, and often those who came temporarily to escape decided to stay. Thanks to its isolation the western portion of the village was spared inclusion in the Manhattan Grid plan and retains its winding 18th-century street layout as well as its village atmosphere. In the late 19th, early 20th centuries Greenwich Village became a haven for writers and artists, becoming America's equivalent of Paris's 'Left Bank'. Today it is too expensive for all but the most successful artists.

A WALK AROUND GREENWICH VILLAGE WEST OF BROADWAY

Start point: Union Square

Walk west on 14th Street and turn left (south) on to Fifth Avenue.

Salmagundi

At No. 47, opposite the First Presbyterian Church, whose tower is said to be modelled on the famous Magdalen Tower of Oxford University, is the SALMAGUNDI CLUB, AMERICA'S OLDEST ARTIST'S CLUB, housed in a rare brownstone with one of the few remaining stoops on Fifth Avenue. The club was founded in the Village in 1871 as the New York Sketch Club and moved here in 1917. Its present name was inspired by Washington Irving's satirical 'Salmagundi Papers'. Past members have included Stanford White, Louis Tiffany, Childe Hassam and William Merritt Chase. Winston Churchill was an honorary member.

First Church

On the corner west of 10th Street is the CHURCH OF THE ASCENSION, consecrated in 1841 and THE FIRST CHURCH ON FIFTH AVENUE. It was designed by Richard Upjohn as one of New York's earliest examples of English Gothic Revival and opened five years before Upjohn's new Trinity Church. Inside, the chancel is decorated with a huge mural by JOHN LAFARGE showing the Ascension of Our Lord. Many of the angels in the mural look remarkably like LaFarge's mistress Mary Whitney.

In 1844 the church hosted THE FIRST MARRIAGE OF A SITTING PRESIDENT when the tenth U.S. President John TYLER secretly married his second wife, JULIA GARDINER, a young socialite from one of New York's oldest families and 30 years his junior. Tyler is best remembered as THE FIRST VICE-PRESIDENT TO ASCEND TO THE PRESIDENCY, which he did in 1841 after William Henry Harrison died of pneumonia caught while delivering his two-hour inaugural speech in freezing weather.

Brevoort

At Nos. 11–15, the Brevoort Apartments stand on the site of FIFTH AVENUE'S FIRST HOTEL, the BREVOORT HOTEL, built in 1851 and famous for NEW YORK'S FIRST SIDEWALK CAFÉ, where village characters such as Eugene O'Neill, Isadora Duncan and Edna St Vincent Millay would congregate. Aviator CHARLES LINDBERGH came here for breakfast in 1927 to collect $25,000 from the hotel's owner Raymond Orteig, who had put up the money as a prize for the first person to fly solo non-stop across the Atlantic.

BUDDY HOLLY lived in the Brevoort Apartments after his marriage in 1958 until his death in 1959. Also CARMINE DESAPIO, the last boss of Tammany Hall.

The name Brevoort comes from Henry Brevoort, a landowner from Dutch stock whose house here was THE FIRST HOUSE ON FIFTH AVENUE.

A short step down West 8th Street, the New York Studio School occupies what in 1931 was the original home of the Whitney Museum of American Art.

Washington Mews

Back on Fifth Avenue, past No. 1, is WASHINGTON MEWS, the ONLY MEWS IN NEW YORK and also THE OLDEST COBBLED STREET IN NEW YORK. It was laid out in the 1830s as stables for the big houses in the area. Some of the stables were converted into studios in 1916, with Gertrude Vanderbilt Whitney as an early tenant. The properties now belong to New York University, and although the street is gated to discourage idle sightseers, the Mews is not private and you can stroll down it if you wish.

Washington Square Park

WASHINGTON SQUARE PARK marks the start of Fifth Avenue and, as the largest green space in Greenwich Village, is a popular meeting place. It also serves as a quadrangle for New York University, THE LARGEST NOT-FOR-PROFIT INSTITUTION IN AMERICA, which owns most of the buildings around the park.

In the early 19th century the park was a 'potter's field', or public burial ground for the indigent, and many of the victims of the yellow fever outbreak of 1822 were buried here. Some 20,000 bodies are thought to still be lying beneath the square.

Washington Square North

In 1826 the potter's field was levelled out as a military parade ground and by the 1830s it had become a desirable place to live. The beautiful houses along the east side of Washington Square North, along what is known as the 'Row', date from this time and form one of the first terraces to be built in New York.

HENRY JAMES's grandmother lived 'in venerable solitude' at No. 18 Washington Square North (now gone). Henry himself was born just around the corner at No. 21 Washington Place in 1843, and between the ages of four and 12 lived at No. 58 West 14th Street. His novel, *Washington Square*, published in 1880, is set in the area during the time he was growing up here.

RICHARD MORRIS HUNT, the architect who designed the pedestal of the Statue of Liberty, the 'Met' and Carnegie Hall, lived at No. 2 Washington Square North from 1887 to 1895.

The artist EDWARD HOPPER and his wife lived in a studio on the top floor of Nos. 1–3 Washington Square North from 1913 until his death in 1967.

Washington Square Arch

In 1889 a wooden arch was raised in Washington Square to celebrate the centenary of George Washington's inauguration. It was replaced in 1892 by a permanent arch made of Tuckenhoe

marble, designed by Stanford White and modelled on the Arc de Triomphe in Paris. Two statues of Washington, one as Commander-in-Chief and one as President, were added on the north side in 1918, along with Washington's motto, *Exitus acta probat* (The end justifies the means), and the Washington family coat of arms, three stars over two stripes, inspiration for the American Stars and Stripes. A small door in the western leg of the arch gives access to a secret spiral staircase of 102 steps leading to the top, from where there would no doubt be a wonderful view, if only one were allowed to see it.

Now walk west through the park, past the statue of Italian patriot Giuseppe Garibaldi, who lived in New York in 1850-51, while in exile, and on into Washington Place, to the Brown Building on the left.

Triangle Shirtwaist Factory Fire

This was the site in March 1911 of the WORST INDUSTRIAL DISASTER IN NEW YORK'S HISTORY, THE TRIANGLE SHIRTWAIST FACTORY FIRE. The factory occupied the top three floors of what was then called the Asch Building, and the afternoon shift was just ending when fire broke out on the eighth floor and quickly swept through the ten-storey building. While most of those on the eighth and tenth floors were able to escape, those on the ninth floor found themselves trapped as the management had locked the doors to the stairwells and exits to prevent pilferages. The elevators soon became inoperable and the poorly maintained fire escape collapsed, sending scores of women plunging 100 ft (30 m) to their death on the street below. When the fire department arrived their ladders couldn't extend above the sixth floor, and the remaining workers were left to either jump or burn to death. One hundred and forty-six people died, most Italian immigrant women. The tragedy prompted legislation for major improvements in safety in the workplace, championed largely by the International Ladies Garment Workers Union. One of those watching in horror as the women fell to their deaths was FRANCES PERKINS, who determined that day that she would fight for improved conditions for workers. She later became THE FIRST WOMAN EVER APPOINTED TO A CABINET POSITION IN AMERICA when Franklin D. Roosevelt made her Secretary of Labour in 1933.

Judson Memorial Church

Now return to Washington Square and walk to the southern exit to see the

Judson Memorial Church on the corner of Thompson Street. This fine Romanesque-style church was built in 1892 by Stanford White and is named after Adoniram Judson, THE FIRST AMERICAN MISSIONARY TO BE SENT ABROAD, in his case to Burma in 1811. The church is mostly renowned for its collection of stained-glass windows by John LaFarge, who did the mural in the Church of the Ascension on West 10th Street. A window on the second stair landing called 'Praying Angel' is another depiction of LaFarge's mistress Mary Whitney.

Provincetown Playhouse

Walk to the south-west corner of Washington Square, where the chess players sit, and where the 1993 movie *Searching for Bobby Fisher* was filmed, and turn left (south) into MacDougal Street, named after New York senator Alexander McDougall. Playwright EUGENE O'NEILL moved into a room in the boarding house at No. 38 on the corner in 1916 when his first work, *Bound East for Cardiff*, was being staged by the Provincetown Players in a converted parlour at No. 139. The Players eventually moved into an old stable at No. 133, which they made into the PROVINCETOWN PLAYHOUSE, and many more of O'Neill's plays were staged there. PAUL ROBESON made an early stage appearance there in 1922, and BETTE DAVIS made her stage debut there in 1929. In 1960 the theatre was

the scene of the first production of Edward Albee's first play, *The Zoo Story*.

Hell Hole

Down at the end of West 3rd Street to your right is GOLDEN SWAN PARK, which marks the former site of the GOLDEN SWAN CAFÉ, a rough, run-down Irish dive with sawdust on the floor better known as the Hell Hole and patronised by gamblers, gangsters, Tammany Hall politicians and assorted misfits. Eugene O'Neill loved to drink there and pick up material for his plays, and he later immortalised the Hell Hole as Harry Hope's saloon in *The Iceman Cometh*. The bar was demolished, or fell down of its own volition, in 1928.

Back on MacDougal Street, LOUISA MAY ALCOTT finished writing *Little Women* while living at Nos. 130–132 between 1867 and 1870.

First Cappuccino

Across from there is the CAFÉ REGGIO, established in 1927 and THE FIRST CAFÉ IN AMERICA TO SERVE CAPPUCCINO. The café featured in a number of films including *The Godfather II*, *Serpico* and the first *Shaft* movie. In 1959 presidential hopeful John F. Kennedy gave a speech on the sidewalk outside.

Café Wha?

The CAFÉ WHA? on the corner of Minetta Lane is where BOB DYLAN

played his debut gig in 1961. Others who began their careers here include Jimi Hendrix, Bruce Springsteen, Peter, Paul and Mary, Kool and the Gang, Richard Pryor and Bill Cosby. Although it has changed hands several times, the Café Wha? remains a groundbreaking venue for up-and-coming performers.

Across Minetta Lane is the MINETTA TAVERN, a popular haunt for Ernest Hemingway, F. Scott Fitzgerald, Dylan Thomas and Ezra Pound. During Prohibition it was a speakeasy called the Black Rabbit. THE READER'S DIGEST was founded in the basement in 1922 by DeWitt Wallace and his wife Lila Bell.

Now walk down Minetta Lane and turn left into Minetta Street – these two roads run along the course of the now hidden Minetta Brook. At the end of Minetta Street cross Sixth Avenue to Bleeker.

Downing Street

DOWNING STREET, running south-west off Bleeker and Sixth, is named after diplomat Sir George Downing who was responsible for arranging the handover of New Amsterdam to the British in 1664. The little square next to it is called Sir Winston Churchill Square in honour of the British Prime Minister who lived in No. 10 Downing Street in London (named after the same Sir George Downing).

Continue north on Bleeker as far as Jones Street, unchanged since Bob Dylan and his girlfriend Suze Rotolo strolled down it in the photo on the cover of his early album *The Freewheelin' Bob Dylan*.

Cross back over Bleeker left and right and go down Morton, then left and right over Seventh Avenue into Leroy, which leads to . . .

St Luke's Place

On its north side St Luke's Place is lined with a row of rather nice 1850s townhouses. No. 10 is the home of the Huxtable family in THE COSBY SHOW, and No. 6, marked by the two tall lamps that identify mayoral homes in New York, was the home of the popular, high-living, 'anything goes' MAYOR JIMMY WALKER, whose hedonistic lifestyle of women, drink and easy money was brought crashing down by Robert Moses and the Great Depression. Walker, after whom the park opposite is named, resigned in 1932 and fled to Europe, while his house was sold to settle his unpaid tax bill.

Morton Street

Now turn right on Hudson and then right again into Morton Street. No. 66, with the distinctive angular bow window, is a favourite movie location, where Harrison Ford lived in *Working Girl*, Winona Ryder lived in *Autumn in New York* and Matthew Broderick lived in *The Night We Never Met*.

Opposite, at No. 65, is where the alleged Soviet spies JULIUS AND ETHEL ROSENBERG lived. Accused during the height of the McCarthy era of passing secrets about the atomic bomb to the Russians, they were executed in 1953, THE FIRST U.S. CIVILIANS EVER TO BE EXECUTED FOR ESPIONAGE.

Film director SOPHIA COPPOLA has lived at No. 46, an Italianate townhouse built in 1854 at a bend in the street. Narrow at the front, the house widens towards the rear and has a huge back garden.

At the junction turn hard left into . . .

Bedford Street

At No. 75½ and marked by a plaque is the 'NARROWEST HOUSE IN THE VILLAGE', just 9½ ft (2.9 m) wide and

built in 1873 to fill an alleyway. The poet EDNA ST VINCENT MILLAY lived here in 1923–4, then the actor JOHN BARRYMORE, and later CARY GRANT.

Next to it, on the corner at No. 77, is the ISAACS-HENDRICKS HOUSE, the OLDEST HOUSE IN THE VILLAGE, dating from 1799. John Isaacs, who built the house, was a wholesale merchant. The second owner, Harmon Hendricks, cornered the colonial copper market along with his associate Paul Revere and provided the copper for the engines of Robert Fulton's steamboat the *Clermont*.

Cherry Lane Theater

Just around the corner in Commerce Street is the CHERRY LANE THEATER. Built in 1836 as a brewery, and then a tobacco warehouse, it was converted into a theatre in 1924 by Edna St Vincent Millay.

BEA ARTHUR, Dorothy in *The Golden Girls*, made her professional debut here in 1947. TONY CURTIS was discovered here by a scout from Universal Pictures in 1948 while playing the lead role in Clifford Odet's *Golden Boy*. In 1958 Samuel Beckett's *Endgame* had its American première here, and in 1961 the theatre staged the world première of Beckett's *Happy Days*.

Chumley's

Return to Bedford Street and continue north. The small unmarked brownstone at No. 86 is the home of CHUMLEY'S, New York's most famous speakeasy, which was founded by Leland Chumley in 1922, and frequented by the likes of F. Scott Fitzgerald, who had a regular table, Edna St Vincent Millay, Eugene O'Neill, Norman Mailer and Allen Ginsberg. Deliberately anonymous, Chumley's closed for repairs after a fire in 2007 and did not re-open until 2013.

Continue up Bedford and cross over the junction with Grove Street. Now turn and look back at the building on the left of Bedford at No. 90. This is the 'Friends' Building, where Rachel, Monica, Phoebe, Joey, Chandler and Ross all live at one point or another, in the television series *Friends*. Although the series was shot in a studio in Los Angeles, the exterior of this building is shown many times in each show to establish that this is where the series is actually set.

On the corner across Grove from the *Friends* building is the gorgeous WILLIAM HYDE HOUSE, the only large wooden house in Manhattan still in private hands. It was built in 1822 by window sash maker William Hyde as a full-size advertisement for his work, and his workshop still stands behind the house on Bedford Street.

Grove Court

Turn left (south) on to Grove Street, leaving the William Hyde House behind on your right and look to your left as the road bends. At the end of a small-gated passageway are six small townhouses constructed in 1854 as infill for the space left by the bend. Officially named GROVE COURT, this became known as 'Mixed Ale Alley' since the houses were built for people too poor to afford ale other than the mixings at the bottom of the barrel. Today you would need to own a whole brewery to be able to afford to live there.

Carry on down Grove and cross Hudson to the Church of ST LUKE IN THE FIELD, an Episcopal church built in open countryside in 1822 for the people of Chelsea and Greenwich Village who couldn't get downtown to Trinity Church. One of the founders was Clement Clarke Moore, owner of much of Chelsea and author of 'Twas the Night Before Christmas'. The church was named after St Luke, the physician evangelist, in recognition of the Village's role as a haven from New York's yellow fever epidemics. The church is surrounded by two acres (0.8 ha) of beautiful gardens laid out in

---

'Speak Easy'

The first 'speakeasy' was a saloon bar outside Pittsburgh run illegally by a woman called Kate Hester, who refused to keep paying for a liquor licence when the price rose from $50 to $500 in 1888. If her customers became too noisy and risked attracting attention to the bar, she would exhort them to 'speak easy, boys, speak easy'.

1950 by Barbara Leighton, a secret oasis of lush greenery and wild plants which, remarkably, is open to the public.

White Horse Tavern

Four blocks north on Hudson Street is one of Greenwich Village's oldest pubs, the WHITE HORSE TAVERN, established for longshoremen in 1880 and the place where DYLAN THOMAS drank himself to death in 1953, knocking back, he claimed, 'eighteen whiskeys' in a two-hour drinking session. However many it was, they didn't sit well with the pills he was taking for his depression, and the next day he collapsed at the Chelsea Hotel and died not long afterwards in St Vincent's Hospital. The White Horse was also a favourite of writer JACK KEROUAC, a leading light with Allen Ginsberg of the 1950s Beat Generation, who rejected the drab conformity of their era and pursued a bohemian lifestyle of drugs, promiscuity and alternative expression through art and writing.

Kerouac was thrown out of the White Horse almost nightly. Other literary figures who drank here were ANAÏS NIN and MALCOLM LOWRY, while NORMAN MAILER got the idea for the free alternative weekly newspaper, VILLAGE VOICE, during a session here.

Retrace your steps down Hudson and turn left back into Grove Street. Walk on past the William Hyde House. The unusual pink-brick mansion at No. 45, built in the 1830s Federal style and the only one of its kind left in the Village, is where John Wilkes Booth plotted the assassination of Abraham Lincoln with his co-conspirators. It also played Eugene O'Neill's house in the Warren Beatty film *Reds*.

At No. 57 is ARTHUR'S TAVERN, established in 1937 and THE OLDEST CONTINUOUSLY OPERATING JAZZ CLUB IN NEW YORK. Charlie Parker and Roy Hargrove played there regularly.

Next door at No. 59 is MARIE'S CRISIS CAFE, on the site of the small wooden farmhouse where political theorist and revolutionary THOMAS PAINE died in 1809. The café, which is also a piano bar, gets its name from a previous owner Marie Dumont and Paine's *American Crisis* pamphlet series (beginning 'These are the times that try men's souls . . .').

Stonewall

Now cross Seventh Avenue to Christopher Park, considered to be the heart of Greenwich Village and named after Charles Christopher Amos, a developer who laid out many of the streets in the

THOMAS PAINE (1737–1809) was born in Norfolk in England and emigrated to America in 1774 so that he could participate in the American Revolution. In January 1776 he wrote a pamphlet called *Common Sense*, urging the colonists to fight for independence, and it became the best selling book in terms of sales per head of population in American history. The future president John Adams wrote, 'Without the pen of the author of Common Sense, the sword of Washington would have been raised in vain.'

area. Confusingly, Christopher Park has a statue of Union General Philip Sheridan in it, while Sheridan Square to the south just has some (very nice) trees. On the other side of Christopher Park, on Christopher Street, is the STONEWALL INN, a gay bar set up in 1967 by a small-time Mafia boss called 'Fat Tony' Lauria. Despite Mafia protection and kickbacks to the local police, gay bars were still subject to occasional raids in those days, and in the early hours of 28 June 1969 eight police officers entered the Stonewall Inn and demanded to see everyone's identification. A scuffle followed that spilled out on to the street and attracted a hostile crowd who pelted the police officers with bottles until they had to barricade themselves in the bar. The policemen were eventually rescued by more police in full riot gear who took the opportunity to beat up some of the crowd. There were similar disturbances over the next few nights between the police and gays demanding their right to congregate freely, and the riots marked the dawn of the Gay Liberation movement. Today New York's annual Gay Pride March, the biggest parade in the city, takes place in June on the Sunday

nearest to the anniversary of the Stonewall riots. The gay lobby group Stonewall takes its name from here, too.

Northern Dispensary

With the Stonewall Inn on your left, continue up Christopher Street to the tip of Christopher Park and turn right in front of the handsome NORTHERN DISPENSARY into Waverley Place, named after the popular 'Waverley' novels of Sir Walter Scott. The dispensary was built in 1831 to provide health care for the poor of Greenwich Village who couldn't make it to the dispensary downtown at City Hall. EDGAR ALLAN

POE was treated there for a head cold in 1837 caught, no doubt, while traipsing around cemeteries looking for plots for his horror stories.

The dispensary occupies a curious triangular plot that means two sides are on one street, Waverley Place, while the other one side is on two streets, Grove and Christopher Streets.

Continue down Waverley Place and take the first left into Gay Street, where in 1926 Mayor Jimmy Walker set up his showgirl mistress, Betty Compson, in an apartment. Turn right on to Christopher Street, then left on to Greenwich Avenue and right on to West 10th Street. Half a block up on your left is one of New York's hidden gems . . .

Patchin Place

PATCHIN PLACE is a gated, tree-lined cul-de-sac with a row of ten brick houses built around 1848 and almost unchanged ever since. At the far end of the alley, and glimpsed only darkly, is a real treasure, NEW YORK'S ONLY SURVIVING 19TH-CENTURY GAS STREETLAMP. It still works but is now powered by electricity.

Located right in the middle of the Village and yet affording privacy, PATCHIN PLACE became a haven for writers. The poet E.E. CUMMINGS lived at No. 4 from 1923 until his death in 1962 and spent much of his time banging on the window of No. 5 to see if his neighbour, the reclusive poet DJUNA BARNES, was still alive. JOHN REED, the communist activist writer, lived at No. 1, with his wife Louise Bryant, during his final few years, while finishing off his

eyewitness account of the Bolshevik revolution, *Ten Days That Shook the World*. He died, aged 33, in 1920. The book, and Reed himself, were the subject of Warren Beatty's 1981 film *Reds*.

Jefferson Market Courthouse

The great Victorian Gothic pile on the corner of West 10th Street and Sixth Avenue that is JEFFERSON MARKET COURTHOUSE is consistently voted one of the top ten most beautiful buildings in New York. It was built in 1876 on the site of a fire bell tower and a produce market named after Thomas Jefferson. The old fire bell was installed in the clock tower and the whole edifice was designed to look like a church, a sort of 'cathedral of justice', complete with tympanum over the doorway showing, not Christ and the Apostles, but the courtroom scene from the end of Shakespeare's *The Merchant of Venice*. In its early days the Courthouse was kept busy dealing with miscreants from the rowdy theatre district at nearby Madison Square, but by the 1950s it had been abandoned and was threatened with demolition. A successful preservation campaign was launched, led by e.e. cummings from nearby Patchin Place, and the Courthouse was reopened in 1967 as a branch of the New York Public Library.

West 10th Street

Now cross Sixth Avenue and continue east on West 10th Street to No. 45, the Peter Warren. This 11-storey apartment block was put up in the 1950s on the site of the Tenth Street Studio Building, built in 1858 by the architect Richard Morris Hunt to house THE FIRST ARCHITECTURAL SCHOOL IN AMERICA, as well as studios for American artists and his own office. This studio and others that sprang up around it were hugely influential in establishing Greenwich Village as a place for artists of all kinds. Actress Julia Roberts has an apartment in the Peter Warren.

On the opposite side of the street, the converted stable at No. 50 was the home in the 1960s of playwright EDWARD ALBEE, who bought it with the proceeds from his hit play *Who's Afraid of Virginia Woolf?* He wrote *Tiny Alice* and his Pulitzer Prize winner *A Delicate Balance* while living here. In 1968 Albee sold the house to composer and lyricist JERRY HERMAN, who bought it with the proceeds from *Hello Dolly* and *Mame*.

Now continue on West 10th, lined with some of New York's loveliest houses, past No. 18, once the home of the poet EMMA LAZARUS, author of the words 'Bring me your poor, your huddled masses', and No. 14, where MARK TWAIN lived from 1900 to 1901.

Cross over Fifth Avenue and continue along East 10th Street to Broadway, where you turn left and finish the walk at Union Square.

Well, I never knew this
about
GREENWICH VILLAGE

Fifth Avenue used to pass through Washington Square to become West Broadway, but in 1952 residents campaigned successfully to have the square made traffic free.

Washington Square Park is where Corrie, played by Jane Fonda, wanted to be *Barefoot in the Park*.

As well as students, budding guitarists,

The last tree before you exit Washington Square Park at the north-west corner is an ancient English elm marked with a green plaque that says HANGMAN'S ELM. Folklore has it that highway robbers and other miscreants were hanged from this tree in the 18th century and then buried in the potter's field. Whether or not this is true, the tree is reckoned to be at least 350 years old and is certainly the most ancient living thing in Greenwich Village.

painters and poets, you may at any time, or more particularly in spring, find yourself sharing Washington Square Park with a red-tailed kite or two. A pair of kites named Bobby and Violet took up residence on a 12th-floor ledge of the Bobst Library on the south-east corner of the square a few years ago. Violet died and was replaced by Rosie, and every year birdwatchers gather in the square to see their new chicks learn to fly. The birds are quite unfazed by people and can often be seen at close quarters grubbing for worms on the grass or perched on the lower branches of a tree, keeping a beady eye out for unwary squirrels. A webcam operated by the *New York Times* keeps an eye on the nest.

Meg Ryan and Billy Crystal meet up under the Washington Arch in *When Harry Met Sally*, and Harold Lloyd drives a horse-drawn trolley through the archway in the silent movie *Speedy*.

In 1954 playwright EDWARD ALBEE was visiting a bar on West 10th Street when he saw scrawled on a cloakroom mirror the words 'Who's Afraid of Virginia Woolf?' and thought the phrase might make a good title for a play about living life without false illusions. He determined from that moment that he was one day going to live on West 10th himself, and fittingly he finally achieved it thanks to the success of *Who's Afraid of Virginia Woolf?*

CHAPTER II

BROADWAY – UNION SQUARE TO TIMES SQUARE

The Flatiron Building

Union Square

UNION SQUARE marks, and its name refers to, the union of Manhattan's two earliest and most important thoroughfares, Broadway and the Bowery. Once a 'potter's field', or public burial place for the poor, it was laid out as a public park in 1839, modelled on the smart residential squares of London.

Union Square witnessed all the different phases of New York's northward development and was, at different times, lined with grand houses, hotels, the shops of Ladies Mile, theatres and concert halls. As one of the larger open spaces in the growing city the square became popular for mass rallies including a huge patriotic gathering in support of the Federal Union at the start of the Civil War in 1861, which attracted half a million people, the largest public assembly seen in America up to that time. Four years later, 300,000 people lined Broadway as Abraham Lincoln's body was brought to Union Square from its lying-in-state in City Hall, for a memorial service.

America's first Labor Day was celebrated in the square in 1882 – and in 2001, following the September 11 terrorist attacks, Union Square became the main gathering place for mourners.

Today Union Square is still a popular meeting place and the setting for MANHATTAN'S LARGEST FARMERS' MARKET, THE GREENMARKET, held on four days each week, where farmers from all across New York State come to sell their fresh produce.

The huge Independence Flagstaff in the centre of Union Square, the largest in New York State, commemorates the 150th anniversary of the Declaration of Independence.

Ladies Mile

Ladies Mile is a name given retrospectively to the next stretch of Broadway between Union and Madison Squares, which in the latter half of the 19th century was home to many of New York's most glamorous department stores, where the ladies of New York society would come to do their shopping.

The ARNOLD CONSTABLE STORE, opened in 1868 at No. 873 Broadway, was one of the stars of Ladies Mile, offering 'Everything from Cradle to Grave'. Started in 1825 on the corner of Canal and Mercer Streets by Aaron Arnold from the Isle of Wight in the UK, it became Arnold Constable when Arnold's daughter married James Constable in 1837, and proudly called

itself 'THE OLDEST DEPARTMENT STORE IN AMERICA'. During the next 100 years or more the company expanded both within New York and across America, merging in 1925 with A.T. Stewart and Company. The last Arnold Constable store, on Fifth Avenue, closed in 1975.

The flamboyant, cast-iron wedding cake structure with an ornamental corner pavilion and French Renaissance cap at No. 901 Broadway, on the corner of East 20th Street, was once the flagship store of LORD AND TAYLOR, AMERICA'S OLDEST UPMARKET RETAILER, founded in 1826 on Catherine Street and moved here in 1870. In 1914 Lord and Taylor became THE FIRST MAJOR STORE TO OPEN ON FIFTH AVENUE.

Flatiron District

A short hop east down East 20th Street, at No. 28, is the birthplace of the ONLY NEW YORK-BORN PRESIDENT, THEODORE ROOSEVELT. The actual brownstone house where Roosevelt was

Monumental Union Square

There are a number of significant statues in Union Square, including:

- GEORGE WASHINGTON (south centre): Unveiled on 4 July 1856, this statue by Henry Kirke Brown originally marked the spot where Washington was welcomed by a deputation of New Yorkers on 25 November 1783, Evacuation Day, the day when the British finally left the city after the Revolution. It was THE FIRST PUBLIC SCULPTURE RAISED IN NEW YORK since that of George III at Bowling Green and THE FIRST AMERICAN BRONZE EQUESTRIAN SCULPTURE. The statue was moved to its present location during the construction of the subway station under the square in the 1920s.

- MOHANDAS GANDHI (south-west corner): The statue of the famous advocate of non-violence was dedicated in 1986 in honour of Union Square's history of peaceful protest.

- LAFAYETTE (east): The statue of the Marquis de Lafayette was dedicated on 4 July 1876, the Centennial of the Declaration of Independence. It was sculpted by Frédéric Auguste Bartholdi to remind New Yorkers of the friendship between France and America and to encourage them to donate towards the pedestal of his most famous work, the Statue of Liberty. Lafayette is shown offering his sword to George Washington, but is unfortunately facing the wrong way and appears to be honouring a tree instead.

- ABRAHAM LINCOLN (north centre): Henry Kirke Brown's statue of the great Union hero, dedicated in 1870, originally stood where the statue of Gandhi now resides, in the south-west corner of Union Square, with a wall around the base inscribed with words from his second inaugural address, 'With malice towards none, charity toward all'. Now tucked away at the back of the square Lincoln goes sadly unnoticed.

born in 1858 was demolished in 1916, but it was rebuilt in 1923 with the rooms restored to how they would have looked when Roosevelt was growing up there. In 1962 the house opened as a public museum.

Flatiron Building

As you walk up Broadway towards Madison Square you come suddenly, and thrillingly, upon everyone's favourite, the glorious FLATIRON BUILDING. Because its lines blend so seamlessly into the line of Broadway, you don't realise its sheer size until you are standing beneath it, gazing up in awe.

The Flatiron is one of those rare buildings that actually exceed expectations or memories. However many times you see it, the sheer beauty and perfection of its design take the breath away. The two broad expanses that meet at an apex of just six feet (1.83 m) wide,

could so easily be dull and monolithic, but exquisite limestone carvings and three lines of shallow bay windows on the middle floors make the whole façade appear to ripple, an illusion enforced if viewing the building from the north, from where it resembles a stately ocean liner forging its way toward Madison Square through streams of traffic either side.

The Flatiron was built in 1902, and is one of the many buildings in New York that has a claim to being the first skyscraper – it was certainly the first skyscraper north of 14th Street. The architect was Daniel Burnham from Chicago, and the Flatiron is his only building in New York, which is hardly surprising – how could he ever design anything better? The distinctive shape of the building is dictated by the triangular plot on which it stands, where Broadway meets Fifth Avenue, one of many such triangles created by the disobedient Broadway as it traverses Manhattan at a jaunty angle to the more sober grid plan.

It was originally to be named the Fuller Building, after George Fuller, founder of the Fuller Company, who commissioned the building as a headquarters, but everyone called it the Flatiron and the name stuck. Another earlier name for the building was Burnham's Folly, so called because many observers were convinced that the Flatiron would be blown over by the wind. In fact the wind did cause problems, but of another kind – eddies of wind caused by the building's unusual shape whipped up the skirts of ladies walking along 23rd Street, and crowds of eager young men would flock to enjoy the spectacle. NYPD officers shouted at them to skedaddle, giving rise to the phrase '23 skidoo', meaning scram or beat it.

Madison Square

The Flatiron provides an appropriately impressive introduction to Madison Square, perhaps the loveliest of New York's big squares. Madison Square was laid out as we see it today in 1870, at a time when it was at the centre of New York society. Like Union Square it began life as a 'potter's field', or public burial ground, was later used as a parade ground, and takes its name from a timber roadhouse that stood where Fifth Avenue now meets 23rd Street, the last stop for stage coaches heading north out of the city in the mid 19th century. The roadhouse was called Madison Cottage after the former President James Madison.

Circus Games

In 1853 the cottage was demolished and replaced by FRANCONI'S HIPPODROME, forerunner of the modern circus, an enormous tented arena where up to 6,000 spectators could watch chariot races and gladiator fights.

Fifth Avenue Hotel

The Hippodrome was taken down in 1856 to make way for wealthy merchant Amos Eno's luxurious FIFTH AVENUE HOTEL, known as 'Eno's Folly', since it was so far north of the city centre it seemed most unlikely that anyone would want to stay there. However, Eno packed the hotel with innovations such as private bathrooms, a fireplace in every room and THE FIRST PASSENGER ELEVATOR TO BE INSTALLED IN AN AMERICAN HOTEL, a steam-powered 'vertical screw railway' designed by inventor Otis Tufts that was propelled upwards by means of a hollow revolving screw that passed through the centre of the car.

The hotel quickly proved a success and for a while became the most exclusive hotel in New York. Edward, Prince of Wales (later Edward VII) stayed there. Ulysses S. Grant began his presidential campaign with a dinner party there, and Chester Arthur maintained a suite in the hotel. Cornelius Vanderbilt, 'Diamond' Jim Fisk, railroad developer Jay Gould and Tammany's Boss Tweed would meet to trade stocks, while the powerful State senator Thomas Collier Platt ran New York from a cubbyhole in the hotel lobby, which became known as 'Amen Corner' because no project in the state could progress unless it had Platt's blessing or 'amen'.

The hotel was also popular with New York's cultural crowd, attracting the likes of Mark Twain, Jenny Lind and Edwin Booth, while Gore Vidal set his novel about the controversial 1876 Presidential election, rather cleverly entitled *1876*, in the Fifth Avenue Hotel.

While the hotel succeeded in luring New York Society north to Madison Square it couldn't keep it there forever, and by the start of the 20th century the crowd had moved further north again, leaving Madison Square to face life as a commercial centre. The Fifth Avenue Hotel was torn down in 1908, and a year later the Fifth Avenue Building, now the International Toy Center, rose in its place.

Met Life Tower

One of the reasons that Madison Square is such a joy is that it is encircled by a variety of beautiful buildings. The Flatiron is one, while on the east side of the square is another one, the Met Life Tower, erected in 1909 as an addition to the original 1893 headquarters of the Metropolitan Life Insurance Company. Seven hundred feet (213 m) tall, 51 storeys high, the Met Life Tower was the tallest building in the world from 1909 until 1913, when it was superseded by the Woolworth Building. The tower, modelled on the Campanile in St Mark's Square in Venice, sports a huge four-faced clock with chimes that play a measure by Handel every quarter hour. Although the original marble facing was replaced with limestone in 1964, the Met Life Tower is one of New York's most pleasing skyscrapers. The cupola at the summit of the tower remains illuminated throughout the night and used to feature in the insurance company's advertising slogan, 'The Light That Never Fails'.

The Tower is connected by a bridge at seventh-floor level to a strangely stunted art deco office block across 24th Street called the North Building, begun in 1928 and intended to be a 100-storey telescoping tower that would have reclaimed 'tallest building in the world' status from the Woolworth Building. The Great Depression set in, however, and the project was never realised. The present North Building of 32 storeys was completed in 1950 and is today occupied mainly by Credit Suisse, while the Met Life Tower is now a hotel.

Appealing

Across East 25th Street is the Appellate Division of the Supreme Court of the State of New York, a grand title for a grand building, which comes as something of a grand surprise lurking amongst all the soaring skyscrapers. This exquisite four-storey marble-faced *beaux-arts* courthouse, with its massive

Holocaust Memorial

One of New York's lesser-known memorials can be found on the north-west corner of the 1950s extension to the Appellate Court on Madison Avenue. The MEMORIAL TO ALL VICTIMS OF THE HOLOCAUST consists of a tall column of Carrera marble, 40 ft (12 m) high and carved with flames, representing a crematorium smokestack, set above an aerial view of Auschwitz modelled on a photograph taken during an air raid in August 1944, five months before the camp was liberated. It was sculpted by Harriet Feigenbaum and unveiled in 1990. The artist deliberately chose a material that would blend into the building, and it is probable that thousands of people pass by the memorial every day without realising that it is there.

entrance portico supported by six great Corinthian columns, is decorated with 30 marble statues fashioned by 16 different sculptors, THE LARGEST NUMBER OF SCULPTORS TO HAVE WORK FEATURED ON ANY ONE BUILDING IN AMERICA. Allegorical figures such as Wisdom (by Frederick Ruckstuhl), Peace (Karl Bitter) and Justice (Daniel Chester French, who later sculpted the figure of Lincoln on the Lincoln Memorial in Washington) jostle with figures from history such as Confucius, Moses and, once upon a time, Muhammad, until the latter was removed after protests from Muslim nations about this graven image of the prophet.

The interior is no less splendid, with murals depicting legal themes, more columns, more marble, chandeliers and a courtroom with a stained-glass dome and ponderous legal furniture.

The court hears appeals relating to both civil and criminal cases for New York and the Bronx, and some famous names have appeared here including Charlie Chaplin, Fred Astaire and Edgar Allan Poe.

Anglo-American

Attached to the back of the courthouse is the 42-storey, 577 ft (176 m) high brown glass Merchandise Mart Building, put up in 1973 as a trade facility and showroom for the tableware industry. It stands on the site of the flamboyant JEROME MANSION, home of the financier Leonard Jerome, friend and sometime partner of Cornelius Vanderbilt, co-founder of the American Jockey Club and founder of one of New York's earliest opera houses the Academy of Music, at the time the world's largest opera house. The Jerome Mansion included a theatre that could seat 600 people, a breakfast room that could seat

70, and a ballroom with fountains that flowed with champagne. Jerome's daughter Jennie married Lord Randolph Churchill, younger son of the Duke of Marlborough, and was the mother of British wartime leader Sir Winston Churchill.

Cocktails

When Jerome moved his family to Brooklyn in 1867, the house was leased out to the Union League Club and later to the Manhattan Club, where Democrat grandees like Grover Cleveland, Franklin D. Roosevelt, New York governor Alfred E. Smith and New York mayor Jimmy Walker would meet, possibly over a Manhattan cocktail – Canadian whiskey, red vermouth, Angostura bitters and a Maraschino cherry – which was invented in the club bar.

Double Act

Next door to the Jerome Mansion was the Madison Square Hotel. Here, while appearing on Broadway in 1934, before they both departed for Hollywood and stardom, JIMMY STEWART and HENRY FONDA rented rooms together and during the day built model aeroplanes. Stewart would later return to Madison Square to film on the roof of the Flatiron for the movie *Bell, Book and Candle* in 1958.

New York Life

Across East 26th Street is the majestic NEW YORK LIFE INSURANCE COMPANY BUILDING, built in 1928 by Cass Gilbert and inspired, apparently, by Salisbury Cathedral in England. The golden pinnacle, which was added in 1967, was lit for the company's 140th anniversary in 1985 and has remained lit ever since. In 1999 New York Life began using the building for a popular TV advertising campaign, making it one of the most recognised buildings in America. New York Life was founded in 1845 and is one of the oldest insurance companies in America. In 2000 it became the FIRST INSURANCE COMPANY IN THE WORLD TO HAVE MORE THAN $1 BILLION OF POLICIES IN FORCE.

Madison Square Garden

The first structure of any note to formerly occupy the site now inhabited by the New York Life Insurance

Company Building was P.T. Barnum's Hippodrome. This was demolished by William Vanderbilt in 1879 to make way for the first MADISON SQUARE GARDEN, where heavyweight boxing champion John L. Sullivan was the main draw.

This in turn was replaced in 1890 by the most famous of all the Madison Square Gardens, a masterpiece of Moorish architecture designed by Stanford White. This featured THE LARGEST AUDITORIUM IN THE WORLD, with seating for 8,000, THE LARGEST RESTAURANT IN NEW YORK, a famous roof garden and a tall tower, modelled on the Giralda bell tower of Seville cathedral. It was the second tallest building in New York at the time and was topped by a nude statue of the Roman goddess, Diana, which caused outrage.

Madison Square Garden II hosted AMERICA'S FIRST CAT SHOW in 1895, AMERICA'S FIRST CAR SHOW in 1900, and in 1924 THE LONGEST Democratic NATIONAL CONVENTION EVER HELD, which took 17 days and 103 ballots to choose John W. Davis as the Democratic nominee for President.

But perhaps the most famous event of all that took place at Madison Square Garden II was the fatal shooting of its architect, Stanford White, in the roof garden in 1906.

Notable New Yorker

STANFORD WHITE was born at No. 110 East 10th Street in 1853 and was a New Yorker through and through. After spending two years studying architecture in Europe he returned to New York and

joined with Charles McKim and William Mead to form McKim, Mead and White, which became one of New York's leading architectural practices in the second half of the 19th century, specialising in the *beaux-arts* style. Aside from Madison Square Garden II, White is particularly known for the Cable Building at No. 611 Broadway, the Judson Memorial Church and the Washington Square Arch.

As well as a love of architecture White also possessed a fondness for women, particularly young women, and he kept a number of love nests around town where he could take them to show his appreciation. One such retreat on West 24th Street possessed a swing upon which the girls would, er, swing for White's delectation.

In 1901 White's roving eye alighted on a beautiful 16-year-old actress and model called EVELYN NESBIT, who was appearing in the musical *Florodora* at the Casino Theater, and he was instantly smitten, as indeed were most men who saw her. Evelyn became a fixture on the swing at West 24th, and there was speculation that the nude statue above Madison Square Garden was modelled on her, but in 1905 Evelyn went and married a millionaire from Pittsburgh called Harry K. Thaw, and White turned his attention elsewhere.

Thaw, however, was the jealous type and resented Evelyn's past with White. On the evening of 25 June 1906, Thaw and Evelyn were dining at Martin's Restaurant before going to see the opening performance of a new musical, *Mam'zelle Champagne*, at the rooftop theatre in Madison Square Garden, when they saw White dining at a nearby table. Thaw became agitated and Evelyn wisely escorted her husband from the restaurant and on to the theatre.

Unfortunately, as it turned out, White decided to catch the show himself and was in his place at his usual table in the roof garden, nodding along to the song 'I Could Love a Million Girls', when Thaw marched up and shot him three times in the head, crying out, 'You've ruined my wife!' Or it could have been 'life!' No one seems sure.

Thaw was tried for murder and sent off to the Matteawan State Hospital for the Criminally Insane, but was declared sane in 1915 and released. Evelyn divorced Thaw and went back to work as an actress. In 1955 she worked as technical assistant on the movie *The Girl in the Red Velvet Swing*, a fictionalised account of her life starring Joan Collins.

Madison Square Garden II was pulled down in 1925 and a third Madison Square Garden was built at Eighth Avenue and 39th Street. The fourth and current Madison Square Garden was built above Pennsylvania Station in 1968.

Worth Square

WORTH SQUARE, a triangular sliver of land west of Madison Square, is named after GENERAL WILLIAM JENKINS WORTH, born in Hudson, New York, in 1794, who fought in the War of 1812, the Seminole Wars and the Mexican American War, and was one time Commandant of Cadets at West Point Military Academy. In 1849 he died of cholera in San Antonio, Texas, and was finally buried here, in the state of his birth, in 1857, beneath a 51 ft (15.5 m) high granite obelisk designed by James Batterson. The Worth Monument is THE SECOND OLDEST MONUMENT IN NEW YORK after the equestrian statue of George Washington in Union Square and one of only two monuments on Manhattan that are also mausoleums – the other being Grant's Tomb.

Great White Way

In 1880 the section of Broadway between Union and Madison Squares became ONE OF THE FIRST STREETS IN

Monumental Madison Square Park

There are a number of interesting statues in Madison Square Park, including:

- WILLIAM SEWARD (south-west corner). This bronze statue, by Randolph Rogers, was dedicated in 1876. Seward was 12th Governor of New York State and U.S. Secretary of State under Abraham Lincoln and Andrew Johnson. He survived an attempt on his life on the same night that Lincoln was assassinated, as did Andrew Johnson – the attacks were a conspiracy to decapitate the Union government. Seward is remembered especially for 'Seward's Folly', the purchase of Alaska from Russia for $7 million in 1867. Seward was THE FIRST NEW YORKER TO HAVE A MONUMENT ERECTED IN HIS HONOUR.

- ROSCOE CONKLING (south-east corner). Conkling was a leading Republican, congressman and senator for New York from 1867 to 1881. In March 1888 he got lost in a snow drift in Union Square while walking home from his office in Wall Street during the Great Blizzard of 1888, the worst snowstorm in New York's history. He managed to make it to the entrance of his club, the New York Club on 25th Street, where he collapsed, succumbing to pneumonia a few weeks later.

- ADMIRAL FARRAGUT (north centre). This statue is by Augustus Saint-Gaudens, with a base by Stanford White. David Farragut was THE FIRST ADMIRAL IN THE U.S. NAVY and a Union flag officer during the American Civil War. He is remembered for his battle cry at the Battle of Mobile Bay in 1864, 'Damn the torpedoes, full speed ahead!'

- CHESTER ARTHUR (north-east corner). Arthur was a lawyer and friend of Roscoe Conkling (see above). His route to becoming 21st President of the United States was as collector of customs at the Port of New York. He assumed the presidency after the assassination of James Garfield in 1881.

- On the west side of the park is the Eternal Light Memorial Flagpole, dedicated on Armistice Day, 11 November 1923, to commemorate the return of American soldiers and sailors from the First World War. The star at the top of the flagpole is perpetually lit as an 'eternal light, an inspiration and a promise of enduring peace'.

AMERICA TO BE LIT WITH ELECTRIC ARC LAMPS, and it wasn't long before Broadway's shops and theatres began to advertise their wares with electric signs. The section between 23rd and 42nd Streets, where most of the theatres were located at that time, was so brightly illuminated that it became known as the GREAT WHITE WAY, a term first applied by Shep Friedman, a columnist for the *New York Morning Telegraph* in 1901.

When the theatre district moved north to Times Square, the name Great White Way went with it and now refers to the area between 42nd and 53rd Streets.

World's First 'Cinema'

Broadway now heads north from Madison Square, and the excitement mounts as we begin to sense in the distance the bright lights of the world's most exhilarating theatre district –

indeed the very name Broadway has become synonymous with theatre. But Broadway is just as important to screen as it is to stage, for it was on the next stretch of Broadway, now somewhat narrow, dark and nondescript, that the cinema was born, on 14 April 1894.

Today No. 1155 Broadway is the address of the Broadway Plaza Hotel, but on that day in 1894 it was the address of THE WORLD'S FIRST 'CINEMA', a Kinetoscope Parlor opened by the Holland Brothers, George and Andrew, in a converted shoe store. The parlour was due to open on Monday the 16th, but such was the excitement among intrigued passers-by that the brothers opened two days early on the Saturday.

The first cinemagoers were greeted at the entrance by a bust of Thomas Edison, inventor of the Kinetoscope, and once inside, by ten machines arranged in two rows of five, each showing a different film. For 25 cents customers could see all five films in one row, for 50 cents all ten films. Each film lasted 20 seconds and was viewed through a peephole at the top of the wooden cabinet, which held the Kinetoscope. Amongst the films on offer were such titles as 'Wrestling', 'Barber Shop', 'Highland Dancing' and 'Trapeze', and some of the films starred celebrated contemporary performers such as the British contortionist Madame Bertholdhi and German strongman Eugen Sandow, one of Florenz Ziegfeld's discoveries.

Five hundred satisfied customers passed through the doors on the first day of the world's first cinema, producing takings of $120, and a billion-dollar American industry was born. On Broadway. There should at least be a plaque.

Tin Pan Alley

There actually is a plaque commemorating TIN PAN ALLEY, set into the sidewalk on the south side of West 28th Street, just east of Broadway, although you could be forgiven for missing it since it's very small and usually covered by street stalls.

During the first half of the 20th century New York's music publishing industry was concentrated on West 28th Street between Fifth and Sixth Avenues, near to the musical theatres that were the biggest markets for their songs. Songwriters would come from all over America to West 28th Street and demonstrate their songs to the various publishers. One of them, Monroe Rosenfeld, composer of 'Johnny Get Your Gun', wrote an article in the *New York Herald* in which he described the sound of umpteen different tunes being pounded out on tinny old pianos in all the different offices as being like the banging of tin pans in an alleyway. The nickname Tin Pan Alley caught on and came to refer to the American music business in general.

Between 1895 and the 1950s Tin Pan Alley dominated American music and produced some of the most memorable songs and songwriters of all time including 'After the Ball' by Charles K. Harris, THE FIRST SONG EVER TO SELL OVER ONE MILLION COPIES, 'Give My Regards to Broadway' by George M. Cohan, 'Shine on Harvest Moon' by Nora Bayes and Jack Noworth, 'Alexander's Ragtime Band' and 'God Bless America' by Irving Berlin and 'Swanee' by George Gershwin. Other names associated with Tin Pan Alley include Cole Porter, Jerome Kern, Richard Rodgers, Oscar Hammerstein and Lorenz Hart.

The rise of rock 'n' roll in the 1950s saw Tin Pan Alley decline, but it has left us with a golden legacy of unforgettable songs.

The Real McCoy

At No. 1200 Broadway on the corner of West 29th Street there is a glorious cast-iron Victorian pile that opened in 1872 as the GILSEY HOTEL, a favourite of Oscars Wilde and Hammerstein – and THE FIRST HOTEL IN NEW YORK TO OFFER GUESTS A TELEPHONE SERVICE. In 1898 boxer 'GENTLEMAN' JIM CORBETT, the first boxer to defeat the world's first heavyweight champion John L. Sullivan, was lunching at the Gilsey Hotel when a young boxer called CHARLES 'KID' McCOY walked in. A fist fight ensued during which McCoy challenged Corbett to a proper fight, and this took place at Madison Square Garden two years later in 1900. Although Corbett won, the result was in doubt, with McCoy suspected of having pulled his punches, perhaps to win a bet. From then on, at any contest in which McCoy was involved, the press would speculate as to whether the 'real McCoy' would turn up.

Let the Music Pay

No. 1204 Broadway, now a jewellery shop, was once Shanley's Restaurant, which holds an important place in the history of popular music. A favourite meeting place of theatre folk, Shanley's was noted for its in-house orchestra, which would entertain diners with hits from the current Broadway shows. One evening in the spring of 1915 VICTOR HERBERT, the Irish-born Tin Pan Alley composer and founder in 1914 of the American Society of Composers, Authors and Publishers (ASCAP), walked into Shanley's Restaurant and heard a song from his hit operetta *Sweethearts* being played. Herbert decided to sue the restaurant for violation of copyright, and in 1917, in the first case of its kind ever brought, Supreme Court Judge Oliver Wendell Holmes found in Herbert's favour, ruling that Shanley's profited not only by its food but by the music it offered.

'If the music did not pay, it would be given up,' said Holmes. Since then performing rights societies have had the right to collect licence fees for any performance of musical works under the copyright act. The ruling is still being tested today with regard to downloads from the internet.

Greeley Square

GREELEY SQUARE fills the southern half of another one of those little bow-tie triangular plots that appear whenever Broadway crosses the Manhattan grid. It is a small but pleasant green space busy with trees, a restaurant kiosk, coffee tables and chairs and is named after HORACE GREELEY, who in 1841 founded the influential *New York Tribune*, which he also edited. Greeley was passionately against slavery and an advocate of the homestead policy of handing over government land to settlers for free – in an editorial in 1865 he famously advised, 'Go West, young man, go West and grow up with the country.'

The bronze statue of Greeley seated here in the square, sculpted by Alexander Doyle, was dedicated in 1890 and is one of two statues of Greeley in New York, the other one being in City Hall Park.

Herald Square

'Remember me to Herald Square,' wrote George M. Cohan in the chorus of 'Give My Regards to Broadway' in 1904, when the square was at the heart of the entertainment district known as the Tenderloin. A lot of people remember Herald Square these days, most of them, perhaps, as the place where Santa Claus is welcomed at the climax of the Macy's Thanksgiving Day Parade.

The square is named after the *New York Herald* newspaper, which had its offices here from 1893 until 1921 in a flamboyant, two-storey arcaded Venetian palace designed by Stanford White. The *Herald* was founded in 1835 by Scottish-born James Gordon Bennett, and within ten years was the most popular paper in America.

Gordon Bennett!

Under Bennett's son, James Gordon Bennett Jr., the *Herald* instigated the Gordon Bennett Motor Races, the inspiration for today's Grand Prix races. Bennett Jr. was something of a

playboy and was always getting himself into some kind of ridiculous scrape, giving rise to the exasperated cry 'Gordon Bennett!', as in 'What the dickens has Gordon Bennett been up to this time . . .?'

Some years after Gordon Bennett Jr.'s death the *Herald* was bought by the *New York Tribune* and became the *New York Herald Tribune*. This in turn was taken over by the *New York Times* and is now the *International Herald Tribune*.

Stuff and Guff

All that remains of the New York Herald Building in Herald Square is the huge JAMES GORDON BENNETT MONUMENT, which incorporates two clocks from the south face of the old building and a sculptural group from the building's pediment, which consists of Minerva, the goddess of wisdom, an owl and two blacksmiths named Stuff and Guff, who rotate and swing their hammers to strike the bell on the hour. In fact they only appear to strike the bell – a pair of mallets hidden inside actually do the heavy work. In 2007 the monument underwent restoration after vibrations from the subway running underneath caused Stuff to shift forward so that his hammer really did start to make contact with the bell, with potentially disastrous consequences.

Macy's

MACY'S, which dominates the west side of Herald Square, covers an entire city block and advertises itself as 'THE WORLD'S LARGEST STORE', which indeed it was until 2009 when the new Shinsengae Centum City Department Store in Busan, South Korea, took the crown.

Macy's began life as a small shop on Sixth Avenue, opened in 1858 by Rowland H. Macy, and quickly established itself with such innovations as clearly marked prices (no haggling), often at one cent under the full dollar, exuberant newspaper advertisements, money back guarantees and AMERICA'S FIRST FEMALE STORE MANAGER, MARGARET GETCHELL, appointed in 1866. Macy's also began the transformation of Christmas into a shopping celebration as well as a religious one by tempting customers with illuminated window displays and, in 1870, THE FIRST IN-STORE SANTA CLAUS in a large department store. By the time Macy died in 1877 his shop was an American institution, occupying 11 different buildings

---

The Tenderloin

The TENDERLOIN was the name given to the entertainment area and red-light district of New York which ran from 23rd Street to 42nd Street, and was centred on Herald Square during the late 19th and early 20th centuries. The name was coined by NYPD Captain Alexander 'Clubber' Williams who commented, when transferred to the district from a somewhat quieter precinct, that thanks to all the pay-offs he would receive from the area's nightclubs and brothels for police protection, he could stop eating chuck steak and start enjoying tenderloin.

with departments selling everything under the sun.

Macy's continued to expand under new owners Isidor and Nathan Straus, licensees of the store's china and glassware department, and in 1902 the Straus brothers moved Macy's into a purpose-built store at its present location at 34th Street and Broadway. Ironically, the only part of the block occupied by Macy's that the store doesn't own is the corner on Herald Square where the giant red Macy's shopping bag sign is displayed. The plot was bought in 1900 by someone acting for another store, Seigel Cooper, who had just finished building what they had hoped would be the largest store in the world on Sixth Avenue. Macy's simply built around the building already there and now lease the space above for their massive banner.

The Big Parade

The first Macy's Thanksgiving Day Parade took place in 1924 with a procession of entertainers, floats, bands and live animals borrowed from Central Park Zoo. They marched from 145th Street in Harlem to Herald Square, where Santa Claus arrived to herald in the unofficial start of Christmas, a tradition that still continues. In 1927 the live animals were replaced with huge animal-shaped balloons such as Felix the Cat, an elephant and a dragon. For a few years, at the end of the parade, the balloons were released into the air to float away – whoever found one and posted it back received a Macy's gift voucher. This excitement was eventually

discontinued for safety reasons. Today, some three million people line the 2½-mile (4 km) route of the parade from 77th Street and Central Park West to Herald Square.

The 1946 parade featured prominently in the 1947 film *Miracle on 34th Street*, a perennial Christmas favourite, which weaves a heart-warming tale around the Santa Claus at Macy's.

The Casino

THE FIRST THEATRE IN NEW YORK TO BE LIT BY ELECTRICITY, THE CASINO THEATER, built in 1882, stood appropriately enough on the Great White Way, at No. 1404 Broadway, on the corner with West 39th Street. The Casino was also THE FIRST THEATRE IN NEW YORK TO HAVE A ROOF GARDEN, and in 1900 introduced BROADWAY'S FIRST CHORUS LINE, in a production of *Florodora*. It was here in 1901 that one of the girls in that chorus line, Evelyn Nesbit, first caught the eye of the architect Stanford White. The theatre closed in 1930.

The Old Met

Located diagonally opposite at 39th and Broadway, and opened at around the same time as the Casino Theater, the METROPOLITAN OPERA HOUSE was funded by New York's new moneyed industrial and merchant families, such as the Vanderbilts, Morgans and Rockefellers, who were unable to get a box at the 'old money' Academy of

Music on East 14th Street. Twice the size of the Academy and open to anyone who wanted to hear opera and good music, the Metropolitan Opera House soon eclipsed the Academy as the place to be seen, and the Academy was forced to cancel its opera season in 1886. CARUSO made his American debut at the Metropolitan Opera House in 1903.

In 1966 the Metropolitan Opera moved to a brand new opera house in the Lincoln Center on the Upper West Side, and the following year the old Met building was demolished so that no rival opera company could take it over. In its place rose the World Apparel Center, a 40-storey tower of showrooms and offices.

A couple more blocks and we have reached 42nd Street – the 'Crossroads of the World'.

Well, I never   *knew this*
about

BROADWAY – UNION SQUARE TO TIMES SQUARE

As one leaves Union Square heading north on Broadway, on the corner of 17th Street, there is a silver statue of artist ANDY WARHOL, set on the sidewalk outside No. 860 Broadway where he had his third studio (or Factory) from 1974 until 1984.

The OLD TOWN BAR at 45 East 18th street, which opened in 1892, still boasts its original 55 ft (17 m) long mahogany bar and the OLDEST DUMBWAITERS IN NEW YORK.

In 1901 TEDDY ROOSEVELT became Vice President to William McKinley, and when McKinley was assassinated six months later Roosevelt became, at the age of 42, the YOUNGEST EVER PRESIDENT OF THE UNITED STATES.

The Flatiron served as the offices of the *Daily Bugle* in the 2002 movie *Spider-Man*.

In the 1958 movie *Bell, Book and Candle* James Stewart and Kim Novak are magically transported on to the roof of the Flatiron, which is also seen in Warren Beatty's *Reds* and the 1998 remake of *Godzilla*.

The NEW YORK KNICKERBOCKERS BASEBALL TEAM, one of the first professional teams, originally played on a sand lot in Madison Square, in the 1840s. One of their team, Andrew Cartwright, known as the 'Father of Baseball', drew up the 'Knickerbocker Rules' on which the modern professional game of baseball is based.

Madison Square is where NEW YORK'S FIRST PUBLIC CHRISTMAS TREE was illuminated, in 1912. The Christmas tree lighting ceremony still takes place here annually.

EDITH WHARTON (1862–1937) the first woman to win the Pulitzer Prize in literature, (*The Age of Innocence*, in 1921), was born just off Madison Square at No. 14 West 23rd street.

Macy's red star logo was inspired by a tattoo that the store's founder Rowland Macy had on his forearm, a souvenir of his days as a whaler.

Part of Macy's is built on the former suite of KOSTER AND BIAL'S MUSIC HALL where, on 23 April 1896, the first moving picture projected by Thomas Edison's Vitascope, the first commercially successful movie projector, was shown to a paying audience for the first time. The film showed a couple of dancers and some breaking waves. As it says on the plaque beside Macy's' entrance on 34th street, 'Here the Motion Picture Began'.

In 1915 sculptor KARL BITTER was coming out of the Metropolitan Opera House, where he had gone to celebrate the completion on that day of his Pulitzer fountain, now located on Fifth Avenue outside the Plaza Hotel, when he was run down by a car and killed.

CHAPTER 12

CHELSEA

Hotel Chelsea

CHELSEA was originally farmland belonging to a Jacob Somerindyck, who sold it in 1750 to retired British army captain called Thomas Clarke. Clarke built himself a fine Georgian house and named the estate Chelsea after the Royal Chelsea Hospital for retired army personnel in London.

The Chelsea estate then passed to Clarke's daughter, who married Dr Benjamin Moore, Episcopal Bishop of New York and President of Columbia University. Their son CLEMENT CLARKE MOORE was born in Chelsea in 1779. In 1821 he donated land from the Chelsea estate for the General Theological Seminary and became their first Professor of Greek, Hebrew and Oriental Languages. He is known for compiling THE FIRST GREEK AND HEBREW LEXICONS EVER PRINTED IN AMERICA.

For the first half of the 19th century Chelsea was a well-to-do neighbourhood of large middle-class houses, but industrialisation along the Hudson and the arrival of the elevated railroad along Ninth Avenue in the 1870s brought music halls, theatres, shops and fashion warehouses in its wake. Residents moved north and Chelsea became a centre of the garment industry, serving the shops along Broadway's Ladies Mile and department stores like Macy's. In the 1960s and 70s the empty warehouses of Chelsea attracted artists and musicians, and today Chelsea is known for its art galleries, while the old 19th-century houses have become fine residences once more.

A WALK AROUND CHELSEA

Start point: Madison Square

Masonic Hall

Walk west from Madison Square along West 23rd Street to No. 71, the MASONIC HALL. This is the home of the GRAND LODGE OF NEW YORK, founded in 1782 and once THE LARGEST FREEMASON'S LODGE IN THE WORLD. Chancellor Robert R. Livingston was Grand Master here for 16 years from 1784 and it was he that arranged for the 1767 Bible owned by St John's Lodge No. 1 to be used at George Washington's inauguration in 1789. That same Washington Inaugural Bible is used to swear in the Grand Master today. Famous New York masons include Cecil B. DeMille, Mayor Fiorello LaGuardia, Norman Vincent Peale, John Jacob Astor, Irving Berlin and Harry Houdini. There are free public tours of the Masonic Hall, Monday to Saturday.

Cross Sixth Avenue and continue west along 23rd, noting the French Catholic

church of ST VINCENT DE PAUL on your right, where Edith Piaf married fellow singer Jacques Pills in 1952, with Marlene Dietrich as her matron of honour.

Turn left on to Seventh Avenue and walk four short blocks to PETER MCMANUS's CAFÉ on the corner of West 19th Street at No. 152. Established in 1936, this is one of New York's oldest family-run bars and has appeared many times in film and television series such as *Seinfeld, Law and Order* and *Saturday Night Live*.

Turn right on to West 19th and walk one block, past the Dance Theater Workshop at No. 219. Actor Whoopi Goldberg is amongst the artists who attended workshops here.

Cushman Row

At Eighth Avenue turn right and then left into West 20th Street, which is lined with fine townhouses. After crossing Ninth look out for Nos. 406–418 on your left. This row of splendid Greek Revival houses is CUSHMAN ROW, built in 1840 for Don Alonzo Cushman, founder of the Greenwich Savings Bank. Note the pineapples on the iron stair railings in front of No. 416, a traditional symbol of hospitality.

General Theological Seminary

Across the road is the GENERAL THEOLOGICAL SEMINARY, THE FIRST EPISCOPAL THEOLOGICAL SEMINARY IN

AMERICA. It was founded in 1817 and moved here, on to land donated by Charles Clarke Moore, once the construction of the campus was completed in 1827. The seminary occupies a whole block called Chelsea Square and comprises a number of fine Gothic Revival buildings surrounding a beautiful garden known as the Close. The whole is dominated by the 166 ft (50 m) high tower of the Chapel of the Good Shepherd, completed in 1888, and containing THE OLDEST SET OF TUBULAR BELLS IN AMERICA. If the college is closed it is possible to get a glimpse of the sylvan campus through the iron railings running along the north side of West 20th Street.

Continue west along West 20th, cross Tenth Avenue and then climb the steps on your left on to the High Line and turn left, heading south.

High Line

In 1999 a group of concerned Chelsea residents formed Friends of the High Line to preserve the remaining sections of the elevated railroad known as the HIGH LINE, which ran for 13 miles (21 km) along the West Side when it was Manhattan's busiest industrial area. Work began on transforming the old railroad tracks into an elevated greenway in 2006, with the first section opening in 2009.

The High Line was built in the 1930s to remove dangerous railroad freight traffic from Tenth Avenue, known then as Death Avenue for all the accidents that occurred along its route. The High Line meant that trains could travel high above the road and pass through the buildings they served, rather than around them, allowing for produce to be unloaded without disruption to other traffic. In the 1950s, however, road transport began to take over from rail, and by the 1960s the High Line was no longer used, and the southern section was pulled down. The last train to run along the High Line was in 1980.

Today the High Line between Gansevoort Street (near West 12th Street) and West 30th Street is a beautifully landscaped elevated urban greenway, providing a unique view of New York and the Hudson River. The foliage is inspired by the natural plants that seeded themselves along the derelict tracks, and sections of track have been left in place to retain something of the flavour of the High Line's previous function. There are places to eat and to sit and admire the view, while a variety of artistic enterprises have sprung up on empty building lots and wall spaces along the way, greatly adding to the experience.

The High Line is a remarkably imaginative example of urban regeneration and has become a much loved attraction for New Yorkers and tourists alike.

Take the High Line south to 16th Street, where the path disappears into the Old Biscuit Factory, and you can exit to street level via an elevator. Enter Chelsea Market at No. 88 on Tenth Avenue.

Chelsea Market

CHELSEA MARKET is a complex of shops, restaurants, offices and television studios located in the old factory, built in 1898, of the National Biscuit Company, or Nabisco. AMERICA'S MOST POPULAR BISCUIT, THE OREO, WAS INVENTED HERE and introduced in 1912. Today the factory building with its exposed piping and bare brick walls hums with galleries, sculptures, a waterfall, and a lobster place that serves mouth-watering lobster rolls the size of hay bales.

Pier 54

Exit Chelsea Market by the same door, cross Tenth Avenue, turn left and then right on to West 15th and go across

Eleventh Avenue. A couple of blocks south are the rusting metal gates of PIER 54, standing gaunt and alone by the river. On the arch above the gates you can just make out the words Cunard and White Star. There is something melancholy here, for this is where the RMS *Carpathia* unloaded survivors from the sinking of the White Star Line's *Titanic* in 1912. And three years later in May 1915 Cunard's RMS *Lusitania* left from Pier 54 on its fateful last voyage before being torpedoed by a German submarine off the coast of Ireland. Pier 54, the southernmost of the Chelsea Piers, is now used as a rather exhilarating open-air performance space.

Chelsea Piers

Titanic was actually heading for Pier 59 in 1912, and that is where we should head for now. Walk north up Eleventh Avenue along the riverside path, past the open water left by Piers 55 and 56, which burned down in 1947, past the dilapidated Pier 57, once home to the Grace Line, and on to the northern Chelsea Piers, which have been transformed into a huge entertainment and sports complex. Pier 59 is home to MANHATTAN'S ONLY MICROBREWERY, THE CHELSEA BREWING COMPANY. The extraordinary building across Eleventh Avenue from Pier 59 is Frank Gehry's 'Sails', headquarters of international media company InterActiveCorp.

Pier 62 houses THE LARGEST CENTRE FOR FILM AND TELEVISION PRODUCTION IN MANHATTAN. The TV situation comedy *Spin City*, starring Michael J. Fox, was filmed here, as is *Law and*

Order, and the CBS Sports Network is based here.

From Pier 62 go across Twelfth Avenue and Eleventh Avenue and proceed straight ahead into West 22nd Street.

Classic Diner

When you reach Tenth Avenue, cross over for the HIGHLINER, an iconic stainless steel and chrome 1920s art deco style American diner previously called the Empire. The Empire, which had been a Chelsea landmark for more than 30 years, was a favourite of the late Bette Davis and helped drive the rejuvenation of the Chelsea area in the 1980s. It appeared in films such as Woody Allen's *Manhattan*, *Home Alone 2*, *Lost in New York* and *Men in Black II*, and is mentioned in the Billy Joel song 'Great Wall of China'.

After the Empire Diner closed in 2010, the place was buffed up and refurbished in the same style by new owners and reopened as the Highliner in 2011.

Now continue east along leafy 22nd

Street and turn left on to Eighth Avenue, then right on to 23rd Street.

Hotel Chelsea

'A rest stop for rare individuals'

The glorious 11-storey red-brick Hotel Chelsea, with its ornate iron balconies and air of raffish decadence, has long been New York's most celebrated bohemian hangout, and you should allow yourself plenty of time to read through all the plaques on the walls outside documenting the hotel's colourful history.

The Chelsea was originally built in 1883, at the heart of what was then the city's theatre district, not as a hotel but as one of the first of New York's famous co-operatives, whereby individual shareholders buy the right to live in one of the apartments, while the cooperative as a whole owns the building and takes care of the maintenance and servicing of the property.

Famous Chelsea Guests

- VIRGIL THOMSON (1896–1989) wrote his Pulitzer Prize-winning film score for the 1948 film *The Louisiana Story* at the Chelsea, where he lived for more than 50 years.

- DYLAN THOMAS completed *Under Milk Wood* while living at the Chelsea in Room 205. In 1953, shortly before *Under Milk Wood* had its première, Thomas collapsed in his room allegedly after drinking 'eighteen straight whiskys' at the White Horse Tavern in Greenwich Village. He was taken by ambulance to nearby St Vincent's Hospital where he died a few days later.

- 'Beat Generation' poets ALLEN GINSBERG, JACK KEROUAC and WILLIAM BURROUGHS lived in a haze of drugs at the Chelsea in the 1950s and Burroughs somehow wrote his seminal work *Naked Lunch* while resident there.

- BRENDAN BEHAN wrote *Brendan Behan's New York* while staying at the Chelsea in 1963.

- ARTHUR MILLER, author of *Death of a Salesman, The Crucible* and other works, lived in Room 614 from 1962 to 1968, while getting over the break-up of his marriage to Marilyn Monroe, and wrote his play *After the Fall* there. According to Miller you could 'get high just by standing in one of the hotel lifts and inhaling the marijuana fumes'.

- BOB DYLAN, who changed his surname from Zimmerman to Dylan in tribute to previous Chelsea resident Dylan Thomas, wrote 'Sad Eyed Lady of the Lowlands' in Room 211 in 1965. Dylan also mentions the Chelsea in his 1976 song 'SARA' with the line 'Staying up for days in the Chelsea Hotel writing Sad Eyed Lady of the Lowlands for you'. (Sara was dedicated to his first wife Sara Lownds.)

- In 1966 ANDY WARHOL shot his first 'commercially successful' film *Chelsea Girls* at the hotel, featuring models from his Factory down the road on East 47th Street. One Chelsea Girl in particular who came to prominence was 'It Girl' EDIE SEDGWICK, 1965's 'Girl of the Year', who had an affair with Bob Dylan and nearly died at the Chelsea by setting fire to her false eyelashes there in 1966.

- ARTHUR C. CLARKE, who invented the communication satellite and in 1974 predicted the Internet, wrote *2001: A Space Odyssey*, based on his short story 'The Sentinel', while living at the Chelsea. Published in 1968, the book was written simultaneously with the film, which was co-written and directed by Stanley Kubrick.

- ROBERT MAPPLETHORPE took his first photographs in Room 1017 at the Chelsea in 1969, using a Polaroid camera lent to him by artist Sandy Daley.

- LEONARD COHEN wrote a song called 'Chelsea Hotel No. 2' in 1974 about a night of passion he spent with Janis Joplin in Room 415, which unsurprisingly included the line 'I remember you well in the Chelsea Hotel'.

- In 1978 NANCY SPUNGEN, the girlfriend of Sex Pistols bass player Sid Vicious, was found lying under the sink of their hotel room at the Chelsea, Room 100, stabbed to death with Vicious' knife. Vicious was accused of her murder but died of a drug overdose before he could be tried.

- Pop star MADONNA lived at the hotel during the 1980s and returned there in 1992 to shoot photographs for her book, *Sex*, in Room 822.

- In 2003 actor ETHAN HAWKE moved into the hotel after breaking up with his wife UMA THURMAN.

Successful at first at attracting artists and actors from the surrounding theatres, the Chelsea suffered as the middle classes and the theatres moved north at the end of the 19th century. In 1905 it became a hotel, offering long-term residences as well as overnight stays. Actors such as Lillie Langtry and Edith Piaf, and writers like Mark Twain, Tennessee Williams and Eugene O'Neill all enjoyed time at the Chelsea and helped to cement its reputation as a place for artists to stay.

In 1912 survivors from the *Titanic* were given rooms in the Chelsea while they recovered from their ordeal.

In the 1930s the hotel was taken over by the Bard family, who for the next 60 years or so ran the hotel with an indulgent eye to the excesses of their guests (see panel).

Continue east on West 23rd and turn left on to Seventh Avenue. Walk three blocks and turn left on to West 26th. The huge concrete building on the corner here is the Fashion Institute of Technology, where Calvin Klein and film director Joel Schumacher both studied.

There is a museum dedicated to fashion here, entrance on Seventh Avenue.

Birthplace of Paramount Pictures

Head west along West 26th and on your right at No. 221 is the CHELSEA STUDIOS, built as an armoury and converted in 1914 into a film studio by ADOLPH ZUKOR for his FAMOUS PLAYERS FILM COMPANY, which evolved into Paramount Pictures. Amongst the classic films made at the Chelsea Studios are *12 Angry Men*, *The Night They Raided Minsky's* and Mel Brooks's *The Producers*. Now a television studio, Chelsea productions have included *Sergeant Bilko*, *Ricki Lake* and *Judge Hatchett*.

Post Office

Continue west along 26th Street and turn right on to Eighth Avenue. Walk north five blocks to the magnificent GENERAL POST OFFICE, now the James A. Farley Post Office Building, so named as a testament to the 53rd U.S. Postmaster General. A broad sweep of steps leads up to 20 Corinthian columns above which runs a 250 ft (76 m) long inscription, 'Neither snow nor rain nor heat nor gloom of night stays these couriers from the swift completion of their appointed rounds.' A noble motto for the Post Office, you might think, but in fact it was filched from the postal service of the Persian Empire, as described in HERODOTUS'S HISTORIES, written in about 440 BC.

New York's main post office was built in 1913 by McKim, Mead and White and its grand façade was designed to complement their equally impressive Pennsylvania Station across the road.

Pennsylvania Station

PENNSYLVANIA STATION, or Penn Station as it is commonly known, is AMERICA'S BUSIEST STATION, serving some 300,000 passengers every day. Today the actual concourse is buried underground beneath the ugly concrete cylinder that is Madison Square Garden, but before 1963 the station was housed in one of the architectural glories of New York, built in 1910 by McKim, Mead and White. It was a vast *beaux-arts* Doric temple, with entrances similar to Berlin's Brandenburg Gate, while its monumental

waiting room, modelled on the ancient Roman Baths of Caracalla, was the size of the nave of St Peter's Basilica in Rome and THE LARGEST INDOOR SPACE IN NEW YORK. The station's destruction in 1963, described in the *New York Times* as a 'monumental act of vandalism', so enraged New York that the city was roused into action and set up a Landmarks Preservation Commission to ensure that such a calamity would never be allowed to happen again. One of their first victories was to prevent the demolition of Grand Central Station in 1967.

Madison Square Garden

Pennsylvania Station was demolished to make way for possibly the least distinguished building in New York, a circular stadium that holds 20,000 and is home to the New York Knicks basketball team, the Liberty women's basketball team, and the New York Rangers hockey team. This is the fourth building to bear the name MADISON SQUARE GARDEN and sits eight blocks away from its original home on Madison Square.

While the building may be dull, some very exciting events have taken place here. Joe Frazier defeated Muhammad Ali here in 1971 in the Fight of the Century. In 1974 John Lennon gave his last ever live performance during a concert here by Elton John, who holds the record for the most concerts played at Madison Square Garden, with 62.

Nadia Comaneci scored perfect 10s in the inaugural edition of the American Cup gymnastics here in 1976.

Now head east on West 31st and turn left on to Seventh Avenue. Note the magnificent marble eagle standing proudly on a granite plinth beneath the flagpoles outside the entrance to Madison Square Garden. This mighty bird guarded the entrance to the old Penn Station and is one of the last remaining vestiges of the much lamented landmark.

Hotel Pennsylvania

His twin sits on the corner of 33rd Street, looking across at the HOTEL PENNSYLVANIA, which was built in 1919 by McKim, Mead and White to serve Penn Station. The hotel's telephone number, said to be THE OLDEST IN USE IN NEW YORK, was immortalised by Glenn Miller in his song 'Pennsylvania 6–5000'. Miller used to play with his orchestra in the hotel's Café Rouge.

Fashion Avenue

Continue north along Seventh Avenue to Times Square and the end of the walk. This stretch of Seventh Avenue is known as FASHION AVENUE, and here you can tread the FASHION WALK OF FAME where fashion designers like Calvin Klein, Ralph Lauren, Bill Blass and Donna Karan are commemorated with plaques of white bronze set in granite and embedded on the sidewalk between 35th and 41st Streets.

Well, I never knew this
about
CHELSEA

CLEMENT CLARKE MOORE (1779–1863), owner of the Chelsea estate, is widely credited as the author of the poem 'A Visit from St Nicholas', better known as 'Twas the Night before Christmas'. In the poem he virtually invented the Santa Claus of modern tradition, transforming St Nicholas, the patron saint of children, into a fat, jolly, fairy-tale character flying about on a sleigh drawn by eight reindeer with names like Donner and Blitzen, who comes down the chimney on Christmas Eve bearing toys for good children. The poem was written in 1822 for his own children and was never intended for publication, but a family friend sent the poem to the *New York Sentinel*, who published it on 23 December 1823. It became a Christmas favourite with children all across America, but Moore, who wished to be known for his serious works, didn't acknowledge authorship until 1844, when he was 65 years old.

Notable alumni of the General Theological Seminary include The RT. REV. GENE ROBINSON, Bishop of New Hampshire, THE FIRST OPENLY GAY BISHOP IN THE EPISCOPAL CHURCH, and THE REV. JEANNETTE PICCARD, a high-altitude balloonist who was THE FIRST WOMAN TO FLY INTO THE STRATOSPHERE. In 1974, after attending the seminary, and at age 79, she became THE FIRST WOMAN EVER TO BE ORDAINED IN THE EPISCOPAL CHURCH.

The Rev. Jeannette Piccard's husband, JEAN PICCARD, was a famous pioneering balloonist like his wife. Gene Roddenberry, creator of *Star Trek*, named the commander of the starship *Enterprise* Captain Jean-Luc Picard in their honour.

During the 1920s and 30s the FASHION DISTRICT, centred on Seventh Avenue, had the LARGEST CONCENTRATION OF GARMENT MANUFACTURERS IN THE WORLD, and remains today the centre of the American fashion industry.

CHAPTER 13

GRAMERCY &
MIDTOWN SOUTH

The Empire State Building

Gramercy

GRAMERCY PARK is the ONLY PRIVATE PARK IN NEW YORK. It was laid out in 1831 by developer SAMUEL RUGGLES, who bought the land, once part of Peter Stuyvesant's huge farm, from New York's first post-Revolution mayor, James Duane. The name of the area in Dutch was Krom Moerasje, meaning little crooked swamp, which was anglicised over time to Gramercy.

Ruggles set up the park as a cooperative, owned and administered by the owners of the houses around it, who would all have keys to the park gates. To provide better access, because the property didn't reach Third or Fourth Avenue, Ruggles built a road running north from the park, which he called Lexington, after the first battle of the Revolution, and one running south, which he called Irving, after his friend Washington Irving.

A Walk around Gramercy & Midtown South

Start point: Union Square

Steinway Hall

Walk east on East 14th as far as Irving Place. At Nos. 71–73 East 14th, on the corner, stood THE WORLD'S FIRST STEINWAY HALL, built behind the piano company's showrooms in 1866 as somewhere for famous pianists to give performances on Steinway pianos. Here Charles Dickens gave a series of readings in 1867, Henry Stanley talked about David Livingstone in 1872, and in the same year Anton Rubinstein gave a celebrated piano concert in front of a record audience of 3,000. Steinway Hall was also home to the New York Philharmonic Orchestra for 25 years before Carnegie Hall opened 1891. In 1925 a new Steinway Hall was opened on 57th Street, and the old building was closed and then demolished the following year.

Academy of Music

Across Irving Place was the site of the ACADEMY OF MUSIC, LARGEST OPERA HOUSE IN THE WORLD when it was opened in 1854 for the elite of New York. In 1860 a celebrated ball was held there for the Prince of Wales, later Edward VII. Only the oldest and most distinguished families were able to buy a box at the Academy, a conceit that

led to its downfall. When the newly moneyed industrial tycoons such as the Vanderbilts and Rockefellers were unable to obtain a box, they simply got together to build the much larger Metropolitan Opera House on Broadway, which was open to all and took away the Academy's audience.

Con Edison

Beyond the Academy on 14th Street was the first headquarters or 'wigwam' of Tammany Hall. Both the Academy and Tammany Hall were demolished to make way for the present CON EDISON BUILDING put up in 1914, with the landmark clock tower added in 1926. The tower, crowned by a bronze lantern, was designed as a 'Tower of Light' and is lit up dramatically at night, both as an advertisement for the company and as a memorial to employees who died in the First World War.

Turn left into Irving Place and walk north. At No. 33 are the offices of AMERICA'S OLDEST MAGAZINE, THE NATION, founded in 1865.

First Lady of Interior Decoration

On the corner of Irving Place and East 17th Street there is a huge bust of WASHINGTON IRVING, sculpted in 1855, and placed here in 1935 outside the Washington Irving High School. Across the road is Irving House, sporting a plaque beside the entrance on East 17th that says Washington Irving lived here. He didn't, although he did frequently visit his nephew who lived nearby on East 21st Street.

Irving House was actually the home in the late 19th and early 20th centuries of ELSIE DE WOLFE, who invented the profession of interior decorating and whose clients included most of New York society and the Duchess of Windsor. Elsie's motto was 'never explain, never complain' and she lived here, in what was called a 'Boston' relationship, with BESSIE MARBURY, theatrical agent to Oscar Wilde and George Bernard Shaw. At the age of 61 Elsie married diplomat Sir Charles Mendl and she is remembered across the road in the Lady Mendl tea rooms of the Inn at Irving Place, which occupies a pair of fine 1841 Greek Revival houses at No. 56.

Pete's Tavern

On the corner of East 18th Street is PETE'S TAVERN, another of New York's oldest bars, which was built in 1829 as

The Portman Hotel and opened as a tavern in 1864. It was a favourite haunt of Tammany Hall bosses, whose 'wigwam' was nearby on 14th Street. Writer O. HENRY, who lived at 55 Irving Place from 1903 to 1907, frequented Pete's Tavern (when it was known as Healy's) and allegedly wrote his most famous story, *The Gift of the Magi*, in booth 2 here. During Prohibition the front of the house functioned as a flower shop while the back room operated as a speakeasy accessed through a dummy refrigerator door. Pete's Tavern has appeared in *Seinfeld*, *Law and Order* and *Sex and the City*, as well as advertisements and numerous other productions.

Block Beautiful

Continue up Irving Place and turn right into East 19th. This leafy street, lined with lovely 1920s townhouses, is known affectionately as Block Beautiful. No. 132 was something of a theatrical digs, a temporary home to Hollywood's first sex symbol Theda Bara, as well as Mrs Patrick Campbell, Lillian Gish, Ethel Barrymore and Helen Hayes.

Return to Irving Place and continue north to Gramercy Park.

Gramercy Park

South

From Irving Place turn right into Gramercy Park South. The house on the corner to your right at No. 19 is the STUYVESANT FISH HOUSE, built in 1845 and expanded in 1887 for railroad magnate Stuyvesant Fish, a descendant, funnily enough, of Peter Stuyvesant. A marble staircase was installed and there was a huge ballroom on the top floor where Mrs Fish lavishly entertained the cream of New York society. For a while in the early 1900s the house became luxury apartments whose occupants included the actor John Barrymore, while he was appearing on Broadway, and playwright Edward Sheldon. In 1931 publicist Benjamin Sonnenberg and his wife moved into the top two floors and finally bought the whole house in 1945, restoring it to its former glory and proceeding to match the sumptuous hospitality of Mrs Fish – at one dinner party in 1967 the guest list included Brooke Astor, Jacob Javits, Jackie Kennedy, Tom Wolfe, Alistair Cooke, Truman Capote, Ethel Kennedy and Bob Dylan. The house remains a private residence.

East

Turn left into Gramercy Park East and admire the awesome brownstone entrance to THE GRAMERCY, opened as NEW YORK'S FIRST COOPERATIVE in 1883 and home to movie stars Margaret Hamilton (the Wicked Witch of the West in MGM's 1939 musical *The Wizard of Oz*), James Cagney and John Carradine.

The white Gothic terracotta extravaganza next door at No. 36 opened in 1910. Residents here have included sculptor Daniel Chester French, actor John Barrymore (again) and circus owner Alfred Ringling.

North

Turn left into Gramercy Park North and on the far corner with Lexington is the GRAMERCY PARK HOTEL, which in 1925 replaced the former homes of architect Stanford White and diarist George Templeton Strong. Humphrey Bogart married his first wife Helen Menken at the hotel in 1926; baseball legend Babe Ruth was a regular patron at the bar in the 1930s; and Joseph Kennedy and his family, including a young JFK, lived on the second floor for several months before moving to London, where Joseph was to be the U.S. Ambassador.

West

Turn left into Gramercy Park West, which is lined with a row of delightful mid 19th century townhouses, the nicest houses on the square. The 23rd U.S. President Benjamin Harrison had his second wedding reception at No. 2 in 1896, when it was the home of Gifford Pinchot, America's first Chief of the Forest Service. Two iron mayoral lanterns outside No. 4 mark the former home of James Harper, New York's mayor in 1844, who established New York's first municipal police force.

Actress Julia Roberts has lived in the penthouse of the condo block at No. 7.

National Arts Club

Turn left into Gramercy Park South. The façade of the large brownstone at No. 15, which was built in the 1840s, was remodelled by Calvert Vaux in the 1870s and sports a number of bas-relief

faces of famous writers, such as William Shakespeare and John Milton, as well as a bust of Michelangelo. This is the NATIONAL ARTS CLUB, founded in 1906 in the former home of Samuel J. Tilden, 25th Governor of New York, who led the fight against the corruption of Tammany Hall and the Tweed Ring. In the controversial 1876 presidential election Tilden was the Democratic candidate running against the Republican Rutherford B. Hayes, and became THE FIRST CANDIDATE TO LOSE THE ELECTION ON ELECTORAL VOTES WHILE WINNING THE POPULAR VOTE.

The National Arts Club, founded to 'stimulate, foster and promote public interest in the arts', was one of the very few private clubs in New York that admitted women as members from the outset. Membership has included three U.S. Presidents, Teddy Roosevelt, Woodrow Wilson and Dwight Eisenhower, and most of the leading American artists and sculptors of the 20th century, who were expected to donate one of their works in return for membership. Present members include Martin Scorsese, Robert Redford, Uma Thurman and Ethan Hawke. The club is open to the public during exhibitions.

Players Club

Next door, in the imposing brownstone at No. 16, is the PLAYERS CLUB, founded in his own home in 1888 by actor EDWIN BOOTH. The club is modelled on London's Garrick Club for the 'promotion of social intercourse between members of the dramatic profession and the kindred professions . . .' Women were not admitted to the club until 1989, when the actress Helen Hayes became the first woman member. Membership has included James Cagney, Gregory Peck, Kevin Spacey, Angela Lansbury, Sidney Poitier, Liza Minnelli, Peter O'Toole, Roger Moore, Lauren Bacall, Harry Belafonte and Humphrey Bogart. In 1906 the architect Stanford White, who was responsible for transforming the house from a townhouse into a clubhouse, took his last luncheon at the Players before going on that evening to Madison Square Garden, where he was shot to death.

Before you walk around the park again to continue north on Lexington Avenue, peer through the iron gates to see the statue of Edwin Booth dressed as Hamlet, which was unveiled in 1918 by Booth's grandson Edwin Booth Grossman.

Lexington

Now begin walking north on Lexington, towards the Chrysler Building in the far distance. The block of flats at No. 7 stands on the site of the home of Peter Cooper, founder of the Cooper's Union. He died here in 1883.

Baruch College at No. 55 stands on the site of the RCA Victor studios where Elvis Presley recorded 'Hound Dog'.

At No. 68, on the corner of 25th Street, is the 69th Regiment Armory, home of the 'Fighting 69th', New York's only Irish regiment, who fought in the Civil War and the two world wars. In 1913 the Armory was the scene of the controversial Armory Show, which introduced modern art to America for the first time.

No. 123, now Kalustyan's Indian Grocery Store, used to be the home of CHESTER ARTHUR, 21st President of the United States. In September 1881 he took the oath of office here after the assassination of James Garfield, becoming THE ONLY PRESIDENT, OTHER THAN GEORGE WASHINGTON, TO TAKE THE OATH IN NEW YORK. Arthur died at this address in 1886. Newspaper baron William Randolph Hearst lived here from 1900 until 1908.

White Wood House

Turn right on to East 29th Street and walk one and a half blocks to see the gorgeous White Wood House at No. 203. Built in the early 19th century, it is one of the few wooden houses left in Manhattan. The brick carriage house beside it is even older, dating from around 1790, one of Manhattan's few surviving 18th-century buildings. These two unexpected little buildings are a joy to behold.

Return along East 29th and continue east towards Fifth Avenue.

The Little Church Around the Corner

Across Madison, at No. 1 East 29th, there is a red-brick church with a copper roof known as THE LITTLE CHURCH AROUND THE CORNER. More properly called The Church of the Transfiguration, it was founded in 1848 by The Rev. George Houghton, who made the church welcome to all, regardless of colour, faith or class, and even to members of the acting profession. In 1870 an actor called Joseph Jefferson, particularly known for playing Rip Van Winkle on the New York stage, tried to arrange the funeral of his friend George Holland at a nearby church but was refused when the priest learned that Holland was an actor. Instead, he could try 'the little church around the corner, where it might be done', the priest suggested. 'Then God bless the little church around the corner!' cried Jefferson. His words are commemorated on a window on the south side of the church.

Now cross Fifth Avenue to the . . .

Marble Collegiate Church

The MARBLE COLLEGIATE CHURCH is one of four Reform Collegiate churches in New York serving THE OLDEST PROTESTANT CONGREGATION IN AMERICA, the Dutch Reform Church, which was founded in New Amsterdam in 1628. The building here dates from 1851 and the 'marble' in the name refers to the façade of Tuckahoe marble.

The church found national fame under the ministry of DR NORMAN VINCENT PEALE, author of *The Power of Positive Thinking*, who served as senior minister here from 1932 to 1984. RICHARD NIXON met Dr Peale during the Second World War while stationed at the Brooklyn Navy Yard. They became firm friends, and the whole Nixon family attended services here in the 1960s, when Nixon was working as a lawyer in New York. In 1968, as Nixon was about to take up office as President, his youngest daughter Julie married Dwight Eisenhower II, grandson of former President Dwight Eisenhower, in the Marble Collegiate Church, with Dr Peale officiating.

There is a fine bronze statue of Dr Norman Vincent Peale, thinking positively, just to the right of the entrance to the church.

Now continue northwards up Fifth Avenue to the towering, dramatic art deco entrance lobby of the Empire State Building at No. 350.

Married at the Marble Collegiate Church

- Tenor ENRICO CARUSO married Dorothy Benjamin here in 1918.
- LUCILLE BALL married her second husband Gary Morton here in 1961.
- DONALD TRUMP married his first wife IVANA ZELNICKOVA here in 1977. He later met MARLA MAPLES here and married her in the church as his second wife in 1993.
- LIZA MINELLI married DAVID GEST here in 2002.

Empire State Building

'The closest thing we have to Heaven in New York City!'

DEBORAH KERR IN
An Affair to Remember

Named as one of the Seven Wonders of the Modern World by the American Society of Civil Engineers, and frequently voted America's favourite building, the EMPIRE STATE BUILDING is the ultimate symbol of not just New York, but America. It is the world's idea of what a skyscraper is and should be.

The Story Begins

The story begins in 1859 when John Jacob Astor III built himself a house at No. 350 Fifth Avenue, starting a trend for building grand houses along the avenue. In 1862 Astor's younger brother William Blackhouse Astor built a mansion next door where his wife CAROLINE SCHERMERHORN ASTOR presided over a huge ballroom that could hold 400 people. The 400 that Mrs Astor deemed worthy to invite into her ballroom became known as MRS ASTOR'S FOUR HUNDRED and represented the epitome of New York Society in the late 19th century.

In 1890 John Jacob Astor III died and his son William Waldorf Astor decided to build a luxury hotel called the Waldorf (named after Walldorf in Germany from where the Astors originated) on the site of his father's house – largely, it is said, in the hope that the noise of the guests would annoy his snobbish aunt Caroline next door, whom he didn't like. Caroline retaliated by tearing down her own house and putting up an even more luxurious hotel called the Astoria, then flouncing off to a new house near Central Park. The two hotels merged in 1897, connected by a corridor across Peacock Alley, and became the Waldorf=Astoria, with the double hyphen representing both the connecting corridor and equality between the two branches of the Astor family.

In 1928 the hotel moved uptown to its present site on Park Avenue, and the old lot was sold to the Empire State Building consortium, headed by former New York governor Alfred E. Smith, his presidential campaign supporter John Jakob Raskob of General Motors and business tycoon Pierre du Pont.

Empire State

When Raskob met the architects, Shreve, Lamb and Harmon, to discuss what the new building should look like, he stood a pencil on end and asked, 'How high can you make it so that it doesn't fall down?'

Empire State Building

Stats and Stories

- The Empire State Building has 102 floors, THE FIRST BUILDING IN THE WORLD TO HAVE MORE THAN 100 FLOORS.

- Upon completion in 1931 it became THE TALLEST BUILDING IN THE WORLD, with a roof height of 1,250 ft (381 m), and 1,454 ft (443 m) to the top of the spire.

- It was the tallest building in the world for longer than any other building in the 20th century, just over 40 years, until the completion of the North Tower of the World Trade Center in 1972.

- In July 1945, in thick fog, a B-25 bomber crashed into the north side of the building, between the 79th and 80th floors, killing 14 people, including the pilot and his two passengers. The impact severed cables on one of the elevators, which plunged 75 storeys with operator Betty Lou Oliver on board. She survived the longest ever survived elevator drop thanks to the successful operation (eventually) of the elevator's safety devices.

- Since 1964 the top of the Empire State Building has been floodlit in colours to match seasonal or special events such as St Patrick's Day and Independence Day, or to celebrate New York's sports teams.

- There are two observation decks, an open one on the 86th floor and an enclosed deck on the 102nd floor, reached by a separate elevator from the 86th floor. The lower observation deck has been the setting for a number of films, most memorably *An Affair to Remember*, starring Cary Grant and Deborah Kerr, and for the denouement in *Sleepless in Seattle*, starring Tom Hanks and Meg Ryan.

The original idea was to call it the GM Building (Raskob and du Pont were on the board of General Motors), but Alfred Smith wanted to recognise the State of New York, of which he had been a popular governor, and so they decided on Empire State, using the nickname that New York had allegedly been given by George Washington in 1783 when he declared New York to be the 'seat of empire'.

Construction began on St Patrick's Day, 17 March 1930, and the building was completed after just 410 days, being officially opened on 1 May 1931 by President Herbert Hoover, who pressed a button in Washington D.C. to turn on the lights.

In order to trounce the Chrysler Building, which in 1930 had beaten the Manhattan Life Building to become the tallest building in the world by fixing a purely decorative spire on top, it was decided to give the Empire State Building a spire that could be usefully employed as a mooring mast for dirigibles. In the end the mast was used only once for that purpose, when the *New York Evening Journal* delivered a parcel of newspapers from the Financial District. The whole rigmarole proved far too dangerous, with updrafts whipping the airship hither and thither and passengers having to leap for their lives on to the gangplank – and all this 1,300 ft (396 m) above the street. The only other time the mooring mast proved useful was as something for the big gorilla to hang on to as he swatted fighter planes in the 1933 movie *King Kong*, starring Fay Wray.

It proved difficult at the start of the Great Depression to find anyone to rent space in the building, which became affectionately known as the Empty State Building. The observation deck, however, made $2 million in the first year and established the Empire State as a lucrative tourist destination. Even today it makes more money from ticket sales for the observation decks than from renting out office space. The building finally became profitable in 1950 and was sold in 1951 for $51 million, the highest price ever paid at that time for a single building.

Fifth Avenue

Cross 34th Street and continue north on Fifth Avenue. The corner lot on your left was the site of A.T. Stewart's mansion,

built in 1867 in marble, like his great store. Despite all his money, Stewart never made it into his neighbour Mrs Astor's ballroom next door as one of the Four Hundred.

The corner lot on the left across 37th Street is the former site of the Brick Presbyterian Church. SAMUEL OSGOOD, THE FIRST U.S. POSTMASTER GENERAL, whose house on Cherry Street served in 1789 as the first presidential mansion, was buried there in 1813. Mark Twain's funeral was held there in 1910.

At Nos. 424–434 is Lord & Taylor, founded in 1826 and one of New York's oldest upmarket retailers. It was the first major store to open on Fifth Avenue, and also the first store to introduce special Christmas window displays.

The block between 39th and 40th, now part occupied by a branch of the New York Public Library, was formerly the site of Dickel's Riding Academy, where in 1876 James Gordon Bennett Jr. organised THE FIRST POLO MATCH IN AMERICA.

New York Public Library

After crossing 40th Street you will come to one of New York's best-loved buildings, the main branch of the NEW YORK PUBLIC LIBRARY, opened in 1911.

This was previously the site of the Croton Aqueduct Distributing Reservoir, contained within vast Egyptian-style fortress walls on top of which there was a walkway offering tremendous views of the city. The foundations of the reservoir

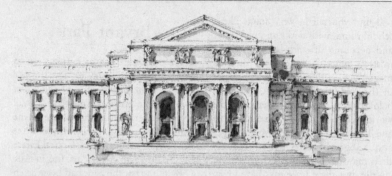

were preserved to create foundations for the library.

The New York Public Library was the inspiration of former governor Samuel Tilden, who left part of his estate to 'maintain a free library and reading room in the city of New York'. It was formed by bringing together the collections of the two biggest private libraries in the city, the Astor Library and the Lennox Library.

The new library building was THE LARGEST MARBLE STRUCTURE IN AMERICA when it was built, its main façade on Fifth Avenue stretching for 390 ft (119 m). The entrance is guarded by two lions made of Tennessee marble, which were originally called Leo Astor and Leo Lennox after the library's founders, but were re-christened Patience and Fortitude by Mayor Fiorello La Guardia in the 1930s, as a tribute to the qualities shown by New Yorkers during the Great Depression. In the 1978 film *The Wiz*, one of the lions comes to life and accompanies Dorothy and her dog Toto on their journey through Oz.

Inside, the main reading room, the Rose Room, is nearly 300 ft (91 m)

long, the length of two city blocks, and lined with some 30,000 reference books. If a reader requires a book from one of the 88 miles (142 km) of bookshelves in the basement, he or she fills in a call slip that is sent by pneumatic tube to a librarian downstairs, who locates the book and sends it up by dumb waiter. On the opening day, the first book requested, N.I. Grot's entertaining study of Nietzsche and Tolstoy, *Ethical Ideas of Our Time*, was retrieved in exactly six minutes.

Today, many visitors come to see the magnificent murals painted by Richard Haas in the Periodicals Room, where DeWitt Wallace, the founder of *Reader's Digest*, spent countless hours in the 1920s reading and condensing material from the library's collection.

Pooh

If you want to see the New York Public Library's greatest treasure you must seek out the Children's Center, hidden away down several gloomy flights of stairs on the north side of the building. Follow the chatter of young voices and you will find yourself in what looks like a school room, with desks and play areas and a couple of stern-looking school mistress types. Press on, for there is magic here, sitting in a small chamber in the middle of the room, the most beloved gang of animal friends in the world – the original WINNIE THE POOH and his friends, Piglet, Eeyore, Tigger and Kanga. Battered and threadbare they may be, and in need of a good cuddle, but these little toys have given untold pleasure to children all over the world.

Winnie the Pooh was bought from Harrods in London as a first birthday present for author A.A. Milne's son Christopher in 1921, and named after Christopher's favourite black bear at London Zoo called Winnie, short for Winnipeg. His companions were added one by one over time. They were all brought over to America by Milne's American publisher E.P. Dutton and donated to the library in 1987.

One of the excitements of being in New York is catching sight of film stars and celebrities almost on a daily basis, but very little can match the thrill of meeting Winnie the Pooh.

Bryant Park

Leave the library by the entrance on to 42nd Street and turn left for BRYANT PARK, the site in 1853 of New York's first World's Fair. An iron and glass Crystal Palace was erected in the middle of the park for the occasion. Like its namesake in London, the New York Crystal Palace burned down in a spectacular fire, in 1858.

By the 1970s the park had been taken over by prostitutes and drug dealers, and in 1980 the Bryant Park Restoration Corporation was formed to clean the park up. Today it is a lively, privately run public park with the LARGEST AREA OF LAWN IN MANHATTAN south of Central Park. As well as being a good space for staging film festivals and music events and being a nice place to relax, the lawn serves as a protective roof for miles of archives belonging to the Public Library that are stored in vaults underneath.

Bryant Park is named in tribute to *New York Evening Post* editor and Central Park champion WILLIAM CULLEN BRYANT, who sits in bronzed splendour gazing over the proceedings from a Greek alcove set against the library wall.

From Bryant Park it is a short walk along 42nd Street to Times Square and the end of the walk.

Well, I never knew this
about

GRAMERCY & MIDTOWN SOUTH

LEXINGTON AVENUE was the scene of New York's FIRST RECORDED ARREST FOR SPEEDING, when cabbie Jacob German was overtaken and flagged down by a bicycle patrolman for racing down Lexington at a reckless 12 miles (19 km) per hour.

WASHINGTON IRVING (1783–1859), who gave his name to Irving Place in Gramercy and wrote such classics as *The Legend of Sleepy Hollow* and *Rip Van Winkle*, was the man who coined the word 'Gotham' as a term for New York. While travelling in England he had visited the little English village of Gotham in Nottinghamshire, where in the 13th century the villagers feigned madness in order to avoid paying taxes to the king. The name Gotham City was later made famous by the Batman comics. Irving was also the source of the term Knickerbocker, referring to any New Yorker who could trace their ancestry back to the original Dutch settlers of New Amsterdam. In his *History of New York*, he narrates under the pseudonym Dietrich Knickerbocker.

CHESTER ARTHUR, who lived on Lexington Avenue, is THE ONLY U.S. PRESIDENT NEVER TO HAVE BEEN ELECTED. He assumed office in 1881 after the assassination of James Garfield but was not nominated for re-election in 1884.

NO. 230 FIFTH AVENUE provides the best view of any open-air rooftop bar in Manhattan.

WALDORF SALAD, diced red-skinned apples, celery and mayonnaise, on a lettuce base, was invented by OSCAR TSCHIRKY, maître d'hôtel of the original Waldorf-Astoria Hotel, and was first presented there in 1893.

In the 1984 movie *Ghostbusters* a destructive ghost haunts the bookshelves in the basement of the NEW YORK PUBLIC LIBRARY on Fifth Avenue. In the 2002 film *Spider-Man* the library serves as a backdrop to a pivotal scene, while in the 2004 disaster movie *The Day After Tomorrow* the main characters seek shelter in the library from flooding caused by a global warming storm surge.

CHAPTER 14

BROADWAY –
TIMES SQUARE TO
COLUMBUS CIRCLE

The Lyceum Theater

Times Square

TIMES SQUARE. The name conjures up theatre, bright lights, New Year's Eve, Great White Way, the Crossroads of the World. Times Square is, by some counts, THE MOST VISITED TOURIST ATTRACTION IN THE WORLD. It has a GREATER CONCENTRATION OF ILLUMINATED ADVERTISING BILLBOARDS THAN ANYWHERE ELSE ON EARTH. It is NEW YORK'S BUSIEST TRAFFIC INTERSECTION and has NEW YORK'S BUSIEST SUBWAY STATION.

Times Square is the heart of New York's Theater District, known to the world as Broadway.

Broadway and the Theater District

Although most people regard Broadway and the Theater District as the same thing, they are not quite. The Theater District is certainly centred on Broadway but extends beyond the Broadway theatres to include smaller venues, concert halls and studios. It is generally agreed that New York's Theater District runs east–west between Eighth and Sixth Avenues and north–south between 40th and 54th Streets.

There are 39 theatres officially called Broadway theatres – a Broadway theatre offers big productions with professional actors, usually big stars, and must have more than 500 seats. An Off-Broadway theatre offers a variety of new or lesser known shows, plays, musicals and revues that producers feel may not be able to fill a large Broadway theatre, and has between 100 and 500 seats. An Off-Off-Broadway theatre showcases low-budget, unconventional and experimental shows, usually with unknown actors, and has fewer than 100 seats.

The first theatre on what is now Times Square, the OLYMPIA, was built in 1895 by opera lover OSCAR HAMMERSTEIN, a German Jewish immigrant who had got rich making cigars. He was encouraged by the success of the Metropolitan Opera House, which had opened on 39th and Broadway in 1883 and had attracted full houses away from the theatre district around Union and Madison Squares to what was then New York's frozen north. Hammerstein, whose first two theatres had been in Harlem, took advantage of the cheap land on offer around Times Square and went on to open three more theatres in the area in quick succession, the Victoria in 1898, the Republic in 1900 and the Lew Fields Theater in 1904, almost single-handedly establishing what would become the world's most famous theatre district.

What's in a Name?

Times Square, at the time that Hammerstein was building his theatres here, was the centre of New York's carriage building industry and was actually called Longacre Square, after Long Acre, the area in London where carriages were built.

In 1904 the publisher of the *New York Times*, Adolph S. Ochs, moved his newspaper to a newly built headquarters on Longacre Square, to take advantage of New York's first subway line, which ran from City Hall, along 42nd Street and north to Harlem. The TIMES TOWER had its own subway station, which meant that the *Times* could be distributed all round New York as soon as it was printed, giving the paper an advantage over its rivals.

In the same way that Herald Square had taken its name from the *New York Herald* after the paper moved there in 1895, so did Longacre Square succumb to the *New York Times* and become Times Square, in April 1904. Three weeks later Times Square got its first electronically lit advertisement, fixed to the side of a bank at the corner of Broadway and 46th Street.

New Year, New Traditions

To celebrate the opening of its new headquarters and to welcome in 1904, the *Times* threw a New Year's Party and 200,000 people gathered in the square to watch a firework display staged 395 ft (120 m) up on the roof of the Times Tower, then the second tallest building in New York and visible from 12 miles (19 km) away. Before then, New York's New Year celebrations had been held at Trinity Church, but ever since then Times Square has been the focus for not just New York's but America's New Year celebrations.

By 1907 the Times Tower was no longer the only tall skyscraper in the district and it was decided that something more than fireworks was needed to make the New Year celebrations memorable. Down at No. 195 Broadway the Western Union building had a time ball on its roof that dropped at exactly noon every day to serve as a chronometer for the ships in New York harbour. It seemed to work, so why not use a time ball to signal the start of the New Year? The first year to be ushered in by the glitzy time ball drop in Times Square was 1908, and every year since

has been so welcomed, save for 1942 and 1943 during the Second World War when New York was blacked out.

Times Square continued to flourish and grow until the 1920s, when it reached its glamorous heyday, with movie palaces springing up amongst the theatres and competing for acting stars and songs from Tin Pan Alley. Then in 1929 the 'zipper' newsreel began to display news of the great stock market crash, and in the Great Depression that followed the theatres emptied and closed or else became cheap restaurants or seedy sex joints showing adult films. The hotels deteriorated and the whole area descended into a red-light area of vice and prostitution, as depicted in films such as *Midnight Cowboy* (1968) or *Taxi Driver* (1976).

Since the mid 1990s, however, the area has benefited from massive redevelopment and concerted efforts to spruce up the neighbourhood, and today Times Square is safer, more vibrant, more brilliantly lit, and more buzzing with shows and all kinds of entertainment, than ever before.

42nd Street

New Amsterdam

Broadway, the street, hits Times Square at 42nd Street. A short detour west along 42nd Street brings you to one of the two oldest surviving Broadway theatres, the NEW AMSTERDAM at No. 214 West 42nd, built in 1903 and THE FIRST THEATRE IN AMERICA TO HAVE AN ART NOUVEAU INTERIOR. Between 1914 and 1928 this was the home of the Ziegfeld

Follies, featuring such top entertainers as W.C. Fields, Eddie Cantor, Josephine Baker, Will Rogers and Sophie Tucker. From the 1930s the theatre fell on hard times until bought and renovated by the Walt Disney Corporation in 1995 as a home for Disney musicals and plays. The musical adaptation of *The Lion King* premièred here in 1997, and other shows have included *Mary Poppins, Beauty and the Beast, High School Musical* and *The Jungle Book*.

New Victory

Right across the street at No. 211 stands the NEW VICTORY THEATER, built in 1899 by Oscar Hammerstein as the Republic and THE OLDEST SURVIVING THEATRE BUILDING IN THE THEATER DISTRICT. In 1931 it was converted by Bill Minsky into MINSKY'S BURLESQUE, BROADWAY'S FIRST BURLESQUE HOUSE, where the famous stripper GYPSY ROSE LEE appeared. In 1942 it became a cinema named the Victory Theater in anticipation of the end of the war, and then in 1972 became THE FIRST THEATRE ON 42ND STREET TO SHOW ADULT FILMS. In 1990 it was taken over by the city of New York and restored as the New Victory, opening in 1995 as NEW YORK'S FIRST DEDICATED THEATRE FOR CHILDREN AND FAMILIES.

One Times Square

The first building on the left as you enter Times Square along Broadway is the TIMES TOWER, now called, appropriately enough, One Times Square. Not that you would know that this was the building that started it all, or indeed that there was a building of any sort in there, for the whole structure is one vast illuminated wedge-shaped electric billboard.

When the Times Tower was completed in 1904 it was the second tallest building in the world, a masterpiece of granite and terracotta based on Giotto's Campanile in Florence. Then, after barely ten years, the Times moved on, most recently to Eighth Avenue between 40th and 41st, and the Times Tower passed through a number of hands before in 1996 it was encased from bottom to top in a giant frame hung with advertisements and TV screens, and transformed into the world's tallest billboard. There are no tenants, but a roster of caretakers ensure that routine maintenance is carried out to keep the building in good shape. The only clues to its former glory are the time ball on top and the zipper newsreel around the base.

Condé Nast

Across Broadway from the Times Tower billboard is the Condé Nast Building, at No. 4 Times Square, home to such magazines as *Vogue, GQ, Vanity Fair* and the *New Yorker*. Author Lauren Weisberger based her bestselling novel *The Devil Wears Prada*, later turned into a film starring Meryl Streep, on her experiences as assistant to *Vogue* editor-in-chief Anna Wintour, whose offices are in this building.

On the south-east corner of Broadway and West 43rd are the offices of NASDAQ, housed in a cylindrical glass tower that serves as an electronic video display showing market quotes and financial news.

Across 43rd Street at No. 1500 Broadway a plaque on the wall of Starbucks commemorates the birthplace of playwright EUGENE O'NEILL, who was born in the Barratt Hotel on this site in 1888, while his father James was performing as Edmond Dantes in *The Count of Monte Cristo* off Broadway.

Directly across the road, in front of the Paramount Building, is a U.S. Armed Forces Recruiting Station, opened in 1946, that has ENLISTED MORE RECRUITS FOR THE MILITARY THAN ANY OTHER WALK-IN STATION IN AMERICA.

Paramount Building

The art deco-style PARAMOUNT BUILDING at No. 1501 Broadway was built in 1927 as the headquarters of Paramount Pictures. The site was previously occupied by the Putnam Building, erected on the spot where General Putnam, commanding American troops in New York, met General Washington at the start of the Revolution in April 1776.

At 431 ft (131 m) in height, the Paramount Building was the tallest building on Times Square at the time of its completion and the illuminated glass globe at the peak could be seen from across the Hudson in New Jersey. The stepped setbacks at the top create the shape of a mountain, while the four clock faces are numbered with stars to replicate the stars in the Paramount mountain trademark.

On the ground floor was the fabled, 3,600-seat Paramount Theater, with its iconic marquee and arched entrance on Broadway, and lobby modelled on the Paris Opera. Paramount Pictures premièred many of its early films here, introducing stars like Gary Cooper, Mae West, Fred Astaire, Bing Crosby and Claudette Colbert to the New York audience. During the Great Depression the theatre was used for live music, showcasing the big bands of Tommy Dorsey, Benny Goodman, Glenn Miller and Guy Lombardo, while later on the likes of Jack Benny, Dean

Martin, Jerry Lewis and Frank Sinatra drew the crowds.

In 1956 Elvis Presley's first film, *Love Me Tender*, premièred at the Paramount Theater, but in 1964, as television accelerated the decline of Broadway, the theatre closed, the arch was filled in and the space was converted into offices.

In 2000 the World Wrestling Federation leased the theatre space, reopened the arch and the Marquee over the Broadway entrance and started a wrestling themed restaurant here. Today the theatre area is occupied by the Hard Rock Café.

No. 1500 Broadway

The American Society of Composers, Authors and Publishers (ASCAP) was founded on 13 February 1914 at the Hotel Claridge, which at that time occupied the corner block at No. 1500 Broadway and West 44th Street. Amongst the founding members were Victor Herbert and Irving Berlin. In the film *Midnight Cowboy* the characters played by Dustin Hoffman and Jon Voight stayed in the Hotel Claridge.

The site is occupied today by the ABC TELEVISION STUDIOS, and Times Square forms the backdrop to the *Good Morning America* studio on the second floor. Early risers in the square can sometimes see the presenters and guests arriving or can even find themselves as part of the backdrop during live outside broadcasts.

West 44th Street

A quick detour west for one block along West 44th Street and back takes you past several notable Broadway establishments.

North Side travelling west:

The SHUBERT THEATER, at No. 225, opened in 1913 and was named after S. Shubert, one of Broadway's three powerful Shubert theatrical producing brothers. *A Chorus Line* ran here for a record-breaking 6,137 performances between 1975 and 1990.

Running along the east side of the Shubert Theater and linking it to the BOOTH THEATER on West 45th Street (named after actor Edwin Booth), is SHUBERT ALLEY, where actors would line up hoping to be cast. Shubert Alley is regarded as the GEOGRAPHICAL CENTRE OF 'BROADWAY'.

The BROADHURST THEATER, at No. 235, opened in 1917 and was named after playwright and theatre manager George Howells Broadhurst. The first song which Tin Pan Alley brothers George and Ira Gershwin wrote together, 'The Real American Folk Song', was performed here for the first time in 1918 in the show *Ladies First.*

The MAJESTIC THEATER, at No. 245, opened in 1927 as BROADWAY'S LARGEST THEATRE with a seating capacity of 1,600. BROADWAY'S LONGEST-RUNNING PRODUCTION, PHANTOM OF THE OPERA, has been housed here since January 1988.

South Side travelling east:

Opposite the Majestic Theater is the ST JAMES THEATER, at No. 246, opened in 1927. Rodgers and Hammerstein made their debut here in 1943 with *Oklahoma!*

The HELEN HAYES THEATER, at No. 240, opened in 1912 as The Little Theater and was renamed in 1983 after Helen Hayes, the 'First Lady of American Theater', one of only four actresses to win an Emmy, a Grammy, an Oscar and a Tony award.

SARDI'S RESTAURANT, at No. 234, has been a Broadway institution since it was opened here by Italian-born Vincent and Eugenia Sardi in 1927. By offering a low cost 'actor's menu' for members of Actors' Equity, Sardi's attracted many impoverished actors, who repaid the favour by returning when they were big stars and giving Sardi's great publicity – James

Cagney and Greta Garbo to name but two. The cast of any new show would be applauded by diners as they came into the restaurant to eat late into the night while they waited for the early reviews. Sardi's is famous for its caricatures of actors who have eaten there.

Sardi's is also THE BIRTHPLACE OF THE TONY AWARD. In 1946 theatrical producer Brock Pemberton was lunching at Sardi's not long after the death of his professional partner, the actor and director Antoinette Perry, when he came up with the idea of a theatre prize to be awarded in her memory, which he called the Tony Award after her nickname. The announcement of the award nominees still takes place at Sardi's every year.

Back on Broadway, the block on the east side of the street between 44th and 45th Streets, now occupied by the Toys R Us flagship store, was the site of the first theatre on Times Square, Oscar Hammerstein's Olympia Theater.

Astor Plaza, opposite, is home to Viacom and the MTV studios. Music fans gather here to try and catch a glimpse of their favourite pop stars, while MTV occasionally stages live concerts in Times Square.

Astor Plaza was built on the site of Times Square's first luxury hotel the Hotel Astor, which opened at the same time as the Times Tower in 1904 and triggered a rush of hotel building in the area, mainly by other members of the Astor family.

Lyceum Theater

A short hop east down West 45th Street is the *beaux-arts* exterior of the LYCEUM THEATER, opened in 1903 at the same time as the New Amsterdam on 42nd Street. Along with the New Amsterdam, the Lyceum is THE OLDEST SURVIVING BROADWAY THEATRE, THE OLDEST CONTINUOUSLY OPERATING THEATRE IN NEW YORK, and one of the few still operating under its original name. In July 1912 THE FIRST EVER FEATURE FILM, QUEEN ELIZABETH, starring Sarah Bernhardt, had its FIRST SHOWING BEFORE AN AUDIENCE at the Lyceum, while in 1974 the Lyceum became THE FIRST BROADWAY THEATRE TO BE GRANTED LANDMARK STATUS.

Dear Ladies

Almost hidden by billboards on the corner of West 46th Street and Seventh Avenue (which fuses with Broadway here) is the I. MILLER BUILDING, opened in 1927 to house Israel Miller's shoe store. Inscribed along the parapet wall along West 46th Street are the words: 'The show folks' shoe shop dedicated to beauty in footwear'. Below are four niches containing sculptures by Alexander Stirling Calder of the four most popular leading ladies of the day depicted in their most famous roles, Ethel Barrymore (representing drama) as Ophelia from *Hamlet*, Marilyn Miller (musical comedy) as Sunny from the musical of that name, Mary Pickford (movies) as Cedric Errol in *Little Lord Fauntleroy*, and Rosa Ponselle (opera) as Leonora from *La Forza del Destino*.

Duffy Square

DUFFY SQUARE occupies the northern triangle of the bow tie created by Broadway and Seventh Avenue, the southern triangle being Times Square. It is named after Father Francis P. Duffy who, as chaplain to the 'Fighting 69th' New York Division in France during the First World War, became the most decorated cleric in the history of the U.S. Army, being awarded both the Distinguished Service Cross and the Distinguished Service Medal. Duffy later served as pastor of Holy Cross Church on 42nd Street in Hell's Kitchen (now known as Clinton), when he helped to clean up what was then a notoriously rough area. In the square there is a statue of him standing before a Celtic cross, which was dedicated in 1937.

In front of Duffy there is another statue, of 'The Man who owned Broadway', producer and entertainer George M. Cohan, composer of 'Give My Regards to Broadway'.

Behind the Duffy statue is the TKTS office where half-price tickets for that day's Broadway shows can be purchased. The roof of the glass TKTS booth is covered by public bleacher seats giving a panoramic view of Times Square – and in particular the annual Tony Awards, which are screened for free on a giant TV screen set up in front of the seats.

Brill Building

The art deco BRILL BUILDING at No. 1619 Broadway was built in 1931. It was originally called the Alan E. Lefcourt Building and served as a stunning memorial to developer Abraham Lefcourt's son Alan, who died young. Abraham Lefcourt started out in life as a shoeshine boy and worked his way to a $100 million fortune in real estate. He was devoted to his son Alan, and drew up plans to take on the Chrysler Building and the Empire State Building in the race to construct the world's tallest skyscraper, which he would then dedicate to his son to mark the boy's 13th birthday. Alas, within a couple of years Alan had died of anaemia, the Great Depression had set in and Abraham had lost much of his fortune. The building was scaled down to just ten storeys, and not long afterwards Abraham Lefcourt himself died broken-hearted. The Alan E. Lefcourt Building was taken over by the landlords, the Brill Brothers, and renamed the Brill Building. There are just two mementoes of its tragic story, a bronze bust of the young Alan Lefcourt set in a niche above the elaborate front door on Broadway and another bust, of either Alan or his father Abraham – no one seems to know – directly above at the very top of the building.

The Brill Building Sound

Because of the Great Depression the only tenants that the Brill brothers could find for their new building were music publishers, and by the beginning of the 1960s, 165 different music businesses had their offices there, from songwriters and arrangers to publishers and record labels, not so much an alley as a Tin Pan Building.

One of the most successful of these was a boy from the Bronx called DON KIRSHNER who, along with partner AL NEVINS, formed Aldon Music and hired a stable of talented songwriters to compose songs for the burgeoning rock market. Aldon Music's first success was 'Stupid Cupid', written by Neil Sedaka and Howie Greenfield, which became a big hit for Connie Francis in 1958. Other household names who got their start with Aldon, and contributed to the 'Brill Building Sound', were Carole King (the Carol from Neil Sedaka's 'Oh! Carol'), Neil Diamond, Burt Bacharach, Phil Spector and Jerry Leiber, who wrote the sublime 'Spanish Harlem' together, and Gene Pitney.

As well as producing some of the greatest popular songs ever written, the Brill Building became something of a musical matchmaker too. Buddy Holly met his future wife Maria Elena Santiago there, when she was working as a receptionist. Husband and wife song-writing team Carole King and Gerry Goffin met while working there, as did Ellie Greenwich (who discovered Neil Diamond) and Jeff Barry ('Leader of the Pack', 'River Deep, Mountain High'), and Cynthia Weil and Barry Mann ('You've Lost That Loving Feeling', 'On Broadway').

More Premières

Paramount Plaza at No. 1633 Broadway sits on the former site of the Capitol Theater, built in 1919, flagship of MGM and the biggest cinema in the world of its time, where *The Wizard of Oz* and *Gone With the Wind* were premièred.

Opposite, at No. 1634 Broadway, is the Winter Garden Theater, built in 1896, when the area was still the centre of carriage building, as the American Horse Exchange. It was converted to a theatre by the Shubert Brothers in 1911, and that year Al Jolson made his Broadway debut here in the Jerome Kern musical *La Belle Paree*.

Talking of Al Jolson, a little further up Broadway, across West 51st Street, is the site of WARNERS' THEATER, where Jolson appeared in THE FIRST TALKING

MOVIE, THE JAZZ SINGER, and uttered those immortal first words, 'Wait a minute, wait a minute, you ain't heard nothin' yet!' None of the four Warner Brothers could be at the gala première of their ground-breaking film, because Sam Warner had died of pneumonia the previous day and the brothers were obliged to return to California for the funeral. The address of the theatre was No. 1664 Broadway, but the site is now taken up by shops and the Manhattan Hotel.

Birdland

No. 1678 Broadway, just north of 52nd Street, was the first home in 1949 of the fabled BIRDLAND JAZZ CLUB, centre of the New York jazz scene through the 1950s and early 60s. Jazz had arrived in New York from Chicago in the 1920s and set up on 52nd Street, a block east of Broadway. Birdland was inspired by one of those 52nd Street musicians, the genius bebop alto saxophonist Charlie 'Yardbird' Parker, known simply as 'Bird', who was one of the club's first headliners. Other jazz legends who played regularly at Birdland were Dizzy Gillespie, Thelonious Monk, Miles Davis

and Count Basie, who made Birdland his New York headquarters and recorded 'Lullaby of Birdland' live at the club. John Coltrane headlined there in the early 1960s. With such talent appearing there on a nightly basis Birdland became the nightlife of choice for a host of celebrities like Gary Cooper, Marilyn Monroe, Frank Sinatra, Marlene Dietrich, Sammy Davis Jr. and Ava Gardner.

In 1965 Birdland closed down, eclipsed by the emergence of rock 'n' roll, but opened up again uptown at No. 2745 Broadway in 1986. Ten years later it moved back to Midtown to its current location on West 44th Street.

Steamboat Willie

The Broadway Theater at No. 1685 Broadway opened here in 1924 as B.S. Moss's Colony Theater, a vaudeville and movie house. Mickey Mouse made his world debut at the Colony in 1928 in STEAMBOAT WILLIE, THE FIRST TALKING CARTOON, and Walt Disney returned 11 years later in 1939 to première his film *Fantasia* at what was by now the Broadway Theater. With its large seating capacity and stage, the Broadway has been a popular venue for musicals since it became a legitimate theatre in 1930 and has hosted record-breaking runs of *My Fair Lady* and *South Pacific*, amongst others.

The Latest Show

THE ED SULLIVAN THEATER at 1697 Broadway was built by Arthur

Hammerstein in 1927 as the Hammerstein, named in honour of his father Oscar Hammerstein, the original Broadway producer. The theatre's first show was a musical called *Golden Dawn*, featuring as second male lead a young British actor called Archie Leach – born in Bristol in 1904 he arrived in the U.S. at the age of 16 with a stage troupe and decided to stay. After appearing in a number of musicals he went to Hollywood in 1931 and changed his name to CARY GRANT.

In 1936 CBS leased the theatre and converted it into a radio studio and later a television studio. One of the first TV shows broadcast from there was THE JACKIE GLEASON SHOW. Ed Sullivan moved there in 1950 with his show *Toast of the Town*, which in 1955 was renamed THE ED SULLIVAN SHOW. When ELVIS PRESLEY appeared on the show the following year it was almost pulled from the air as his gyrations were considered obscene. On 9 February 1964, just 77 days after President Kennedy had been assassinated, *The Ed Sullivan Show* made television history when a record 73 million people, 40 per cent of America, tuned in to see the first appearance on American TV

of THE BEATLES. In terms of population percentage this was the HIGHEST RATED REGULAR SCHEDULED TV PROGRAMME OF ALL TIME. Ray Block, the show's musical director, was quoted in the *New York Times* as saying of The Beatles that night, 'I give them a year.'

In 1967 the theatre was renamed the Ed Sullivan Theater, but the show began to fall in the ratings and was taken off the air in 1971 after a 23-year run. CBS moved out, but in 1993, having poached David Letterman from NBC, CBS bought the theatre for *The Late Show with David Letterman*, which has been broadcast from here ever since.

At No. 1740 Broadway is the Mutual of New York or MONY Building, once famed for its Weather Star, a tower of lights crowned with a star on top of the building which forecast the weather – the star would glow green if the forecast was fair, orange for cloudy, flashing orange for rain, and flashing white for snow. The tower lights would rise or fall as the temperature was forecast to rise or fall. Until 2007 the building sported a sign on the parapet reading Mutual of New York, with the first letter of each word enlarged and lit in red neon, spelling out MONY. This sign was a recurring motif in the film *Midnight Cowboy* and the inspiration for the 1968 hit single 'Mony Mony' by Tommy James and the Shondells. The MONY sign was eventually replaced by one reading 1740, the building's address. To date, no one has been inspired to write a song called 1740.

Columbus Circle

COLUMBUS CIRCLE, previously the Great Circle, is a busy intersection and one of New York's rare roundabouts, where Broadway breaks free from Midtown and meets Eighth Avenue, West 59th Street and Central Park. It is the gateway to the Upper West Side and THE POINT FROM WHICH ALL OFFICIAL DISTANCES TO AND FROM NEW YORK ARE MEASURED.

In 1892 the Great Circle was renamed Columbus Circle to mark the 400th anniversary of Columbus's discovery of the Americas. At the centre of the Circle a marble statue of Christopher Columbus by Gaetano Russo, erected in 1894, surveys the scene from on top of a 70 ft (21 m) high column of Carrara marble, donated by the readers of *Il Progresso*, the newspaper of New York's Italian community.

Columbus Circle was extensively renovated and redesigned in 2005 with flower beds and new fountains by Water Entertainment Technologies (WET), who designed the musical fountains of Bellagio in Las Vegas.

No. 2 Columbus Place, at the junction of Broadway and Eighth Avenue on the south side of the Circle, is home to the MUSEUM OF ARTS AND DESIGN, which moved there in 2008 following a controversial redesigning of the modernist, marble-clad building already on the site since 1964, which housed the Huntington Hartford Gallery of Modern Art.

The western side of Columbus Circle is taken up by the TIME WARNER

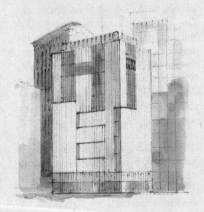

CENTER, consisting of two slender 750 ft (229 m) twin towers rising from an atrium containing an upmarket shopping mall. Also within the complex are the Mandarin Oriental Hotel, the CNN studios and a 1200-seat theatre for 'Jazz at the Lincoln Center', part of the Lincoln Center for the Performing Arts and THE FIRST PERFORMING ARTS FACILITY DEDICATED SOLELY TO JAZZ ANYWHERE IN THE WORLD.

The two graceful towers mirror the sky so effectively that they blend into the background and are at times almost invisible, allaying the fears of some New Yorkers that they would cast a shadow over Central Park.

Well, I never *knew this*
about

BROADWAY —
TIMES SQUARE TO COLUMBUS CIRCLE

Oscar Hammerstein's grandson, Oscar Hammerstein II, had huge successes on Broadway as a producer and lyricist of musicals, including *Show Boat*, written with Jerome Kern, and *Oklahoma!*, *Carousel*, *The King and I*, *South Pacific* and *The Sound of Music*, all written with Richard Rodgers.

THE LINCOLN HIGHWAY, THE FIRST ROAD TO CROSS THE UNITED STATES, begins in Times Square, at the junction of 42nd Street and Broadway. Dedicated in 1913 as THE FIRST NATIONAL MEMORIAL TO ABRAHAM LINCOLN (the Lincoln Memorial in Washington opened in 1922), the highway today covers 3,142 miles (5,055 km) and ends at Lincoln Park in San Francisco.

THE WORLD'S FIRST ELECTRONIC NEWS CRAWL, or 'zipper', appeared on the Times Tower in Times Square in 1928, displaying reports of the election contest between the Democratic candidate, New York governor Alfred E. Smith, and the Republican Herbert Hoover.

42ND STREET gives its name to a 1933 musical film choreographed by Busby Berkeley about the struggles to put on a Broadway musical during the Great Depression.

At 7.45 p.m. every evening the clocks on the Paramount Building in Times Square chime out 'Give My Regards to Broadway' to alert theatre-goers that it's 15 minutes to curtain up.

CARNEGIE HALL, at No. 154 West 57th Street, was New York's first great concert hall. It was built in 1891 by steel magnate Andrew Carnegie, and the

Columbus Circle was trampled over by the Stay Puft Marshmallow Man while he was making his way to 55 Central Park West in the 1984 film *Ghostbusters*.

THE INTREPID SEA AIR SPACE MUSEUM at Pier 86 on the Hudson River is THE ONLY AIRCRAFT-CARRIER-BASED MUSEUM IN THE WORLD. Highlights include the USS *Growler*, the first guided missile submarine ever opened to the public, *Concorde*, the world's only commercial supersonic airliner, and *Enterprise*, the first Space Shuttle orbiter.

guest conductor on opening night was Tchaikovsky.

ACTORS' EQUITY was founded in 1913 at a meeting in the Pabst Grand Circle Hotel, which occupied No. 2 Columbus Circle from 1874 until 1960.

CHAPTER 15

MIDTOWN &
THE UPPER EAST SIDE

St Patrick's Cathedral

A Walk around Midtown

Start point: Grand Central Terminal

Grand Central Terminal

Covering 48 acres (19 ha), with 67 tracks and 44 platforms, GRAND CENTRAL TERMINAL IS THE LARGEST RAILWAY STATION IN THE WORLD. The first station was built here by Cornelius Vanderbilt

in 1871, at the southernmost point on Manhattan that steam trains were permitted to go. His terminal was replaced by the present *beaux-arts* masterpiece in 1913.

The wonderfully spacious main concourse revolves around a central information booth crowned by the station's iconic four-faced clock, a traditional New York meeting place. The vaulted ceiling, 125 ft (38 m) high, is painted with a zodiac and over 2,500 stars from a design by French artist Paul Helleu. The zodiac is shown in mirror

image because the artist based his mural on a medieval map depicting the heavens as they would be seen from the outside.

Whispering Gallery

There are two magnificent staircases sweeping up and out from the concourse, which are modelled on the grand staircase of the Paris Opera, while ramps lead down to the lower levels where there are restaurants and a food court. The oldest and most famous of these eating places is the GRAND CENTRAL OYSTER BAR, which has been here since the terminal was rebuilt in 1913. Its vaulted ceiling is covered in Guastavino tiles, like those in the City Hall subway station, and just outside the entrance there is a small, tile-covered vaulted space that acts as a perfect whispering gallery – if you stand in one corner you can hear perfectly what someone in the opposite corner is saying, no matter how softly they speak.

Campbell Apartment

Hidden away in the north-west corner of the terminal, up another imposing staircase, is a spectacular room designed to resemble the galleried hall of a 13th-century Florentine palace. Now an elegant cocktail lounge known as the CAMPBELL APARTMENT, this was the opulent private office and salon of financier John Campbell, one of the directors of Grand Central, who would relax here in the evening with up to 60 friends, enjoying private music recitals and other entertainments.

Outside the terminal, over the main entrance on 42nd Street, is Jules-Félix Coutan's massive sculpture of Mercury, flanked by Minerva and Hercules, surmounting a clock face 13 ft (4 m) in diameter, which incorporates THE LARGEST EXAMPLE OF TIFFANY GLASS IN THE WORLD.

Turn left on to 42nd Street and walk east to the . . .

Chrysler Building

The fabulous art deco CHRYSLER BUILDING, many people's favourite New York skyscraper, was the first building in the world to exceed a height of 1,000 ft (305 m). Upon its completion in 1930 it was the tallest building in the world at 1,046 ft (319 m), until overtaken by the Empire State Building just 11 months later in 1931. It is still THE TALLEST BRICK BUILDING IN THE WORLD (although encased in steel).

The building was designed by Walter Chrysler as a homage to the golden age

of the motor car, its spire resembling a car radiator grill, the setbacks adorned with wheels and 1929 Chrysler radiator caps, and projecting stainless steel gargoyles modelled on the bonnet ornaments of the 1929 Chrysler Plymouth.

The ravishingly ornate lobby, entered from Lexington, glows amber in a riot of art deco patterns and decoration with angular curves, plenty of chrome trim and artistic triangular shapes. The walls are covered in African marble and the ceiling adorned by an enormous Edward Trumbull mural showing 1920s transportation themes. Measuring 100 ft (30.5 m) by 98 ft (29.8 m), it is reputed to be the LARGEST MURAL IN THE WORLD.

As you walk past the building on 42nd Street you can see that the east side is aligned slightly askew to the street grid. This is because the plot follows the line of the old East Post Road to Boston, which ran past the original property.

Daily News Building

Continue east past a rare surviving 19th-century townhouse and the New York Helmsley Hotel, where owner Leona Helmsley's dreadful treatment of her staff earned her the soubriquet 'Queen of Mean'. At No. 220 is the DAILY NEWS BUILDING, erected in 1930 for New York's first gossipy tabloid newspaper, founded in 1919 and famous for its punchy headlines, glossy photographs and celebrity tittle-tattle – it broke the news of Edward VIII and Mrs Simpson, for instance. Although the paper moved out in the 1990s, the building is a landmark and retains the name – and is instantly recognisable as the home of the *Daily Planet* from the 1980s *Superman* films. The intricate frieze over the entrance is lit by neon at night.

Inside the lobby, under a black glass dome, sits THE LARGEST INDOOR GLOBE IN THE WORLD, rotating slowly and tilted to the Earth's axis. Set in the floor are brass plates giving the distances to various cities of the world, while clocks and thermometers on the walls tell their times and temperatures.

Tudor City

Continue along 42nd to Tudor City, a 1920s housing development of 3,000 apartments built in Tudor Gothic.

Once you have passed under Tudor
City Place, where Matt Damon arranges
to meet with the CIA boss who is
pursuing him in *The Bourne Ultimatum*,
cross First Avenue and turn around to
see a great view of the Chrysler
Building. The Tudor Tower you can see
on the left is the home of the evil Green
Goblin in *Spider-Man* and also where
Tom Hanks lives in the 1984 film *Splash*.
Note how the windows looking in this
direction are so small – when Tudor
City was built, the view (and stench)
would have been of slaughterhouses,
breweries and gasworks.

Turn back to face the river, walk
down the slope, past the ventilation
building for the Queens Midtown
tunnel and follow the sidewalk round
to the right – on your right is ROBERT
MOSES PLAYGROUND, named after New
York's 'Master Builder'. Set along the
top of the fence are models of some of
the projects for which he was responsible, including the Metropolitan
Opera House, Verrazano Narrows
Bridge and Central Park Zoo.

Now return to First Avenue and
the . . .

United Nations

Robert Moses was also largely responsible for bringing the United Nations
headquarters to New York (when it
seemed to be heading for Philadelphia),
persuading John D. Rockefeller Jr. to
buy the 18-acre (7 ha) East River site
from developer William Zeckendorf for
$8.5 million and donate it to the city in
1945. The complex was then designed by

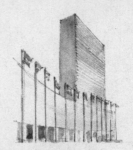

a multinational team led by Rockefeller's
own architect William K. Harrison.

The United Nations complex is international territory administered by the
U.N. itself and has its own security
force and fire department, but is subject
to city, state and federal laws. Special
U.N. stamps are valid on items mailed
from within the complex.

The whole complex is fronted with a
line of flagpoles in which the flags of all
193 member countries fly in English
alphabetical order, the first one being
Afghanistan and the last, by 42nd Street,
being Zimbabwe. Behind the flags towers
the slim, modernist, Le Corbusier-
inspired Secretariat building, 39 storeys
and 504 ft (154 m) high, with New York's
earliest glass curtain wall and the U.N.
Secretary-General's office on the 38th
floor. Controversial when erected in 1950,
the Secretariat Building is now a celebrated landmark. Next along is the
General Assembly Building, seating
1,800, where representatives of all
member states gather every three months,
where world leaders pontificate from the
rostrum, and where Soviet leader Nikita
Khrushchev famously banged on the desk
with his shoe to get attention in 1960.

Hidden behind these buildings, on

the waterfront, sits the Conference Building, home of the real powerhouse of the U.N. the Security Council, which consists of five permanent members, China, France, Russia, the UK and the U.S. and ten non-permanent members elected every two years.

Peace Park

Opposite the U.N. on the north side of U.N. Plaza is NEW YORK'S FIRST PEACE PARK, dedicated to RALPH BUNCHE, a U.N. mediator who brokered a peace agreement between the Arabs and Israelis in 1949. For this he became THE FIRST AFRICAN–AMERICAN TO WIN A NOBEL PEACE PRIZE, in 1950. The 50 ft (15 m) high stainless steel shaft at the north end was sculpted by Bunche's friend Daniel Larue Johnson and is called Peace Form One. It was unveiled in 1980. The granite steps leading up to Tudor City are named the Sharansky Steps in honour of the Russian dissident Anatoly Sharansky and are inscribed with words from the Book of Isaiah, 'They shall beat their swords into plowshares.'

Glamour

Most of the larger buildings in the area are UN offices, but it is impossible to miss the astonishingly precarious-looking bronze glass Trump World Tower, at 861 ft (262 m) the tallest residential building in the world when it was completed in 2001 – spookily it is oddly reminiscent of the monolith from *2001: A Space Odyssey.*

Just behind the tower in 48th Street is a parking lot where there was once

a silent film studio, established in 1916 by JOSEPH SCHENCK, future first president of United Artists, for his wife NORMA TALMADGE. BUSTER KEATON made his first film here in 1917, for Fatty Arbuckle's Comique Film Company, which was based here. Keaton also met his future wife here, Norma's sister Natalie Talmadge.

Across First Avenue is Nos. 860–870 UN Plaza, where TRUMAN CAPOTE bought a brand new apartment with the royalties from his book *In Cold Blood* in 1967. He lived there until his death in 1984. Other residents have included Johnny Carson, Robert Kennedy, Cliff Robertson and Yul Brynner.

Sutton

As you continue north on First Avenue you are entering SUTTON, one of New York's most exclusive residential neighbourhoods. The name comes from Effingham B. Sutton, a shipowner who in 1875 built a row of brownstones on a stretch of Avenue A between 57th and 58th Streets, overlooking the river. In the 1920s Anne Vanderbilt, widow of William K. Vanderbilt, Anne Morgan, daughter of J.P. Morgan, and the society interior decorator Elsie de Wolfe all moved into the brownstones and remodelled them as townhouses, shifting the social centre of New York east from Fifth Avenue.

Beekman

At the art deco Beekman Tower Hotel turn right on to East 50th Street and walk one block to Beekman Place, which occupies the former site of the Beekman family mansion, Mount Pleasant, built in 1784. Wilhelm Beekman was one of the original Dutch settlers who sailed with Peter Stuyvesant.

While most of the apartments and houses here don't look particularly special, their superb river views and proximity to Midtown have rendered them extremely desirable.

IRVING BERLIN lived on the corner, at No. 17, from 1947 until his death in 1989 aged 101, but No. 1 Beekman Place was considered the prime address here and has boasted as tenants John D. Rockefeller III and Prince Aly Khan.

Dead End

Turn left at the end of Beekman Place, then right on to First Avenue and right into 52nd Street, which comes to a dead end on a terrace high above the river. This is the dead end that inspired Sidney Kingsley's Broadway play DEAD END. In the 1930s, when these luxury apartment blocks were built to take advantage of the river views, this area was still teeming with tenement slums, and the story is about the interaction between the rich new tenants in their airy towers and the 'dead end kids' skylarking about along the filthy river front. In 1936 *Dead End* was made into a hit film starring HUMPHREY BOGART – good casting because Bogart had once lived right here on 52nd Street, at No. 434.

No. 450, on the south side of the dead end, is called the CAMPANILE and was referred to by noted wisecracker

Dorothy Parker, who had friends living there, as 'Wit's End'. GRETA GARBO lived here quietly for 40 years.

The north side of the dead end, once the Cremo factory, is now occupied by RIVER HOUSE, built in 1931 and described as 'arguably the city's, if not the world's finest apartment building'. ADELE ASTAIRE, sister of Fred, CORNELIUS VANDERBILT WHITNEY, founder of Pan Am, and his cousin GLORIA VANDERBILT must have thought it was, because they all lived here. HENRY KISSINGER, SIR EVELYN DE ROTHSCHILD and BARBARA TAYLOR BRADFORD still do. The view, however, did nothing to stop FM radio inventor EDWIN HOWARD ARMSTRONG, depressed by long-running litigation over his radio patents, from jumping to his death from his apartment on the 13th floor in 1954, dressed in his hat, gloves and overcoat.

Sutton Place

Go back to First Avenue and turn right and then right again into 53rd Street. Go left into Sutton Place South and cross 57th Street to No. 1 Sutton Place, which is the brownstone Anne Vanderbilt had remodelled as a Georgian townhouse in

1920. This is the start of the original SUTTON PLACE, a quite ravishing row of townhouses made all the more striking by their being surrounded by ordinary, bland New York tower blocks.

No. 3 was designed for Anne Morgan and is now the official residence of the Secretary-General of the United Nations, who can walk to work from here. No. 13 was the final home of Oscar Wilde's agent, Elisabeth Marbury, who died there of a heart attack in 1933.

At the end of the row turn right into Sutton Square and admire the fine view of the Queensboro Bridge, star of an iconic scene in Woody Allen's film *Manhattan*, in which his and Diane Keaton's characters relax on the bench here in the twilight with the bridge in the background.

On your left is Riverview Terrace, a private road of brownstones, once owned by Jack Warner of Warner Brothers. The houses here, unusually for New York, have large gardens, in this case built out over the FDR East River Drive. They were paid for by the city as compensation for digging up their former gardens to make way for the road.

Go back to Sutton Place, turn right and continue north. Just before the bridge turn left up 59th Street and walk to Second Avenue, where you will see the terminal for New York's only cable car.

Roosevelt Island Tramway

The ROOSEVELT ISLAND TRAMWAY is THE ONLY AERIAL COMMUTER TRAMWAY

IN AMERICA. It began operating in 1976 to serve commuters from the newly built apartments on Roosevelt Island and is part of the MTA system, accepting ordinary Metro Cards. The journey takes four minutes and crosses the East River alongside the Queensboro Bridge at a height of 250 ft (76 m), giving passengers what the *New York Times* has described as 'the most exciting view in New York City'.

ROOSEVELT ISLAND, previously Blackwell Island, is mainly residential now but still has the remnants of the 18th-century Blackwell Farmhouse which gave the island its name, a 19th-century lighthouse, the ruins of a smallpox hospital and a jailhouse where Mae West was held in 1927 after a 'lewd performance'. It can also boast sensational views of the city and a relaxed atmosphere, five minutes from the mayhem and excitement of the city but far removed from the noise and stress. Not many New Yorkers seem to know about the tramway or much about the island – which, I suppose, is part of its charm.

Once you have returned on the tramway, walk east on 59th Street to Bloomingdale's.

Bloomingdale's

Brothers Lyman and Joseph Bloomingdale opened their East Side Bazaar on Third Avenue and East 56th Street in 1872, selling a variety of women's fashions and working on the principle of buying in bulk and selling cheap to attract the blue-collar workers of the Upper East Side, who couldn't afford the larger stores downtown. The receipts on their first day totalled $3.66.

The store moved north to its present location at the heart of the East Side transport hub in 1929. The Third Avenue Elevated Railway brought customers from all over Manhattan, giving rise to the slogan 'All cars transfer to Bloomingdale's' – and Bloomingdale's WAS THE FIRST STORE IN NEW YORK TO MAKE DELIVERIES BY MOTOR VEHICLE.

Bloomingdale's next began to move upmarket and specialise in promoting European fashion. It was THE FIRST STORE TO INTRODUCE THE DESIGNER SHOPPING BAG, created by artist Joseph Kinigstein in 1961, to promote the store's 'Esprit de France' promotion. Bloomingdale's was also known for discovering new fashion talent, and amongst the designers who opened their first boutiques in Bloomingdale's were Calvin Klein, DKNY and Yves St Laurent.

During her visit to New York in 1976, Queen Elizabeth II went shopping at Bloomingdale's, cementing the store's image as one of America's most glamorous department stores. In the TV series *Friends*, Rachel Green (played by Jennifer Aniston) achieves her dream job working at Bloomingdale's.

Lexington Avenue

After Bloomingdale's, turn left on to Lexington. Just before 52nd Street, on the north-west corner of the junction, is the grating where MARILYN MONROE stood during the filming of *The Seven Year Itch* to shoot perhaps the most iconic scene in movie history. Thanks to advance publicity some 5,000 photographers and spectators turned up to watch as she came out of what was then the Trans-Lux Theater and stepped on to the grating. The breeze from a passing subway train (in reality a huge special effects fan located underground) then billowed her skirt up around her waist, while she exclaimed, 'Oh, can you feel the breeze from the subway? Isn't it delicious?'

Egged on by the appreciative roars of the crowd, the director Billy Wilder shot and re-shot the scene several times, much to the annoyance of Marilyn's then husband Joe DiMaggio, who was watching. He divorced Marilyn just a few weeks later. In the end the censor insisted that a less revealing version of the scene had to be shot in the studio.

The grating is still there, but there is no marker or plaque, and thousands of New Yorkers pass over it every day without realising they are following in the footsteps of a legend.

Continue south on Lexington, past the magnificent art deco General Electric Building at No. 570, erected in 1931. Its slender tower, 640 ft (195 m) high, is crowned with spikes as an allegory of wireless communications and the whole building was designed to complement the Byzantine St Bartholomew's Church next door on Madison Avenue. Now turn right down East 50th Street to Park Avenue with St Bartholomew's Church on your right and the Waldorf-Astoria Hotel on your left.

Waldorf-Astoria

When it opened here in 1931, having moved from Fifth Avenue, the WALDORF-ASTORIA WAS THE LARGEST AND TALLEST HOTEL IN THE WORLD. It was also THE FIRST HOTEL IN THE WORLD TO OFFER ROOM SERVICE.

In the mezzanine above the Park Avenue entrance sits a battered 1907 Steinway piano that belonged to Cole Porter. He composed many of his acclaimed songs on this piano while living in Suite 33a in the Waldorf Towers, a self-contained boutique hotel occupying some of the upper storeys of the main hotel. Porter lived there from 1934 until his death in California in 1964.

The Royal Suite in the Waldorf Towers was home to the Duke and Duchess of Windsor in the 1950s, while Prince Rainier of Monaco and Grace Kelly celebrated their engagement at the hotel in 1956.

Since 1931 every sitting U.S. President has stayed at the Waldorf-Astoria as a guest, while in 1964 Herbert Hoover, 31st President, died there.

Secret Station

The Waldorf-Astoria sits above the Grand Central Railroad tracks and is rumoured to have its own underground platform and spur, Track 61, first used by General Pershing in 1938 and later by Presidents Franklin D. Roosevelt and Harry Truman. It was accessed by a freight elevator large enough to accommodate President Roosevelt's Pierce Arrow limousine and the brass doors of the elevator can still be seen on 49th Street. When President George W. Bush was staying at the hotel a train was apparently kept permanently idling on Track 61 in case he had to escape quickly.

Now cross Park Avenue and walk along East 50th Street to Fifth Avenue and . . .

St Patrick's Cathedral

When New York was declared an arch-diocese in 1850, the then Bishop of New York John Hughes decided that the city's expanding Catholic congregation deserved a new cathedral to replace the old St Patrick's on Mulberry Street. The site he chose was on land set aside for a cemetery in countryside well to the north of the city. The project was initially termed 'Hughes' Folly' because most people thought it mad to build a cathedral so far out, but Hughes was anticipating, correctly as it turned out, that the city would expand north, and St Patrick's now occupies a prime spot on New York's most glamorous avenue.

The architect chosen for the new cathedral was James Renwick Jr., who had just completed the much admired Grace Church on Broadway. The corner-stone was laid in August 1858, and although work was interrupted by the Civil War, the main body of the cathedral was finished by 1878 and the cathedral was dedicated on 25 May 1879. Built in Gothic Revival style, St Patrick's was then THE LARGEST CATHEDRAL IN AMERICA, able to accommodate a congregation of 2,200 people, and the first to compare in any way with the cathedrals of Europe. The lovely, slender spires, completed in 1888, are 330 ft (100 m) high. In 1901 James Renwick's original apse was removed to a church in Harlem to make way for the Lady Chapel.

Among the treasures in the cathedral are the rose window, 28 ft (8.5 m) in diameter, which was designed by Charles Connick, the Great Organ, which has more than 7,000 pipes, and the baldachin over the high altar, which is made entirely of bronze.

The great bronze doors of the cathedral, which open on to Fifth Avenue, are adorned with the figures of notable New Yorkers such as ST ELIZABETH ANN SETON, KATERI TEKAKWITHA, 'Lily of the Mohawks', a Roman Catholic convert who was THE FIRST NATIVE AMERICAN WOMAN TO BE VENERATED BY THE CATHOLIC CHURCH, and ST FRANCESCA XAVIER CABRINI, THE FIRST AMERICAN SAINT.

The sense of peace and quiet that descends as you pass through the great doors of St Patrick's, leaving behind the noise and lusty hedonism of Fifth Avenue, is extraordinary, and a few moments of contemplation in his cool and tranquil space is a real tonic.

St Patrick's Cathedral has received visits from two Popes, Paul VI in 1964, during the first ever Papal visit to America, and John Paul II in 1979. Funeral masses held in the cathedral have included those of New York governor Alfred E. Smith in 1920, baseball player Babe Ruth in 1948, maestro Arturo Toscanini in 1957 and Senator Robert F. Kennedy in 1968.

Right across Fifth Avenue from St Patrick's Cathedral is the . . .

Rockefeller Center

THE ROCKEFELLER CENTER, which consists of 19 buildings and covers 22 acres (9 ha), is THE LARGEST PRIVATELY OWNED COMMERCIAL COMPLEX IN THE WORLD. John D. Rockefeller Jr. leased the site from Columbia University in 1928, originally to develop as a new home for the Metropolitan Opera, but with the onset of the Great Depression the opera pulled out and Rockefeller went ahead with a purely commercial development, providing jobs for some 40,000 people. Work started in 1931 and the first phase of 14 art deco buildings was completed in 1939.

Radio City Music Hall

The first part of the centre to open was the RADIO CITY MUSIC HALL. The name Radio City was taken from the centre's first tenants the Radio Corporation of America (RCA). When it opened on Sixth Avenue in 1932, Radio City Music Hall was THE LARGEST THEATRE AND MOVIE HOUSE IN THE WORLD, with over 6,000 seats. Amongst the acts appearing on the theatre's opening night was a high-kicking dance troupe from St Louis who took the name *Rockettes*. They have since become an emblem of New York entertainment, performing five shows a day at Radio City Music Hall, seven days a week. *The Radio City Christmas Special*, a spectacular singing and dancing revue first presented in 1933, has become a New York Christmas tradition. The Mighty Wurlitzer organ installed at Radio City Music Hall in 1932 is THE LARGEST WURLITZER EVER MADE.

30 Rock

The Rockefeller Center was officially opened in 1933 with the completion of the centre's main building 30 Rockefeller Center, known as 30 Rock, which is set back from Fifth Avenue in the middle of the complex. Known first as the RCA Building, it was renamed the General Electric Building after GE reacquired RCA, which it had itself founded in 1919.

The original fresco in the lobby of 30 Rock, painted by Mexican socialist Diego Rivera, was dismantled when it was found to contain a portrait of Lenin, and was replaced by a vast mural called 'American Progress' by Spanish artist Josep Cert.

In 1934 the RAINBOW ROOM restaurant opened on the 65th floor, THE FIRST RESTAURANT IN NEW YORK TO BE LOCATED AT THE TOP OF A SKYSCRAPER. It featured a revolving dance floor and a live big band orchestra, where acts such as Noël Coward and Duke Ellington entertained, and quickly established a reputation for fine dining amongst New York's elite. The name was derived from an organ in the building that translated music into different colours of the rainbow.

30 Rock is the headquarters of the broadcaster NBC and home to their news operations as well as *Saturday Night Live*. The building gives its name to an NBC television comedy series called *30 Rock*, based on writer Tina Fey's experiences of working on *Saturday Night Live*.

30 Rock has an observation deck called TOP OF THE ROCK, located on the 70th floor of the building, which is 872 ft (266 m) high. From here there are spectacular 360-degree views of New York and in particular of Central Park and the Empire State Building.

Plaza

In 1933 the first Rockefeller Center Christmas Tree was put up in the sunken plaza in front of 30 Rock and lit up, in a ceremony that became an annual tradition. In 1936 a skating rink was opened in the plaza, which has become a favourite New York institution. During the summer the plaza is occupied by a restaurant and café.

The plaza is overlooked by the most famous piece of art in the centre, a bronze gilded statue of Prometheus bringing fire to mankind, sculpted by Paul Manship.

Now continue north on . . .

Fifth Avenue

This stretch of Fifth Avenue between 49th and 60th Street is often ranked as 'the most expensive shopping street in the world', and contains the flagship branches of many of the world's most prestigious stores.

Fifth Avenue was first an upmarket residential street, and the next few blocks north were occupied almost entirely by mansions belonging to the Vanderbilts (*see* page 199).

The Plaza Hotel

Located where Fifth Avenue meets Central Park, THE PLAZA HOTEL was designed by architect Henry J. Hardenbergh to resemble a French château. (Hardenbergh was also responsible for the Dakota and the original Waldorf-Astoria). The Plaza was opened in 1907 when the first guest, Alfred Gwynne Vanderbilt, was signed in by a grand welcoming committee. F. SCOTT FITZGERALD, who lived there with his wife Zelda in the 1920s, was advised by

51ST–52ND STREET

Across on the east side of the avenue VERSACE occupies No. 647, the last Fifth Avenue Vanderbilt home still standing, built in 1905 for William Henry's son George Vanderbilt.

Next to it at No. 651 is CARTIER, here since 1915, when Pierre Cartier bought the house from Morton F. Plant, Commodore of the New York Yacht Club, for $100 and a string of pearls. In 1904 Louis Cartier, the founder's grandson, created THE FIRST MEN'S WRISTWATCH, the Santos, designed for his friend the Brazilian aviator Alberto Santos-Dumont. In 1934 Cartier created THE WORLD'S FIRST WATERPROOF WATCH.

53RD STREET

Above 53rd Street is ST THOMAS EPISCOPALIAN CHURCH, built here in 1870 and rebuilt after a fire in 1905. Consuelo Vanderbilt married the Duke of Marlborough here in 1895, and former President Benjamin Harrison married Mary Dimmick here in 1896.

MoMA

A two-minute walk west down 53rd Street brings you to the appropriately modern glass MUSEUM OF MODERN ART, reopened in 2004 and home to the world's greatest collection of modern art. Highlights include Paul Cézanne's *The Bather*, Van Gogh's *Olive Trees* and Picasso's *Les Demoiselles d'Avignon* as well as some 10,000 rare films and photographic stills.

54TH–55TH STREET

Back on Fifth Avenue, across 54th Street is the grandest clubhouse in New York, a splendid granite Florentine palazzo built in 1899 for the UNIVERSITY CLUB, founded in 1865 to promote the arts. All members must have a college degree.

At No. 700 on the south-west corner with 55th Street is the PENINSULA HOTEL, built in 1905 as the Gorham Hotel and bankrupt within three years because it was too close to the Presbyterian church across 55th to be allowed a liquor licence – at the time no liquor could be served within 200 yards (183 m) of a church. It reopened as the Peninsula in 1988.

Across Fifth Avenue at No. 703 is the ST REGIS HOTEL, built in 1904 and just far enough away from the church to get a liquor licence. The St Regis was THE FIRST HOTEL IN NEW YORK WITH AIR-CONDITIONING. Marilyn Monroe and Joe DiMaggio stayed here and had noisy rows while she was filming *The Seven Year Itch*. DE BEERS, the world's dominant diamond company, occupies the ground floor.

55TH–56TH STREET

No. 718 is HARRY WINSTON, the jeweller mentioned in the song 'Diamonds are a Girl's Best Friend' from the film *Gentlemen Prefer Blondes* – 'Talk to me, Harry Winston, tell me all about it!' Winston owned the accursed Hope Diamond for ten years before donating it to the Smithsonian in 1958.

56TH–57TH STREET

At No. 721 GUCCI's flagship store occupies the ground floor of the Trump Tower, where Michael Jackson and Lisa Marie Presley spent part of their honeymoon in 1994.

No. 727 is TIFFANY & Co, founded on Broadway in 1832 and moved here in 1940. This was the address of railroad magnate Collis P. Huntington's mansion of 1892. Above the entrance is a wooden statue of Atlas holding a clock, which has survived from the very first Tiffany's jewellery store. Tiffany's most celebrated moment came at 5 a.m. on the morning of 2 October 1960, when Holly Golightly, played by Audrey Hepburn, stepped out of a cab and gazed into the window during the filming of the iconic first scene from the film of Truman Capote's novella *Breakfast at Tiffany's*.

Ernest Hemingway to give his liver to Princeton and his heart to the Plaza. Fitzgerald set some scenes in *The Great Gatsby* at the hotel.

FRANK LLOYD WRIGHT designed the Guggenheim Museum while living in suite 223 at the Plaza in the 1950s, THE BEATLES stayed there on their first visit to America in 1964 and TRUMAN CAPOTE gave his legendary Black and White Ball at the Plaza in 1966, the 20th century's answer to Mrs Astor's Four Hundred Ball.

KAY THOMPSON lived at the hotel while writing *Eloise*, her classic children's tale published in 1955 about a little girl who lives on the top floor of the Plaza.

In 1959 the Plaza became NEW YORK'S FIRST EVER OUTDOOR MOVIE LOCATION when Alfred Hitchcock filmed parts of *North by Northwest* there. The Plaza has also appeared in *The Great Gatsby*, *Barefoot in the Park*, *Funny Girl*, *The Cotton Club*, *Crocodile Dundee* and *Home Alone II: Lost in New York*.

In front of the hotel, on Grand Army Plaza, is the Pulitzer Fountain, unveiled in 1916 and paid for by Joseph Pulitzer.

The statue on the north part of Grand Army Plaza is of General William Tecumseh Sherman, sculpted in bronze with a gold leaf covering by Augustus Saint-Gaudens and unveiled in 1903.

A WALK AROUND THE UPPER EAST SIDE

The UPPER EAST SIDE is an affluent mix of museums, fashionable clubs and old-money mansions and apartments, becoming more middle class as you progress east towards the East River. The trend for building large mansions facing Central Park across Fifth Avenue was started by Caroline Astor when she moved here from 34th Street in 1893, and within ten years the Schermerhorns and the Vanderbilts had houses here too.

*Start point: Fifth Avenue
at 59th Street: Grand Army Plaza*

No. 1 East 60th Street, built in 1894 by Stanford White on a site owned by the Duchess of Marlborough, houses the METROPOLITAN CLUB, founded by the Vanderbilts and others in 1891 with J.P. Morgan as first president. U.S. Presidents Nixon, Ford, Reagan and Clinton have been members here, and writer Salman Rushdie.

No. 2 East 62nd Street is the glorious pink-brick neo-Georgian clubhouse of the KNICKERBOCKER CLUB, formed in 1871 by former members of New York's oldest club, the Union Club, at 69th and Park, who thought the Union

Club's admission standards had been allowed to drop.

No. 1 East 65th Street is the TEMPLE EMANU-EL, built in 1929 and THE LARGEST SYNAGOGUE IN THE WORLD. It stands on the site of the palatial home of Caroline Astor. Her wine cellar and marble fireplaces remain intact inside the synagogue.

No. 1 East 70th Street houses the FRICK COLLECTION in the opulent mansion of steel magnate Henry Clay Frick (1849–1919). Frick left not only his priceless art collection to the nation but also his entire house, one of the few surviving grand early 20th-century mansions on this stretch of Fifth Avenue. Highlights of the collection include Whistler's *Lady Meux* (1881), Vermeer's *Officer and Laughing Girl* (1660) and Hans Holbein's celebrated portrait of *Sir Thomas More* (1527).

No. 991 Fifth Avenue is a fine, bow-fronted townhouse occupied by the IRISH AMERICAN HISTORICAL SOCIETY, founded in Boston in 1897 with Theodore Roosevelt amongst its founding members. The Society moved here in 1940 and notable members have included New York governor Hugh Carey and composer George M. Cohan. In 2009 the Society held a wake here for actress Natasha Richardson, who died in a skiing accident.

Museum Mile

The Metropolitan Museum of Art at Fifth and 82nd Street marks the beginning of MUSEUM MILE, which runs from here to 105th Street and features nine museums.

An annual Museum Mile Festival has been held every June since 1979 to promote awareness of and support for the museums, during which the museums are open for free in the evening.

Metropolitan Museum of Art

The METROPOLITAN MUSEUM OF ART, or 'Met', is AMERICA'S LARGEST ARTS MUSEUM and one of the largest art galleries in the world in terms of area. Since it was founded in 1870 by members of the Union Club, including William Cullen Bryant and railroad executive John Taylor Johnston, whose own art collection formed the nucleus of the museum, the Met has acquired some two million works dating from prehistoric times to the present. Highlights include Picasso's portrait of *Gertrude Stein* (1906), *Cypresses* by Van Gogh (1889), a Rembrandt self-portrait from 1660, *Astor Court*, a Ming-style Chinese garden of meditation, and a Roman temple built by the Emperor Augustus in 15 BC.

Sculpture Garden

Hidden away in the south-west corner of the museum on the hard-to-find fifth floor is a magical roof garden with a terrace bar and restaurant that also serves as a Sculpture Garden, with constantly changing exhibits. The views of the Manhattan skyline across the green sward of Central Park from here are sublime, with a sea of foliage rolling away in waves to the tall white cliffs of Midtown's skyscrapers. To get to the roof garden you have to enter the museum, for which there is a charge, then make your way to the Modern Art wing, take an elevator to the fourth floor, go through an unmarked door and climb a bare staircase before emerging on to the most romantic view in New York.

The garden was a gift from B. Gerald Cantor of securities firm Cantor Fitzgerald and opened in 1987. Merely to know it is there is to feel part of New York. To actually find it is to be a New Yorker.

No. 1048 Fifth Avenue at 86th Street is the NEUE GALERIE NEW YORK, a museum of German and Austrian art and design, opened in 2001 in what was once the house of Mrs Cornelius Vanderbilt III. The highlights include works of the Bauhaus, Paul Klee and

Otto Dix. In 2006 the museum paid a then world record price of $135 million for Gustav Klimt's *Portrait of Adele Bloch-Bauer*, which is on display in the museum.

No. 1071 Fifth Avenue at 89th Street is the GUGGENHEIM MUSEUM, Museum Mile's most distinctive building and a cultural icon designed by Frank Lloyd Wright and opened just after his death in 1959. Solomon R. Guggenheim, from a wealthy mining family, founded Alaska's Yukon Gold Company and was an avid collector of modern art. Highlights of his collection include Chagall's *Paris Through the Window* (1913), Manet's *Before the Mirror* (1876), and Picasso's *Woman with Yellow Hair* (1931).

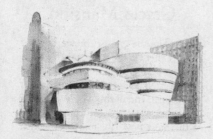

Continue along Fifth Avenue as far as East 97th Street, turn right and walk along to ST NICHOLAS RUSSIAN ORTHODOX CATHEDRAL, an unexpected eastern baroque vision of onion domes and crosses built in 1902 to serve New York's first Russian Orthodox parish. If you can get to see inside, there are marble columns, gold painted wooden screens and the aroma of incense.

No. 2 East 91st Street is the COOPER-HEWITT NATIONAL DESIGN MUSEUM, housed in the former home of steel tycoon Andrew Carnegie. One of two Smithsonian Museums in New York, and the first outside Washington D.C., it is THE ONLY MUSEUM IN AMERICA DEVOTED TO HISTORICAL AND CONTEMPORARY DESIGN. It was founded in 1896 by Peter Cooper's granddaughters, and moved into the Carnegie Mansion in 1970.

Turn right (south) on to Madison Avenue and walk for two blocks to admire the crenellated, castle-like façade of the Squadron A Armory, built in 1894 for what was originally a ceremonial cavalry unit called the New York Hussars, used as escort for presidents and other dignitaries. The squadron went on to fight with great distinction in the Spanish–American War and the two world wars. A plaque on the wall of the south tower recalls the squadron's motto 'Boutez en Avant' ('Charge!'). Behind the walls today is a school playground.

Continue south on Madison and turn left (east) on to East 92nd Street. Cross Park Avenue and shortly, on the right, you will see two delectable wooden houses of a kind now almost extinct in Manhattan. The first, No. 120, was built in 1871, while No. 122 dates from 1859.

Walk along to Lexington, turn left and then right into East 93rd Street. A short way along on the left, at No. 179, is the modest, tenement-like house where the MARX BROTHERS, Chico, Harpo, Groucho, Gummo and Zeppo, were brought up at the end of the 19th century.

Continue to Third Avenue and turn right (south). Walk for five blocks and turn left (east) on to East 88th Street. Continue to the end and enter CARL SHURZ PARK, named after the first German-born American to be elected to the Senate and 13th U.S. Secretary of the Interior. The park has lovely wide views across the East River towards Hell Gate, where the East River meets the Long Island Sound.

Gracie Mansion

It feels like the end of the world here, and yet there is the unmistakable hum of power in the air. Hidden away behind high hedges on a promontory at the north end of this windswept park is GRACIE MANSION, official residence of the most powerful mayor on earth, the Mayor of New York. You can't see very much other than a barrier, a sleepy guardhouse and a tantalising glimpse of yellow-painted weatherboarding – all very discreet. This must be one of the least likely and most lovely locations for an official residence anywhere.

Gracie Mansion is a two-storey Federal-style wooden house built in 1799 for Scottish-born shipping magnate Archibald Gracie, on the site of a fort overlooking Hell Gate. It was the first home of the Museum of the City of

Henderson Place

New York from 1924 to 1936 and became the mayoral residence in 1942, although a number of mayors have refused to live there as there are strict rules as to who can stay overnight – only the mayor's family or public officials, no girlfriends.

Leave the park at 86th Street and walk past HENDERSON PLACE, a charming row of 24 red-brick Queen Anne houses built in 1882 for 'persons of moderate means', by hat-maker John Henderson. The houses turned out to be so desirable that from the start they attracted persons of considerable means, and they still form a delightful little enclave amongst the high-rise apartment blocks.

Now return along 86th Street to Fifth Avenue and the end of the walk.

Well, I never knew this
about
MIDTOWN & THE UPPER EAST SIDE

GRAND CENTRAL TERMINAL is littered with carvings of oak leaves and acorns, a reference to Cornelius Vanderbilt's motto, 'From a little acorn a mighty oak shall grow!'

AMERICA'S FIRST COLOUR TELEVISION BROADCAST was made from a CBS transmitter on top of the CHRYSLER BUILDING on 28 August 1940, and was received at the CBS Building on Madison Avenue.

Although the United Nations has appeared in countless films and television broadcasts, the only movie to be filmed actually in the United Nations complex itself, with special permission from the Secretary-General, was the 2005 movie *The Interpreter* starring Nicole Kidman and Sean Penn.

The QUEENSBORO BRIDGE is the subject of Simon and Garfunkel's '59th Street Bridge Song (Feelin' Groovy)', while the view from the bridge is mentioned in chapter four of F. Scott Fitzgerald's novel *The Great Gatsby*: 'The city seen from the Queensboro Bridge is always the city seen for the first time, in its first wild promise of all the mystery and the beauty in the world.'

The ROOSEVELT ISLAND TRAMWAY was attacked by the Green Goblin in the 2000 film *Spider-Man*.

THE WALDORF-ASTORIA is also the only hotel in America to have had three five-star generals as residents, Dwight Eisenhower, Douglas MacArthur and Omar Bradley.

The first Tony Awards were presented in the Grand Ballroom of the Waldorf-Astoria Hotel in 1947.

Also to be found on Museum Mile:

The JEWISH MUSEUM, housed in the former home of banker Felix Warburg at Fifth Avenue and 92nd Street, with THE LARGEST COLLECTION OF ART AND JEWISH CULTURAL ARTIFACTS OUTSIDE ISRAEL.

THE MUSEUM OF THE CITY OF NEW YORK, founded in 1923 and housed in a fine neo-Georgian building at Fifth and 103rd Street, with superb exhibitions about the history of New York.

EL MUSEO DEL BARRIO, at Fifth and 105th Street, New York's leading museum of Latin American culture.

CHAPTER 16

THE UPPER WEST SIDE

The San Remo

The UPPER WEST SIDE is glorious, an area of wide boulevards and river views, with the green of Central Park on one side and the breezes of the mighty Hudson River on the other. This was once the Dutch village of Bloomingdale, meaning 'vale of flowers', and Broadway here was the Bloomingdale Road. Development didn't really begin until the 1870s with the building of the Ninth Avenue elevated railway, but once the success of the Dakota building proved that you could live this far north and west and survive, the Upper West Side blossomed.

Broadway
59th to 110th

San Juan Hill

In the early 20th century, before the Lincoln Center was built, the area between 59th and 65th Streets to the west of Broadway was home to New York's largest African–American community, among them black veterans of the Spanish–American War of 1989, who had fought with Teddy Roosevelt at the Battle of San Juan Hill on Cuba, from which the area took its name. Many black musicians lived in San Juan Hill, which became a centre of ragtime and early jazz. One such musician, THELONIOUS MONK, lived for 45 years in the Phipps House complex on West 63rd Street and the area has since been named Thelonious Monk Circle in his memory.

In 1940 San Juan Hill was described as 'the worst slum in New York City', and in the 1950s plans were drawn up by Robert Moses to redevelop the area. Leonard Bernstein's *West Side Story* was set in the San Juan Hill of the 1950s, and the movie of the musical was filmed in the streets there just before the area was demolished to make way for the Lincoln Center in 1960.

Lincoln Center

THE LINCOLN CENTER FOR PERFORMING ARTS was largely the vision of John D. Rockefeller III, who raised most of the funding and was the first president and chairman. The site was chosen by Robert Moses as part of his urban renewal plan. In May 1959 President Eisenhower dug the first shovelful of soil to start construction, while the New York Philharmonic Orchestra and the Juilliard Choir performed the *Hallelujah Chorus*, conducted by Leonard Bernstein.

The first building completed, in 1962, was the PHILHARMONIC HALL, the new home of America's oldest orchestra, the New York Philharmonic Orchestra, who moved there from Carnegie Hall. In 1973 the name was changed to the AVERY FISHER HALL after audio and acoustics pioneer Avery Fisher donated $10 million to the orchestra.

Next came the METROPOLITAN OPERA HOUSE in 1964, replacing the Old Met at Broadway and 39th, which had played such an important part in luring cultural New York north.

In 1966 the NEW YORK STATE THEATER opened as a home for the New York Ballet and the New York Opera. In 2008 this was renamed the DAVID H. KOCH THEATER after oil billionaire David H. Koch pledged $100 million to renovate and maintain the building.

These three buildings all face on to a central plaza, where outdoor exhibitions and art shows are held around the fountain. There is also a bowl-style amphitheatre for outdoor concerts called the GUGGENHEIM BAND SHELL.

Today the Lincoln Center boasts 29 indoor and outdoor performance facilities, including a concert hall for the centre's chamber orchestra, a large

'Broadway' style theatre, the VIVIAN BEAUMONT THEATER, an Off-Broadway style theatre, the MITZI NEWHOUSE, and an Off-Off-Broadway theatre, the CLAIRE Tow. The Lincoln Center is now America's leading cultural venue and receives over half a million visitors every year.

The Pythian

If you take a short detour from Broadway east down West 70th Street to No. 135, then you are sure of a big surprise, for here is the PYTHIAN, an extraordinary Egyptian palace decorated with columns and brightly coloured terracotta figures. It could easily be mistaken for a movie palace – an easy mistake to make in fact for the Pythian was designed in 1927 by Thomas W. Lamb, whose day job was designing movie theatres. Above the elaborate door are the words

IF FRATERNAL LOVE
HELD ALL MEN BOUND
HOW BEAUTIFUL
THIS WORLD WOULD BE

which, as anyone knows, are the words of Justus H. Rathbone, the founder, in 1864, of the ORDER OF KNIGHTS OF PYTHIAS, THE FIRST FRATERNAL ORDER EVER TO BE CHARTERED BY AN ACT OF CONGRESS.

The inspiration for the Knights of Pythias is the Greek myth of Damon and Pythias. Pythias was sentenced to death for allegedly plotting against Dionysius, the ruler of Syracuse, but was given permission to return home to put

his affairs in order. His companion Damon volunteered to stay and be executed in place of Pythias if Pythias failed to return. Just as the executioner was licking his lips and raising his axe, Pythias reappeared. Dionysius was so impressed that he released both Pythias and Damon and their tale became symbolic of true friendship. Three U.S. Presidents were Pythian Knights – Warren Harding, William McKinley and Franklin D. Roosevelt – as well as jazz musician Louis Armstrong.

The Pythian was built to serve as a meeting place and Temple for the 120 New York Pythian lodges, but when membership began to decline part of the building was leased to Decca Records, and in 1954 Bill Haley and the Comets recorded 'Rock Around the Clock' here. Buddy Holly, Sammy Davis Jr. and Billie Holiday also recorded here.

In 1983 the building was converted into a condominium and now contains 84 residential apartments. In 1993 seven-year-old Stefani Germanotta moved into an apartment at the Pythian with her parents and spent much of her childhood there before becoming an entertainer and changing her name to Lady Gaga.

72nd Street

The Upper West Side is liberally studded with monumentally ostentatious late 19th-century apartment blocks, and two of the finest and most opulent can be found around 72nd Street where Broadway crosses Amsterdam Avenue.

The Dorilton

You can't miss the DORILTON, at West 71st Street, a monster of *beaux-arts* flamboyance in dark red brick and limestone, which might frighten even the French with its gargoyles, strutting statues and nude figures holding up wrought-iron balconies. It has the tallest courtyard entranceway you have ever seen on West 71st Street, bridged by an arch at the ninth floor and with gates that would grace a château. The building was unveiled in 1902 and the *Architectural Record* at the time said, 'The sight of it makes strong men swear and weak women shrink affrighted.'

Once you have recovered your composure, walk on by Sherman Square, which was named after William Tecumseh Sherman, the Civil War Union general who lived in a townhouse near here at 71st Street from 1886 until his death in 1891. Then on past the landmark 1902 subway kiosk which serves the 72nd Street subway, and have a rest in VERDI SQUARE. The square is

presided over by a marble statue of the composer Giuseppe Verdi, which was dedicated in 1906 and paid for by the much put-upon subscribers of *Il Progresso*. In the 1960s and 70s this place was a well-known drug haunt called 'Needle Park', as portrayed in the 1971 film noir *The Panic in Needle Park*, starring Al Pacino, but like all of the Upper West Side it has undergone a commendable rehabilitation.

The Ansonia

From Verdi Square you can look to the north-west and see the ANSONIA, another ebullient *beaux-arts* apartment block, slightly less overwhelming than the Dorilton, but still a riot of turrets and balconies festooned with carvings and ornamental marble. It was built as a grand hotel in 1899 by William Stokes, heir to the Phelps Dodge mercantile fortune, and was named after his grandfather the New York industrialist Anson Greene Phelps. Originally there was a farm on the roof with ducks, goats, chickens and a bear. The chickens provided fresh eggs for the hotel guests, and the goats, milk, but the bear was purely decorative. The Department of Health closed the farm down in 1907 and the animals were moved to the Central Park Zoo. The Ansonia also sported THE WORLD'S LARGEST INDOOR SWIMMING POOL, no doubt appreciated by baseball star Babe Ruth and boxer Jack Dempsey when they lived there.

The thick, soundproof walls of the hotel suites attracted many musicians, and in the Ansonia's heyday residents included Caruso, Toscanini, Stravinsky, Ziegfeld and the soprano Lily Pons. The Ansonia was converted to a condominium in 1992, but the musical heritage of the Ansonia is honoured in Verdi Square, where Caruso and Toscanini once took the air, with an annual series of free September Sunday afternoon concerts.

Both the Ansonia and the Dorilton were built at this location to take advantage of the new 72nd Street subway station, which is the first express station north of 42nd Street.

Pomander Walk

Now continue north on Broadway and then take a short walk west down 94th or 95th Street and you will find yourself in London – or at least you can peer through a locked iron gate and imagine yourself in London. Here is POMANDER WALK, a secret pedestrian

street lined on either side with a row of tiny, Tudor-style houses, all with miniature cottage gardens and steps leading to brightly coloured front doors. They were built in 1921 by an Irish restaurant owner and theatre buff called Thomas Healy as a temporary development until he could raise the money to put a 16-storey hotel on the site – thank heavens he never did, for this place is a real gem. The attractive little walkway replicates, New York-style, a London street scene from the set of a play called *Pomander Walk*, which opened on Broadway in 1910 after a successful run in London. The set called for 'a retired crescent of five very small, old-fashioned houses near Chiswick, on the river bank of the Thames'. Ignore the surrounding high-rises and you could indeed be in Chiswick. Pomander Walk proved very popular with the acting fraternity, as Healy had hoped, and former residents include Rosalind Russell, Paulette Goddard and Nancy Carroll – and possibly Humphrey Bogart.

At 96th Street Broadway dips slightly to form the western boundary of

Manhattan Valley, a shallow depression that runs west from Central Park to Broadway as far north as 110th Street, where Broadway climbs again toward Morningside Heights.

Straus Park

At 106th Street, where Broadway swerves to take over from West End Avenue, is STRAUS PARK, a small wooded area landscaped in memory of ISIDOR AND IDA STRAUS, owners of Macy's, who died on the *Titanic* in 1912. They lived not far away at No. 2747 Broadway just below 106th Street. At the southern end of the park is a bronze figure of a young woman reclining in contemplation above the words: 'Lovely and pleasant were they in their lives and in their death they were not parted' – a reference to Ida's choice to stay and die with her husband rather than escape into a lifeboat. Straus Park is one of New York's most romantic places, a fitting tribute to a couple who loved each other and were clearly much loved. A poignant way to end this stretch of Broadway.

East of Broadway

Central Park West

CENTRAL PARK WEST, known as CPW, is an extension of Eighth Avenue that runs all the way up the west side of Central Park, starting at Columbus Circle and ending at 110th Street at the north-west corner of the park. It is the most exclusive residential street in the neighbourhood and is sometimes referred to as the Fifth Avenue of the Upper West Side.

The Century

At No. 25 sits the art deco CENTURY APARTMENTS, one of the four tall twin-towered apartment blocks that give Central Park West its distinctive skyline when seen from Central Park. It was put up in 1931 by Irwin Chanin on the former site of the old Century Theater, a fine *beaux-arts* building once described as 'New York's most spectacularly unsuccessful theatre'. A six-bedroom apartment in the Century costs around $20 million.

Ghostbusters Building

Just beyond Holy Trinity Lutheran Church at West 65th Street is No. 55, the first fully authentic art deco building on CPW. The colour of the brickwork changes from a deep purple hue at the bottom to a pale yellow shade on the water tank enclosure at the top, creating the impression that the sun is always shining on the building. No. 55 is perhaps better known as the Ghostbusters Building or 'Spook Central', where Sigourney Weaver lives in the 1984 film *Ghostbusters*. Two-bedroom apartments here retail at $5 million, and residents past and present have included musician Rudy Vallee, designers Calvin Klein and Donna Karan and actresses Ginger Rogers and Marsha Mason.

Hotel des Artistes

A short hop from CPW at No. 1 West 67th Street is an artist's studio building with the very bohemian name of HOTEL DES ARTISTES. The first artist's studio building on West 67th Street had gone up in 1903 at No. 27, a co-op built by a syndicate of artists, with double height windows facing north to catch the artists' favoured northern light. Within ten years the street had become a nest of studios, and in 1917 the painter Penrhyn Stanlaws, an occupant of the second studio to be built, decided to get together a syndicate and build THE BIGGEST STUDIO COMPLEX IN THE WORLD, with 72 apartments – and call it the Hotel des Artistes. It was never a hotel as such, more a combination of co-op and rental, nor was it confined to artists, since stockbrokers and bankers were needed to pay the rent. None of the studios had kitchens because the artists were not meant to bother with such mundane activities as cooking. Instead they would order their meals from the communal kitchens downstairs, kitchens that eventually became the celebrated CAFÉ DES ARTISTES, where New York's finest could dine amongst cavorting naked wood nymphs painted on the walls in the 1930s by one of the co-op's first residents, Howard Chandler Christy. (He was responsible for the magnificent mural above the grand staircase of the Capitol in Washington D.C., *The Signing of the Constitution of the United States*.)

Amongst the artists who have resided at the Hotel des Artistes are the film director ALAN CROSLAND, who directed Al Jolson in *The Jazz Singer*, GEORGE FITZMAURICE, who directed Greta Garbo in *Mata Hari* in 1931, NOËL COWARD, RUDOLPH VALENTINO, NORMAN ROCKWELL and dancer ISADORA DUNCAN.

Shearith Israel

On the corner of West 70th Street is the imposing neo-classical synagogue of America's oldest Jewish congregation, SHEARITH ISRAEL, complete with two millstones from the old horse mill in New Amsterdam where they first congregated in 1654.

The Majestic

The art deco MAJESTIC at No. 115 CPW is another of CPW's twin-towered apartment blocks and is the sister building to the Century at No. 25. It was erected by Irwin Chanin in the same year, 1931, on the site of the Majestic Hotel, where composer GUSTAV MAHLER lived in a suite on the 11th floor between 1907 and 1911 while director of the Metropolitan Opera and New York Philharmonic. The muffled sound of a beating drum from the funeral procession of a fireman passing beneath his window inspired the transition between the fourth and fifth movements of Mahler's *Tenth Symphony*, written in 1910.

Another tenant was the Pulitzer prize-winning writer EDNA FERBER, author of *Show Boat*, which was turned into a successful musical by Jerome Kern in 1927.

As an apartment block the Majestic was home to some slightly less salubrious characters, such as LOUIS 'LEPKE' BUCHALTER, head of the Mafia hit squad Murder Inc., who lived in apartment 17J. Lepke was 'dobbed in' to FBI chief J. Edgar Hoover by one of his neighbours at the Majestic, WALTER WINCHELL, originator of AMERICA'S FIRST SYNDICATED GOSSIP COLUMN, the *New York Daily Mirror*'s 'On Broadway' column. Some other mobsters who lived there were Mafia bosses LUCKY LUCIANO, MEYER LANSKY and FRANK COSTELLO, the latter being the model for Marlon Brando's character Vito Corleone in the movie *The Godfather*. In 1957 Costello was walking through the lobby of the Majestic to the elevator when Mafia shooter Vincent 'The Chin' Gigante shot him in the head. Costello survived the assassination attempt with just a scalp wound.

Amongst the more wholesome inhabitants of the Majestic past and present are the first major star of American television MILTON BERLE, comic actor ZERO MOSTEL, fashion designer MARC JACOBS, who lived there as a teenager in the 1980s with his grandmother, and talk show host CONAN O'BRIEN, who in 2010 sold his apartment to Discovery CEO DAVID ZASLAV for $20 million.

The Dakota

Probably the most famous apartment building in New York, and the city's first truly luxurious apartment block,

the Dakota was completed in 1884 for Edward Clark, head of the Singer Sewing Machine Company. The Upper West Side was at that time considered so remote and inaccessible that Clark was told he might as well put up an apartment building in Dakota. Nonetheless every one of the 85 apartments was sold before the building was finished and the success of the Dakota encouraged the building of more and more apartment blocks, not just on the Upper West Side but all over New York.

Over the years the Dakota has attracted a glittering array of stars from the art and entertainment worlds including Lauren Bacall, Leonard Bernstein, Rosemary Clooney, Roberta Flack, Judy Garland, Lillian Gish, Boris Karloff, who is said to haunt the place, Rudolph Nureyev, Jack Palance, Jason Robards and Judy Holliday, as well as

Strawberry Fields Forever

On 8 December 1980 former Beatle JOHN LENNON was shot dead outside the entrance to the Dakota as he was returning home from a late night recording session. His killer was a deranged 'fan' called Mark Chapman, who remained at the scene of the crime reading J.D. Salinger's *The Catcher in the Rye* until the police arrived.

On 9 October 1985, on what would have been Lennon's 45th birthday, a landscaped area of Central Park directly across the road from the Dakota Building was named Strawberry Fields after the Beatles song 'Strawberry Fields Forever', and dedicated to Lennon by Yoko Ono and New York Mayor Ed Koch. The focal point of the memorial is a round mosaic designed by Italian artists from Naples featuring the word 'Imagine', the title of another of Lennon's songs, evoking a world without war or violence. A bronze plaque lists the more than 120 nations who contributed to the memorial, which has become a place for peace vigils and is permanently decorated with flowers and candles left by Lennon's fans.

New York Jets footballer 'Broadway' Joe Namath and, most pertinently, former Beatle John Lennon with his wife Yoko Ono.

San Remo

The SAN REMO is the tallest and perhaps the most distinctive of the four twin-towered buildings on CPW. It was built in 1930 on the site of the San Remo Hotel and boasts an exhaustive cast list of resident celebrities, including the likes of Rita Hayworth, Steven Spielberg, Tiger Woods, Demi Moore, Steve Martin, Bono, Dustin Hoffman, Dodi Fayed and Aaron Spelling.

Michael Douglas and Catherine Zeta-Jones live next door in the KENILWORTH at No. 151 Central Park West.

New-York Historical Society

The NEW-YORK HISTORICAL SOCIETY at No. 170 CPW is the OLDEST MUSEUM IN NEW YORK – the clue is in the name, for in 1804, when the museum was founded by amongst others Mayor DeWitt Clinton, New York was commonly spelt with a hyphen. The aim of the society is to collect, preserve and explore the political, social and cultural history of New York and its contribution to the development of the United States as a nation. Among the highlights of the museum's collections are the surviving pieces of the statue of George III from Bowling Green, George Washington's camp cot from Valley Forge, the pistols used in the duel between Aaron Burr and Alexander Hamilton, the world's largest collection of Tiffany lamps, all 435 of John James Audubon's preparatory watercolours for *The Birds of America* (infuriatingly only one or two are shown at a time) and, my personal favourite, a first-class portrait of an 'unidentified woman' in a beautiful silk blue dress, circa 1700–25, bearing an uncanny resemblance to the royal governor of His Majesty's Colonies of New York from 1701 to 1708, LORD CORNBURY, later 3rd Earl of Clarendon. His Lordship was, apparently, partial to dressing up in women's clothes.

American Museum of Natural History

The AMERICAN MUSEUM OF NATURAL HISTORY, established in 1868 and moved here to Central Park West at 79th Street in 1874, is THE LARGEST MUSEUM OF ITS KIND IN THE WORLD, containing over 32 million specimens, including THE WORLD'S LARGEST COLLECTION OF DINOSAUR FOSSILS, THE WORLD'S LARGEST IRON METEOR, a blue whale and the 563-carat STAR OF INDIA, THE LARGEST BLUE STAR SAPPHIRE IN

THE WORLD, donated by J.P. Morgan in 1900.

Incorporated in the museum is the ROSE CENTER FOR EARTH AND SPACE, where you can learn about the universe in a giant globe structure that lights up in a spectacular fashion after dark.

Eldorado

The ELDORADO is the most northerly of the four twin-towered apartment buildings on CPW and was built in 1931. Alec Baldwin, Faye Dunaway, Michael J. Fox and musician Moby are amongst the more colourful residents here, past and present.

West of Broadway

Riverside Park

RIVERSIDE PARK stretches for four miles (6.4 km) along Manhattan's west side, rising and falling with the natural landscape. It was mostly laid out by Calvert Vaux and Frederick Law Olmsted in the 1870s along the cliff top, and there was no access to the river until the 1930s when Robert Moses instigated the creation of an esplanade over the railway tracks that ran along the shoreline. The views of the Hudson River from the park, and from the luxurious apartments that line Riverside Drive, Manhattan's only 'winding road', are exhilarating.

The park, with its hills and valleys, twists and turns, makes a delightful open air gallery, and is studded with monuments and statues that can be enjoyed while engaged on a bracing walk. To begin with, at the south end of the park, at 72nd Street, you can find THE FIRST EVER PUBLIC STATUE OF A PRESIDENT'S WIFE, a bronze of Eleanor Roosevelt by Penelope Jencks.

Then at 83rd Street there is a prominent rock called Mount Tom. EDGAR ALLAN POE, who lived in a farmhouse near here, would come to Mount Tom to write – he composed his poem 'To Helen' here.

At 89th Street, standing proudly at a curve in the road, is the magnificently Corinthian SOLDIERS' AND SAILORS' MONUMENT, commemorating those who died in the Civil War. Designed by Charles and Arthur Stoughton, architects of the Ansonia, it is 96 ft (29 m) high, and made out of granite and marble. It was unveiled on Memorial Day in 1902 and is the focus of an annual Memorial Day observance.

In the middle of her own round-about at 93rd Street is JOAN OF ARC, standing in the saddle of her horse with her sword arm aloft, sculpted in 1915 by Anna Huntington and THE ONLY FEMALE EQUESTRIAN STATUE IN NEW YORK. Embedded in the pedestal are fragments of the cathedral at Rheims, where she was honoured, and from the dungeon of the tower at Rouen where she was executed, encapsulating forever her moments of triumph and tragedy.

Well, I never knew this about
THE UPPER WEST SIDE

At No. 256 West 71st Street is NEW YORK'S SMALLEST PARK, SEPTUAGESIMO UNO PARK, just 0.04 of an acre (162 sq m), created out of the space left by a condemned brownstone.

One block west of Broadway, on 77th Street, in the vestibule of the WEST END DUTCH REFORM PROTESTANT COLLEGIATE CHURCH, there are four millstones from the dawn of New York – in fact they are older than New York itself, for they come from New Amsterdam. The millstones are from the horse mill, built in New Amsterdam in 1628, where the early Dutch Protestants worshipped in an upstairs room before their first church was built in 1633. There are two more millstones in the Shearith Israel synagogue on Central Park West.

The Dakota was the setting for the 1968 Roman Polanski film *Rosemary's Baby*, starring Mia Farrow, a one-time resident of the building.

In 1899 HENRY BLISS got out of a streetcar on Central Park West at 74th Street and was knocked down by a taxi, becoming THE FIRST PERSON IN AMERICA TO BE RUN OVER AND KILLED BY A MOTOR CAR.

Legendary movie star HUMPHREY BOGART (1899–1957) lived at No. 245 West 103rd Street, a modest brownstone just a short hop west of Broadway, from when he was born until his early 20s – his formative years.

In 1905 German immigrant RICHARD HELLMAN opened a delicatessen at No. 490 Columbus Avenue in the Upper West Side. His wife's recipe for mayonnaise was so popular that customers began to ask Hellman to bottle some so that they could take it home. Eventually demand became so great that in 1912 Hellman decided to open a factory to jar the mayonnaise and today Hellman's mayonnaise is sold worldwide.

CHAPTER 17

CENTRAL PARK

The Delacorte Clock

CENTRAL PARK was opened to the public in the winter of 1859, THE FIRST LAND-SCAPED PUBLIC PARK IN THE UNITED STATES. It was designed and created by FREDERICK LAW OLMSTED (1822–1903) and CALVERT VAUX (1824–95), out of 700 acres (283 ha) of public land made up of swamps, rocky outcrops and scrubland deemed unsuitable for other types of development. The park now covers 843 acres (341 ha) and measures 2½ miles (4 km) in length north to south and half a mile (800 m) in width east to west.

Central Park contains a variety of environments and natural landscapes, each of them different. There are over 50 monuments and statues, and 36 bridges, all designed by Vaux, but no two of them are the same. The purpose of the bridges is to take one kind of path over or under another so that different park users can be kept separate, pedestrians from cyclists, horse riders from motorists and so on, while cross-city traffic is routed through sunken roadways screened by trees and shrubs.

Central Park is now perhaps the most famous urban park in the world. It is certainly the most visited – some 25 to 30 million visitors a year make it the second most visited tourist attraction in America after Times Square.

A WALK THROUGH CENTRAL PARK

Start Point: Maine Memorial

We enter Central Park through the Merchants' Gate at Columbus Circle on the south-west corner of the park. The gate was so named in 1862 in recognition of the importance of business and commerce to New York – in fact most of the park gates bear the name of a particular trade or profession that has contributed to the rise of New York: Artisans, Artists, Scholars, Inventors, Miners, Engineers, Pioneers, Warriors, Hunters and Explorers.

Maine Memorial

To the right of the Merchants' Gate is the MAINE MEMORIAL, honouring the 258 sailors who died when the USS *Maine* exploded in Havana Harbor off Spanish controlled Cuba in 1898, setting off the Spanish–American War.

The memorial was sculpted by Attilio Piccirilli and unveiled in 1913. The names of the sailors who died are inscribed on the large base pedestal of Maine granite, which stands in front of a fountain and is encircled by nine heroic sculpted marble figures. On top of the pedestal is a gilded figure of the goddess Columbia rising from the sea in a shell-shaped chariot drawn by three horses, all cast in bronze recovered from the guns of the *Maine*, which were lifted off the seabed in 1911.

Sheep Meadow

On entering Central Park head north beside the West Drive until you reach the SHEEP MEADOW, 15 acres (6 ha) of lush grass encircled by a chain-link fence where a flock of Southdown sheep once grazed. Today it is reserved for picnics and sunbathing. The sheep were removed to Prospect Park in Brooklyn in 1934 on the instructions of Robert Moses, who was worried they might be stolen for food by the impoverished victims of the Great Depression who were living in the park. At the same time the sheepfold, standing on a bluff to the west of the meadow, adjacent to 67th Street, was converted into an 'affordable' restaurant called the Tavern on the Green.

Tavern on the Green

With its unique position in the park, its rustic setting and elegant design, which even included a Tiffany stained-glass window, the TAVERN ON THE GREEN quickly became popular with the celebrities living along Central Park West, and equally quickly ceased to be affordable. In 1974 the lease was taken on by Warner LeRoy, grandson of Harry Warner of the Warner brothers, who had an apartment in the nearby Dakota. His neighbours John Lennon and Yoko Ono liked to take their son Sean to the Tavern on his birthday.

During LeRoy's reign the Tavern on the Green was frequently the highest grossing restaurant in America. When he died in 2001 his daughter Jennifer took on the lease, but in 2009 the Parks Department refused to renew the lease any further and the restaurant held its last seating on New Year's Eve 2009. Today it operates as a park visitor centre and gift shop.

The Carousel

From the Tavern head east, keeping the Sheep Meadow on your left. You are now in the Children's District of the park and ahead is a red-and-white banded brick pavilion that houses what is possibly AMERICA'S LARGEST CAROUSEL, formed of 58 hand-carved and hand-painted wooden horses that canter round and round while rising and falling to the music of a huge mechanical organ. The smiles on the faces of the children clinging on as they bob up and down on the ride is testament to the magic of this piece of American folklore.

There has been a carousel here since 1871, when it was turned by a horse and a blind mule plodding patiently around the basement, attached to the turntable by a rope. They were replaced by an electrified carousel in 1924, which famously featured in J.D. Salinger's novel *The Catcher in the Rye*, when the lead character Holden Caulfield watches his sister enjoying a ride. After this second carousel was destroyed by fire in 1950, the Parks Department came across the present carousel disused and in storage on Coney Island, and had it restored and installed here.

The Dairy

The Children's District is centred on a Victorian Gothic structure designed by Calvert Vaux called THE DAIRY, because it was a place where 'perfectly fresh milk should be sold' for the children to drink. When it was first built in 1871 there were actually cows grazing in the fields in front of the Dairy to provide that fresh milk. By the 1950s fresh milk has become freely available everywhere and so the Dairy became redundant and was closed and used as a garden shed. In 1979 it was restored to its original splendour and unveiled as the park's first visitor centre.

Ice Skating

Across from the Dairy is the much photographed WOLLMAN ICE RINK, opened in 1949 with funds donated by stock-broking philanthropist Kate Wollman. Here you can skate into the night from October to April, with the Plaza Hotel and a parade of New York skyscrapers as a backdrop. The ice rink has been seen in countless films and featured prominently in the movies *Love Story* and *Home Alone 2: Lost in New York*. In the summer months the space is occupied by the Victorian Gardens Amusement Park.

Zoo

If you continue east, passing in between the Dairy and the Wollman Rink, you come to the CENTRAL PARK WILDLIFE CENTER, AMERICA'S SECOND PUBLIC ZOO. This was founded in 1864 from a collection of animals donated to the park over the years. The animals were housed in cages from the Arsenal, formerly a munitions dump for the New York National Guard located just behind where the zoo is now. The collection of animals included deer, buffalo, a wolf, an alligator, a porcupine and the star turn, THE FIRST CHIMPANZEE EVER SHOWN IN AMERICA, brought back from Africa by an American consul and given the name MIKE CROWLEY. Proper zoo facilities were built to house the menagerie as part of Robert Moses' renovations of the park in 1934.

Delacorte Clock

Located above the arcade that links the Wildlife Center to the Children's Zoo is one of the park's best-loved features, the DELACORTE CLOCK, donated by publisher George Delacorte in 1965. Every hour on the hour between eight and six it plays nursery rhyme tunes while a parade of sculptured animals playing musical instruments rotate around the clock on a carousel.

American Elms

A few steps north-west from the clock, a statue of Christopher Columbus marks the beginning of THE MALL, the only straight path in the park. The Mall is lined with THE LARGEST STAND OF AMERICAN ELMS IN AMERICA. The original elms were planted when the park was first opened, but they died, as did a second planting, probably from a lack of suitable soil. The present trees were planted in 1920 and have survived the Dutch Elm disease that has decimated elms in the rest of America, thanks to their isolation and the constant tending and vigilance of the park's woodsmen.

The Indian Hunter

Nearby is one of the park's oldest and most treasured statues, THE INDIAN HUNTER, which depicts a Native American hunter with his bow and his hunting dog. Dedicated in 1869, it is the work of JOHN QUINCY ADAMS WARD and was THE FIRST SCULPTURE BY AN AMERICAN ARTIST TO BE ERECTED IN CENTRAL PARK. John Quincy Adams Ward (1830–1910) was known as 'the dean of American sculptors' and is responsible for more sculptures in New York than any other artist, a total of nine in all, four of which are in Central Park including, right here, the statue of William Shakespeare that introduces us to the Literary Walk.

William Shakespeare

WILLIAM SHAKESPEARE, whose statue was unveiled here in 1872, is a powerful presence in Central Park, with a Shakespeare Garden in the centre of the park and an annual Shakespeare Festival held in the Delacorte Theater.

In 1890 drug manufacturer and Shakespeare aficionado EUGENE SCHIEFFELIN, a member of the American Acclimatization Society, released 60 starlings imported from England into Central Park, as part of an attempt to introduce into America all the species of birds mentioned in Shakespeare's plays. The finches, nightingales and skylarks he released did not survive, but the starlings thrived. At first, New Yorkers were thrilled when a starling's nest appeared in the eaves of the Museum of Natural History on Central Park West. Then the birds began to spread their wings and 'go west', reaching the Mississippi within 30 years and California within 50 years. There are now thought to be 200 million starlings in the U.S. displacing native American birds such as bluebirds and woodpeckers. All thanks to Mr Schieffelin. As Shakespeare might have said, 'Oh, what have you done?'

Bonnie Scotland

A little further up the Mall two Scotsmen, the poet ROBERT BURNS and the novelist SIR WALTER SCOTT, sit in companionable silence on either side of the path. Both statues were donated by

Scottish–Americans and were carved by Sir John Steell, with Scott unveiled in 1872 and Burns in 1880.

An American Poet

The next statue, of American poet and social commentator FITZ GREENE HALLECK (1790–1867), was unveiled in 1877 by President Rutherford B. Hayes, in front of his entire cabinet and a crowd of about 10,000 people. Halleck, while popular and well respected, was a fairly minor poet, but he was friends with Washington Irving and personal secretary to John Jacob Astor, and so there was no shortage of eminent New Yorkers, such as J.P. Morgan and William Cullen Bryant, editor of the *New York Evening Post*, who were willing to fund his statue.

Music in the Park

The Mall then goes past the beautiful limestone NAUMBURG BANDSHELL, donated by music-loving banker Elkan Naumburg in 1923. It stands near to the site of the park's original 1862 cast-iron bandstand, where free public classical concerts were staged for over 50

years until the 1920s, when popular music concerts were introduced as well. Both Martin Luther King Jr. and Fidel Castro addressed large crowds from the stage, while John Lennon's eulogy was given here in 1980.

Bethesda

The Mall ends at a wide staircase that leads down to BETHESDA TERRACE AND FOUNTAIN, designed as the climax to the only formal section of the park. The stonework of the terrace is a riot of symbolic carvings and mini sculptures, and there is much fun to be had looking for the most intriguing of the carvings, found on one of the stone posts at the top of the stairs, a flying witch on her broomstick above a jack-o'-lantern pumpkin. This may be a reference to the Irish immigrants who built the terrace and brought Halloween to America with them.

Or then again it may be a tribute to the bewitching view from the upper terrace, over the lake to the park's largest area of woodland, the Ramble.

Angel of the Waters

The fountain at the centre of the round pool on the lower terrace is called THE ANGEL OF THE WATERS, and was created by EMMA STEBBINS (1815–82) in 1868 and installed in 1873, THE FIRST PUBLIC WORK OF ART BY A WOMAN IN NEW YORK. It celebrates the opening in 1842 of the Croton Aqueduct, which brought fresh water to the city. The health-giving properties of that water are reflected in the name of the terrace, which comes from a healing pool named Bethesda in Jerusalem, mentioned in St John's Gospel.

From the terrace head west, keeping the water on your right, until you reach the elegant BOW BRIDGE, which crosses the narrow channel linking the two parts of the lake. It is the oldest of the seven original cast-iron bridges in the park, and THE SECOND OLDEST CAST-IRON BRIDGE IN ALL OF AMERICA. The view from the bridge of the buildings lining both sides of the park is breathtaking, especially the distinctive twin towers of the apartments along Central Park West.

Daniel Webster

Retrace your steps off the bridge and head south, keeping the water on your right, and then go round the bottom of the lake to the junction of the West Drive and the 72nd Street Transverse where you will find the huge statue of DANIEL WEBSTER (1782–1852), celebrated orator and two-time U.S. Secretary of State.

Across the ring road from here is a sign pointing towards Strawberry Fields, and if you follow the path up the hill you will come to the Imagine mosaic.

Weddings and Marionettes

Return to Daniel Webster and head north beside the lake, with the water on your right. This glorious 15-minute

stroll takes you past the LADIES PAVILION, a delicate cast-iron structure with a slate roof that was once used as a shelter for waiting trolley passengers at the Columbus Circle entrance. It was relocated here in 1912 and is now often used for weddings. At the end of the lake is the SWEDISH COTTAGE, home of the park's marionette theatre, one of the last public marionette companies in America. Puppet shows have been held here since 1947.

Belvedere Castle

Turn right past the cottage and continue up the hill through the SHAKESPEARE GARDEN, planted with flowers and shrubs mentioned in the works of William Shakespeare, until you reach the BELVEDERE CASTLE, a turreted folly built partly out of the same schist as the Vista Rock on which it stands, so that it gives the impression of growing out of the rock itself. The castle now houses a visitor centre and the Henry Luce Natural Observatory where you can learn about the park's birds and wildlife. At certain times you can climb to the top of the turret and enjoy the ravishing views north across the Turtle

Pond and Great Lawn from the highest viewing point in Central Park. There is also a weather station here from where the National Weather Service records the temperature in the park.

Vista Rock itself, 130 ft (40 m) high, is actually the second highest natural point in Central Park. THE HIGHEST NATURAL POINT IN CENTRAL PARK is SUMMIT ROCK, at Central Park West and 83rd Street, which is 137.5 ft (41.9 m) above sea level.

Return down the hill through the Shakespeare Garden and follow signs to the DELACORTE THEATER, built in 1962 as a summer home for the Public Theater, founded by Joseph Papp in 1954 to produce the plays of William Shakespeare. The first performance at the Delacorte Theater was a production of *The Merchant of Venice* starring George C. Scott and James Earl Jones. During its annual summer season the Public Theater puts on not just Shakespeare's plays but also classics by other playwrights, such as Chekhov's *The Seagull* and Leonard Bernstein's *On the Town*. Every performance is free – you just have to join the queue for tickets.

The Great Lawn

To the north of the theatre is the magnificent oval GREAT LAWN, the geographical centre of Central Park and recognised throughout the world as the location for countless films, legendary concerts by the likes of Simon and Garfunkel, Diana Ross and the New York Philharmonic and, in 1995, a Papal Mass.

The Great Lawn fills the site of the lower Croton Receiving Reservoir, where fresh water collected from the Croton Aqueduct was stored before being distributed to homes and businesses around the city. In the early years of the 20th century a new water supply system was developed whereby water was stored in upstate reservoirs and distributed through underground tunnels, and this meant that the Croton Reservoir was no longer needed. In 1931 it was drained and filled in, with landfill from excavations for the Rockefeller Center. For the next few years it became a notorious shanty town for homeless victims of the Great Depression until, in 1934, Robert Moses had the shanty town razed and the site levelled off to create the Great Lawn.

The drainage area of the old reservoir was landscaped and transformed into the TURTLE POND, which today provides a tranquil setting between the Great Lawn and the base of the Vista Rock. It is filled, appropriately enough, with five kinds of turtle, examples of which can be seen sunning themselves on the rocks in fine weather. A magical spot.

Go North

At this point you can either exit the park, to the west through the Hunters' Gate or to the east through the Miners' Gate, or you can strike north across the Great Lawn and head for the idyllic and undiscovered northern section of the park where, you can wander undisturbed through quiet glades and balmy meadows and completely forget that you are in the middle of a city of eight million people.

Shortly after you have reached the end of the Great Lawn, you come to the JACQUELINE KENNEDY ONASSIS RESERVOIR, which covers 106 acres (43 ha) and holds over a billion gallons of water. It was built in the 1860s as a temporary holding reservoir while the Croton Water system was being repaired, and was decommissioned in 1993 once construction had got underway on New York's Third Water Tunnel.

The reservoir is encircled by a wide bridle path and a 1½-mile (2.4 km) jogging track, much enjoyed in their time by President Clinton, Madonna and Jackie Kennedy Onassis. You can go round the reservoir either way and on either path, but if you decide to use the jogging track, which provides marvellous views of New York that get better and better as you go further north, then you would be wise to follow the arrows that direct you counter-clockwise. Those who choose to go round the other way may incur the wrath of the joggers, who do not shrink from robust comment on your parentage and physique if you get in their way.

About halfway round the jogging track, on the east side of the reservoir, fixed to an ornamental wall and set back in a little lay-by adjacent to 90th Street, is a gilded bronze portrait bust of JAMES PURROY MITCHEL who in 1913, at the age of 34, became NEW YORK'S SECOND YOUNGEST MAYOR and is credited with cleaning up corruption at Tammany Hall. He was killed in an air training accident during the First World War in 1918.

Great Hill

When you get to the end of the reservoir, turn left and head west along the line of the 102nd Street Transverse with the reservoir on your left. Cross the West Drive, turn right and head north along the line of the West Drive. After you pass the Pool on your left, take the first path you come across on the left and climb to the top of the GREAT HILL, the third highest point in Central Park.

Blockhouse

Continue north over the crest of the hill and follow the path across the West Drive and on through the woods to where the roofless remains of THE BLOCKHOUSE stand on top of a rocky bluff called The Cliff. Built in 1814 to defend the northern approaches to New York from a possible British attack during the War of 1812, the Blockhouse is THE OLDEST BUILDING IN CENTRAL PARK.

Harlem Meer

Locate the path to the west of the Blockhouse and follow it north down to the ring road. Turn right and follow the road east to HARLEM MEER, which was given the Dutch word for lake as a tribute to the Dutch founders of the village of Harlem, on the edge of which we now find ourselves. This lovely, fresh, watery setting is balm in the heat of the summer and a great place for fishing.

Across on the north shore of the meer is the CHARLES A. DANA DISCOVERY CENTER, opened in 1993 and the first purpose-built visitor centre in Central Park. South of the meer is the LASKER RINK AND POOL, two ice rinks in winter and a popular public swimming pool in summer.

A Secret Place

Walk on eastwards with the meer on your left and the ice rink on your

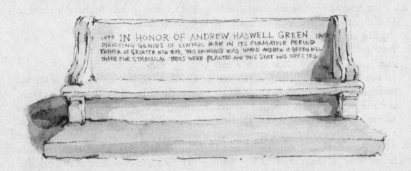

right, and follow the path as it curves southwards to meet the East Drive. Heading west now, cross the road and, if you can find it, follow the narrow path up the hill to the ANDREW HASWELL GREEN MEMORIAL BENCH. Here is New York's only memorial to the man who oversaw the amalgamation of the five boroughs, Manhattan, the Bronx, Queens, Brooklyn and Staten Island, into the one city of New York, creating at the time the second largest city in the world after London. In a park full of romance this is perhaps the most romantic spot of all, a lonely glade at the top of a hill in a part of the park where almost no one comes.

Now head back down the hill, cross over the East Drive again, and keeping the high rocky outcrop of Fort Clinton to your left (you can climb to the top for a fine viewpoint) head east and down into the Conservatory Garden.

The Conservatory Garden

The CONSERVATORY GARDEN was opened in 1898 as the first and only formal garden in Central Park, and was named after a large e-shaped conservatory that formerly stood here. This was demolished in 1934 and the present gardens were laid out by husband and wife team Gilmore D. Clarke and Betty Sprout and opened to the public in 1937.

The garden covers 6 acres (2.4 ha) and is divided into three distinct national styles, French, Italian and English. The FRENCH GARDEN at the northern end nearest the meer is centred around a beautifully life-like and energetic fountain called THREE DANCING MAIDENS. This is a cast of the original, which was sculpted in 1910 by the German sculptor Walter Schott in Berlin, and was donated by the family of New York lawyer Samuel Untermyer from his Greystone estate in Yonkers.

The ITALIAN GARDEN in the middle has a large rectangular lawn bordered by pink and white blossoming crab-apple trees with a 12 ft (3.6 m) high geyser fountain at the western end. Behind the fountain, steps lead up to a crescent shaped wrought-iron wisteria pergola with the names of the original 13 states inscribed on the walkway.

The ENGLISH GARDEN is slightly less formal and more reminiscent of a cottage garden, with trees, shrubs and flower beds arranged around a lily pool. At the centre of the pool is a fountain sculpted by Bessie Potter Vonnoh in memory of FRANCES HODGSON BURNETT, which depicts a boy and a girl based on the characters Mary and Dickon from Burnett's story *The Secret Garden*.

Few tourists venture this far north and the Conservatory Garden is rarely over-crowded. To sit amongst the flowers and trees, listening to the tinkling of the fountains while just yards away from the bustle of Fifth Avenue, is a uniquely soothing New York experience.

Access to the Conservatory Garden from Fifth Avenue is through the magnificent wrought-iron VANDERBILT GATE, forged in Paris in 1894 and orig-inally forming the entrance to the Vanderbilt Mansion at Fifth Avenue and 58th Street. The mansion was knocked down in 1926 to make way for the Bergdorf Goodman department store, and the gate was given to the city by Gertrude Vanderbilt Whitney in 1939.

From here it is a gentle half-hour walk back to the south section of the park. When you reach the Metropolitan Museum of Art, pass to the rear of the building so that the museum is on your left and the Great Lawn on your right. On the west side of the East Drive is a larger-than-life statue of the first U.S. Treasury Secretary ALEXANDER HAMILTON, donated by his son John C. Hamilton in 1880. The statue, carved entirely from durable granite, was made as a replacement for the very first work of marble carved in the U.S., the marble statue of Hamilton that stood in the Merchants' Exchange on Wall Street and was destroyed in the Great Fire of 1835.

A little further south, following the line of the East Drive, is THE OBELISK, nicknamed Cleopatra's Needle, THE OLDEST MAN-MADE OBJECT IN CENTRAL PARK. This pink granite monolith is one of a pair made for the Egyptian Pharaoh Thutmosis III in around 1430 BC, and originally stood in the sacred city of Heliopolis on the River Nile. The other one of the pair can now be found beside the River Thames in London. The two obelisks were given to Britain and America by the Khedive of Egypt in return for foreign aid. The London obelisk was raised in 1879, the New York one two years later in 1881.

Further south, beside the Turtle Pond, is THE LARGEST SCULPTURE IN CENTRAL PARK, an equestrian statue of KING JAGIELLO, who was King of Poland in the 14th and 15th centuries. The statue commemorates Poland's greatest military triumph, the Battle of Grunewald in 1410, when Jagiello led Poland and Lithuania to victory over the Teutonic knights of Germany. It was chosen for the Polish pavilion at the New York World Fair of 1939, but later that year the Nazis invaded Poland

and the statue could not be sent back to its homeland. In 1945 it was placed in Central Park as a symbol of Polish courage and valour.

proved to be one of the most popular attractions in Central Park.

Once the boat racing is done the children can walk round to the west side of the pond and snuggle into the lap of HANS CHRISTIAN ANDERSEN to listen to a free story hour. The much-loved Danish author is depicted here in bronze, reading his tale of The Ugly Duckling to, funnily enough, a rather cute ugly duckling.

Conservatory Water

Continue south along the line of East Drive, past 'Cat Hill', graced by STILL HUNT, Edward Kemeys's frighteningly life-like representation of a crouching feline that gives joggers a scare as they climb the hill, past the LOEB BOATHOUSE, where you can dine by the water's edge, at a price, and you eventually come to Conservatory Water or the Model Boat Pond, where every weekend in summer, children and adults alike come to race model boats. It was originally planned to build a conservatory here for tropical plants, hence the formal name, but money was scarce and the boating pond was put here instead, and has

Or perhaps, if they still have the energy, the children can go and play with ALICE IN WONDERLAND. She sits on a mushroom on the north side of the pond conversing with the Cheshire Cat, the White Rabbit with his pocket watch, the timid little dormouse and the Mad Hatter, the latter being a real-life caricature of the philanthropist GEORGE DELACORTE, who donated the statue in 1959 as a tribute to his late wife Margarita. She used to love reading *Alice in Wonderland* to their own children. The bronze sculpture, created by José de Creeft, has been worn smooth by the hands and feet of countless happy children clambering all over it, just as Carrie (Sarah Jessica Parker) did in Season One of the TV series *Sex and the City*.

In fact Conservatory Water and its statues have been quite a lure for film-makers over the years, featuring in *Breakfast at Tiffany's*, *The Object of My Affection*, *Jungle 2 Jungle*, *F/X* and *The Mirror Has Two Faces*.

E.B. White used Conservatory Water as the setting for the boat race in his novel *Stuart Little*, a scene that was recreated on the actual pond in the 1999 film of the book. And in J.D. Salinger's *The Catcher in the Rye*, the lead char-acter Holden Caulfield confides in the ducks on Conservatory Water.

Continue south past the Zoo to the park exit opposite the Plaza Hotel and the finish of the walk.

Well, I never knew this about
CENTRAL PARK

One of the reasons why Central Park is so famous across the world is because it has BEEN FILMED MORE OFTEN THAN ANY OTHER LOCATION IN THE WORLD. The first film to be shot in Central Park was the very first film version of *Romeo and Juliet*, made by Vitagraph Studios in 1908. Since then over 300 films have been shot in the park, including such classics as *Breakfast at Tiffany's*, *Barefoot in the Park*, *Love Story*, *Annie Hall*, *Kramer vs. Kramer*, *Wall Street*, *Fatal Attraction*, *Home Alone 2*, *You've Got Mail*, *Vanilla Sky* and *The Devil Wears Prada*.

Like Central Park itself, the TAVERN ON THE GREEN has been often used as a film location, appearing in *Wall Street*, *Ghostbusters*, *An Unmarried Woman*, *Edward Scissorhands*, *The Out-of-Towners* and the 2011 film *Mr Popper's Penguins*, in which Jim Carrey plays an estate agent who tries to buy the Tavern from owner Angela Lansbury so that it can be torn down.

The Tavern on the Green also marks the finishing line of the New York Marathon.

The 700 acres (283 ha) of land that was acquired by the city for the creation of Central Park was mostly uninhabited swamps, marshland or rocky hills. There was, however, a well-established community built and run by free African–Americans called SENECA on the west side of the proposed park, roughly centred on a block where 82nd and 89th Streets would now intersect with Seventh and Eighth Avenues. The village was founded around the time when slavery was abolished in New York in 1827, and was the first signifi-cant property on Manhattan Island owned by African–Americans. It had three churches, schools and houses for about 250 people. In 1857 the entire population was evicted and the village razed to the ground. There is no knowledge of where the villagers resettled, no descendants have been traced and the only physical evidence to be seen is the corner of a foundation, thought to be of a church, near the Spector playground at the 89th Street entrance.

In August 1997 one of the largest concerts on record was held in Central Park when nearly one million people attended a free concert by Country superstar GARTH BROOKS. In 1986, 800,000 people attended THE LARGEST CLASSICAL CONCERT ON RECORD when the New York Philharmonic gave a performance in Central Park to mark the rededication of the Statue of Liberty.

CHAPTER 18

UPPER BROADWAY – 110TH TO THE HARLEM RIVER

Riverside Church

Harlem and the Heights

The far north of Manhattan Island is an area of hills and valleys quite unlike any other part of Manhattan. Broadway runs straight as a die up the west side, passing through the various breezy suburban residential heights, Morningside, Hamilton, Washington and Hudson, to Inwood at the northern tip. To the east is Harlem, founded by the early Dutch settlers in the 17th century and named after the northern Dutch city of Haarlem. Then a quiet village, today it is a colourful and vibrant centre of African–American and Latino culture.

Morningside Heights

MORNINGSIDE HEIGHTS starts at West 110th Street, which marks the northern border of Central Park.

On the corner of Broadway and 112th Street is TOM'S RESTAURANT, the subject of Suzanne Vega's 1987 song 'Tom's Diner'. Tom's Restaurant is also Monk's Café in the television show *Seinfeld*, where the lead characters regularly gather to eat, although it is only used for exterior shots, the interior shots being filmed on a sound stage in California. Tom's Restaurant is popular with students from nearby Columbia University, and President Barack Obama used to drop in there when a student at Columbia.

The Cathedral of St John the Divine

One block east on 112th Street the west face of New York's Episcopalian CATHEDRAL OF ST JOHN THE DIVINE looms at the end of the road like a cliff face. It is enormous and impressive, even though the north tower is uncapped, giving the whole edifice a strange, lopsided look.

The cathedral was started in 1892 as the Episcopalian answer to the Roman Catholic St Patrick's Cathedral on Fifth Avenue, and this site was chosen because the land was relatively cheap and the elevated position meant that the cathedral would be visible for miles around, although with no tower and the surrounding area now built up, this hasn't quite worked out as planned. The original architects were Heins and LaFarge, who designed New York's first subway stations, and their vision was for a Romanesque building. In 1911, however, after the choir had been consecrated, Ralph Adams took over and built the nave in a Gothic style, so that the result is something of a

hotchpotch, with a Gothic nave and Romanesque crossing beneath a dome of Guastavino tiles. Work was interrupted by the two world wars and, apart from an addition to the south tower and some exterior carving, has never been resumed since 1941.

St John the Divine is THE LARGEST CHURCH IN AMERICA and potentially the largest church in the world when, if ever, it is finished. Even now, upon entering the cavernous nave, 601 ft (183 m) long, 146 ft (45 m) wide and 124 ft (38 m) high, the sense of space is breathtaking. The huge polished columns of the Romanesque choir, 55 ft (17 m) tall, are said to be THE BIGGEST GRANITE COLUMNS IN THE WORLD and came from Vinalhaven in Maine, the only quarry in the world deep enough to mine them. The magnificent space is well used for concerts and festivals as well as services.

Two blocks north up Amsterdam Avenue, on a high terrace above the surrounding streets, and entered via College Walk, is the campus of . . .

Columbia University

COLUMBIA UNIVERSITY, an Ivy League school, is NEW YORK'S OLDEST EDUCATIONAL ESTABLISHMENT and was founded in 1754 as King's College, by a charter of George II. Early students were Alexander Hamilton, John Jay, Robert 'Chancellor' Livingston and Gouverneur Morris. After the Revolution it was reborn as Columbia College and became a university in 1896, the same year that it moved here to its purpose-built 32-acre (13 ha) campus designed by Charles McKim.

The largest building on the campus is the neo-classical BUTLER LIBRARY on the south side, which now houses all the books from the LOW LIBRARY, facing it across the square. The Low Library, at the centre point of the complex, is based on the Pantheon in Rome and fronted by a statue called ALMA MATER by Daniel Chester French, which in 1968 became the focus of student demonstrations against the Vietnam War. In a nice touch, a wise owl peers out from the folds of Alma Mater's gown.

Immediately east of the library is ST PAUL'S CHAPEL, built in 1904 in red brick to blend in with the other campus buildings. The Byzantine interior is gorgeous, with a red-brick dome that rises to 91 ft (28 m). The acoustics of the chapel are outstanding and the organ is said to have the finest tone of any organ in New York. Both can be enjoyed at one of the regular-free organ concerts given in the chapel.

Continue across the campus on College Walk to Broadway and turn right. Just past the steps to the domed Earl Hall, on the wall of the Math Building, is a plaque commemorating an early American victory over the British at the BATTLE OF HARLEM HEIGHTS, which was fought near here in September 1776.

Walk north on Broadway, turn left on to West 120th Street, go down to Riverside Drive and turn right for . . .

Riverside Church

RIVERSIDE INTERDENOMINATIONAL CHURCH is THE TALLEST CHURCH IN AMERICA, with an extraordinary tower 392 ft (119 m) high, which overwhelms not just the rest of the church but the whole neighbourhood. The tower is in fact a 22-storey skyscraper, with the stone exterior hung on a steel frame. Unlike the nearby cathedral of St John, the church really *can* be seen for miles, a source of satisfaction, no doubt, to John D. Rockefeller who paid for Riverside, having been rebuffed by the Episcopalian cathedral for being a Baptist. Inside the tower hangs the LAURA SPELMAN ROCKEFELLER CARILLON, named in honour of Rockefeller's mother. It is THE LARGEST CARILLON IN THE WORLD and THE FIRST IN HISTORY TO ACHIEVE A SPAN OF FIVE OCTAVES. The bronze hour bell, called the BOURDON, weighs 20 tons and

is THE LARGEST AND HEAVIEST TUNED BELL EVER CAST. For unsurpassed views of the Hudson and the whole of Manhattan, take THE WORLD'S LOFTIEST CHURCH ELEVATOR to the 20th floor, and then some stairs to the windy observation deck, 355 ft (108 m) up. Alas, since 9/11 the deck has been closed to the public but it is possible to arrange a special tour. And well worth it.

The marble floor of the huge nave downstairs, which holds over 2,000 people, is inlaid with a labyrinth, modelled on that in the nave of Chartres Cathedral.

Grant's Tomb

A little further along Riverside Drive, Ulysses S. Grant, Union General and 18th President of the United States, lies entombed with his wife Julia inside THE LARGEST MAUSOLEUM IN AMERICA, the ONLY PRESIDENT TO BE BURIED IN NEW YORK. The tomb, which is inspired by the original mausoleum of King Mausolos at Halicarnassus in Ancient Greece, was dedicated by President William McKinley on 27 April 1897, the anniversary of Grant's 75th birthday. New York State was so chuffed at having procured the prestigious tomb that the day was declared a holiday and over one million people turned up for the ceremony, while it took seven hours for the flotilla of 15 ships to pass by on the Hudson River in review. In the early years of the 20th century the tomb was NEW YORK'S MOST VISITED ATTRACTION, more popular even than the Statue of Liberty.

An Amiable Child

A short walk north of Grant's Tomb, beside the southbound carriageway of Riverside Drive, there is a somewhat less imposing, but no less heartfelt monument, a small urn resting on a pedestal, shaded by trees and fenced in by iron railings. There is a plaque that reads: 'Erected to the memory of an amiable child, St. Claire Pollock, died 15th July 1797 in the fifth year of his age'. Little St Claire was playing on rocks by the river when he fell in and drowned. His father, linen merchant George Pollock, sold the land a few years later and asked that the new owner should respect and take care of the grave, and it has been looked after ever since.

125th Street Station

Continue north on Riverside Drive until you reach the viaduct, take the steps down to 125th Street, and walk east towards Broadway to where you will find the gloriously elevated 125TH STREET SUBWAY STATION, suspended 100 ft (30 m) in the air on the Manhattan Valley Viaduct, which keeps the Line 1 track on the level between 122nd and 135th Streets. Built in 1904, the station is a glorious concoction in iron and steel and is, with the possible exception of the grand City Hall station no longer in use, the most interesting subway station on Manhattan.

Hamilton Heights

Now walk up the ramp to Broadway, go over 136th Street, and bear right into the gently sloping Hamilton Place. Take this to 138th Street, turn right and go to the impressive hilltop grounds of . . .

City College of New York

The quite lovely brown and white neo-Gothic buildings of the school's original quadrangle, which were built between 1903 and 1907, are all made of Manhattan schist excavated during the construction of the city's first subway. The main building, SHEPARD HALL, with its huge four-square tower, is particularly impressive. Newer, less attractive buildings have been added over time and the campus now covers 35 acres (14 ha) – it's larger than Columbia University.

The school used to offer free tuition to all New York residents, but today they must pay a reduced fee.

Make your way through the campus to the east until you reach St Nicholas Terrace, high on a bluff overlooking Harlem. Turn left (north) and continue around the front of Shepard Hall until you see, down a slope on your right . . .

Hamilton Grange

This was Alexander Hamilton's country home, where he lived with his family for the last two years of his life from 1802 until 1804, before his untimely death at the hands of Aaron Burr. It was designed in Federal style by John McComb Jr. and named after Hamilton's

ancestral family estate in Scotland. If the house looks uncomfortable here it is because it has already been moved twice from further up the hill where it got in the way of the Manhattan Grid. Although Hamilton Grange is open to the public, few people seem to know it is here, tucked away incongruously behind a modern office building, but it is worth seeking out for its flavour of elegant early 19th-century country living, and as a tangible link with one of New York's greatest Founding Fathers.

Now, with your back to the Grange, cross the road to Hamilton Terrace straight opposite and walk along the road until it turns sharp left into 144th Street. Take 144th back to Broadway and turn right for a ten-minute walk to Washington Heights and the last active cemetery in Manhattan.

Trinity Church Cemetery

Broadway divides TRINITY CHURCH CEMETERY into east and west, the entrances to each side being on 155th Street. The cemetery was laid out in 1842, in what was then pleasant countryside at the far northern boundary of the city, for Trinity Church parish, on land belonging to the ornithologist and painter, JOHN JAMES AUDUBON (1785–1851), author of *The Birds of America*. He is buried beneath a tall Celtic cross elaborately carved with birds and animals, just inside the gates of the eastern cemetery.

Down the hill in the western cemetery are the vaults of the Astor family, which contain the remains of John Jacob Astor himself and seven of his family, including Caroline Schermerhorn Astor, of Mrs Astor's Four Hundred fame, and John Jacob Astor IV, who died on the *Titanic*. Others who are buried here – and a diverting few moments can be spent looking for them all – include RALPH WALDO ELLISON, author of *Invisible Man*, CLEMENT CLARKE MOORE, who wrote 'Twas the Night Before Christmas', the actor JERRY ORBACH and ALFRED TENNYSON DICKENS, son of Charles Dickens, who died in New York while on a lecture tour about his father.

Next up on Broadway, across 155th Street is . . .

Audubon Terrace

This extraordinary architectural outpost, consisting of eight superb *beaux-arts* buildings facing each other across a tiled plaza, was built in 1906–8 on John Audubon's land by the railroad heir Archer Huntington, who wanted to establish a cultural centre in what was then an exclusive part of town. He was a devotee of all things Hispanic, and the first grand classical building to open on Audubon Terrace housed the HISPANIC SOCIETY OF AMERICA, which is still open to the public there today, and displays Huntington's collection of paintings by Goya, El Greco and Velazquez. In time were added the AMERICAN ACADEMY OF ARTS AND LETTERS, the AMERICAN NUMISMATIC SOCIETY, the AMERICAN GEOGRAPHICAL SOCIETY and the MUSEUM OF THE AMERICAN INDIAN.

The statue of Spanish knight El Cid that stands on the Terrace was sculpted by Huntington's wife Anna.

As the nature of the Washington Heights area changed fewer people came to visit the museums and apart from two, The Hispanic Society and the Academy of Arts and Letters, the institutions moved on, leaving this majestic group of buildings rather stranded. The unexpected thrill of suddenly coming across such an incongruous treasure only adds to the slightly surreal atmosphere of the place.

Sugar Hill

When you step back into the real world, return to 155th Street and walk east as far as Edgecombe Avenue at the bottom of the hill. Across the junction at the beginning of the bridge stands the delightful Hooper drinking fountain and horse trough, bequeathed by businessman John Hooper in 1894.

This area of Harlem is known informally as SUGAR HILL, where, from the 1920s on, wealthy African–Americans came to live the 'sweet life', as immortalised by local resident DUKE ELLINGTON in his song 'Take the "A" Train (to go to Sugar Hill way up in Harlem)'.

Coogan's Bluff

Turn left on to Edgecombe Avenue and walk up to the top of the hill. You are now standing on COOGAN'S BLUFF, named after 19th-century local land-owner James Coogan, which overlooks the POLO GROUNDS, where 100 years ago baseball came of age at the stadium of the New York Giants.

The stadium was demolished in the 1960s after the Giants moved to San Francisco, and is now high-rise housing, but there is still one intriguing relic of those glory days to be seen, the JOHN T. BRUSH STAIRCASE, which leads down to the Polo Grounds from the end of 158th Street.

John T. Brush, whose fortune was made through sports department stores, owned the New York Giants from 1890 until his death in 1912, and the stairway was constructed in his memory by the Giants in 1913. A hopeful ticket booth was installed at the top of the stairs on Edgecombe Avenue, but the view of the stadium from here was so good that crowds preferred to gather on the stairway and the bluff to watch the action for free.

The stairway has been beautifully restored, but something of the atmosphere has been lost from when it was abandoned and rusting and still barely clinging to the cliff face. There was a certain thrill in climbing down it while precariously hanging on to the wobbly railing, to read the plaque on the concrete platform midway down which says, succinctly, 'The John T. Brush Staircase, presented by the New York Giants'.

Continue north along Edgecombe Avenue until you come to THE OLDEST HOUSE IN MANHATTAN, the . . .

Morris-Jumel Mansion

To find the entrance to the MORRIS-JUMEL MANSION turn left on 160th Street and right on Jumel Terrace. Actor and political activist PAUL ROBESON lived here, at No. 16. In 2008 the singer ALICIA KEYS bought his house for her mother.

The Morris-Jumel Mansion is undoubtedly the nicest old house in Manhattan. I am sure the Mayor does himself very nicely in the Gracie Mansion down in Yorkville, but the stunning hilltop position here is unassailable, even though much of the view has been obscured by apartments.

The house itself is beautiful, with a huge classical portico and an unusual octagonal wing. It was built in 1765 for British army colonel Roger Morris, who was a loyalist and had to vacate the house and return to England at the onset of the Revolution. His former colleague George Washington then used the house as a temporary head-quarters during his defence of

Manhattan in 1776. Washington returned here as President in 1790 and enjoyed a formal dinner with John and Abigail Adams, their son John Quincy Adams, Thomas Jefferson and Alexander Hamilton. Mrs Astor would have been green with envy.

In 1810 the house was bought by French Caribbean merchant Stephen Jumel and his wife Eliza, who decorated it in Empire fashion. After her husband died in 1832, Eliza was briefly married to former Vice President Aaron Burr until his death in 1836. She continued to live in the house for the rest of her life and died there, aged 90, in 1865. She is buried in the Trinity Church Cemetery at Washington Heights.

The house then passed through a number of hands and is today run as a museum of the decorative arts. Unlike a lot of museums it feels lived in and loved. There are young parents and children playing in the garden, and when you go in a nice lady asks you apologetically for $4 'just to help keep the place going'. The rooms are laid out, decorated and furnished as Eliza Jumel had them. Particularly fine is the drawing room in the octagonal wing, where Washington and his friends would have gathered for drinks before dinner.

On leaving the mansion cross over Jumel Terrace into SYLVAN TERRACE, a street of perfectly preserved wooden houses as lovely as its name. The street is cobble-stoned and still has a number of old carriage lights, while the houses are all painted white with green shutters. They were built in 1882 along the line of the original carriage drive to the mansion.

Return to Jumel Terrace, turn left and go around the grounds of Morris-Jumel back to Edgecombe Avenue. Turn left and enter the High Bridge Park at the end of 165th Street. Take the obvious track past all the basketball courts and this will lead you through trees to the . . .

Croton Aqueduct High Bridge

Built in 1848 to bring fresh water across the Harlem River as part of the Croton Aqueduct System, the CROTON AQUEDUCT HIGH BRIDGE is THE OLDEST MAJOR BRIDGE IN NEW YORK. It was built to resemble a Roman aqueduct and originally had 15 stone arches but in 1927 the central arches were replaced with a single steel arch to allow larger ships to pass underneath.

Now make your way up the steep stairway to the HIGH BRIDGE WATER TOWER, which was built in 1872 to serve the communities of Upper Manhattan. At weekends in summer you can climb to the top for outstanding views.

Thinkonomics

Now walk around the swimming pool, cross Amsterdam Avenue and take 173rd Street back to Broadway. Turn right (north) on Broadway and pause to wonder at the Byzantine splendour of the magnificent 1930 LOEWS MOVIE PALACE on the corner of 175th Street, the grandest surviving movie house from the Golden Age of Hollywood in Manhattan.

That it has survived is thanks to the irrepressible FREDERICK 'REV IKE' EIKERENKOETTER, who in 1969 rescued the abandoned palace and restored it to its full glory as the United Church Science of Living Institute. Throughout the 1970s and 80s he broadcast motivational radio and television programmes from here, preaching the blessings of material prosperity and urging his flock to send in money so that he might bless them. They did, enough money in fact for the Reverend Ike to buy a fleet of cars sizeable enough for him to be able to drive a different Mercedes or Rolls-Royce every day of the week. 'My garages runneth over,' as he put it.

George Washington Bridge

Continue along Broadway to 181st Street, where you turn left. Walk all the way up the hill and down the other side on 181st until you reach the viewpoint, with sensational views of the GEORGE WASHINGTON BRIDGE, opened in 1931 and the BUSIEST BRIDGE IN THE WORLD, carrying over 106 million vehicles every year. It is 600 ft (183 m) high and 3,500 ft (1,065 m) long and on major holidays sports the LARGEST FREE FLYING AMERICAN FLAG IN THE WORLD.

Now turn right, take the footbridge across the Henry Hudson Parkway and follow the winding footpath under the road and over the railway down to Fort Washington Park and Jeffrey's Hook where, perched on a rock promontory above the river and looking very small under the 'great gray bridge', is . . .

The Little Red Lighthouse

The small, cast-iron, 40 ft (12 m) high little red lighthouse was built in 1880 and originally stood on the tip of Sandy Hook by the Lower Bay in New Jersey. It was moved here in 1921 to warn ships on the Hudson of the rocks where the river narrows at Jeffrey's Hook. In 1931, when the bridge opened, the lighthouse became obsolete since there was a light on the bridge pier.

In 1942 local author Hildegarde Swift wrote a children's book called *The Little Red Lighthouse and the Great Gray Bridge*, about a lighthouse who worries that it is no longer useful. The book became a children's favourite and in 1951, when the lighthouse was threatened with demolition, thousands of children started a nationwide campaign to save their beloved Little Red Lighthouse. Thanks to their efforts there was a happy ending: the threat was lifted and the lighthouse was taken over by the New York City Department of Parks and Recreation.

If you want to get a closer look there

is usually a park ranger nearby, who may or may not be persuaded to let you climb the tower. Do if you can. Best before lunch, because the climb up the iron stairs to the lantern room is steep and you have to squeeze through a tiny trapdoor out on to the balcony, but the windy views down the foam-flecked river are exhilarating – and, of course, unique, for the Little Red Lighthouse is THE ONLY REMAINING LIGHTHOUSE ON MANHATTAN.

Now retrace your steps up to the viewpoint at the end of 181st Street. On the way look up at the cliff face on your right and you may be able to see the remains of a redoubt where cannons from Fort Washington were sited to fire on English ships coming along the Hudson River in 1776.

Hudson Heights

Go back up 181st and after passing, or better still visiting, one of the best bars in New York, the *Ceile* (an Irish word for 'party'), located on the corner of Cabrini Boulevard, you will come to some steps on your left. Take these and at the top walk along Pinehurst Avenue, then go right and left to find the entrance to BENNETT PARK. There is a plaque here, raised by James Gordon Bennett, proclaiming that this was the site of Fort Washington, 'constructed by the Continental troops in the summer of 1776, taken by the British after a heroic defense November 16 1776, and repossessed by the Americans in 1783'.

Highest Point

Just across the park an outcrop of rock marks THE HIGHEST POINT IN MANHATTAN, 265 ft (81 m) above sea level, and the second highest point in all the five boroughs after Todt Hill on Staten Island. Alas, the park is entirely surrounded by massive apartment blocks and so there are no views from the highest point at all.

Exit Bennett Park and turn left on to Fort Washington Avenue and walk for ten minutes until you reach a small roundabout. Go straight over and take the pedestrian entrance into . . .

Fort Tryon Park

This must be one of the loveliest spots in all Manhattan, with unrivalled views across the mighty Hudson to the New Jersey Palisades and the most beautiful gardens, laid out on terraces by Frederick Law Olmsted Jr. and gifted to the city by John D. Rockefeller in 1917.

The fort here was an outpost of Fort Washington and when the British took possession in 1776 they named it after

Sir William Tryon, the last colonial governor of New York.

Now walk through the park following the signs to . . .

The Cloisters

JOHN D. ROCKEFELLER donated the land for THE CLOISTERS and funded the purchase, by the Metropolitan Museum of Art, of sculptor George Grey Barnard's collection of medieval art and sculpture in 1925. The museum here is now a branch of the 'Met' and focuses on Romanesque and Gothic art from Europe.

The medieval-style buildings that house the treasures are part of the museum themselves. The complex was designed by Charles Collins who built Riverside Church, and assembled in 1933 from elements of a number of French abbeys transported across the Atlantic and rebuilt here on a hilltop overlooking the Hudson.

Amongst the highlights are the 12th-century CUXA CLOISTER from the Pyrenees, a 12th-century Romanesque apse from Spain and a 13th-century Gothic chapel, as well as doorways and statuary from 14th- and 15th-century European castles. Particularly fine is the museum's collection of tapestries,

the 14th-century Nine Heroes tapestries from the French royal court and the seven wonderful Hunt of the Unicorn tapestries from 15th-century Brussels.

Outside, the cloister gardens are planted with the trees, herbs, shrubs and flowers that were grown in the Middle Ages.

The view across the Hudson from the terrace of the Cloisters is sublime, and not by accident. John D. Rockefeller bought 700 acres (283 ha) of New Jersey directly across the river from the museum, so that the prospect could never be despoiled.

Exit the museum and follow one of the many paths that lead down through the trees to Broadway. Turn left (north) and walk three blocks to 204th Street and . . .

The Dyckman Farmhouse

Rebuilt by William Dyckman in 1784 after being burned down by the British in the Revolutionary War, and opened in 1916 as a museum, this is THE ONLY REMAINING COLONIAL FARMHOUSE IN MANHATTAN. It stands quietly, high above bustling Broadway, surrounded by lush gardens and redolent of a time when this part of Manhattan was nothing but fishing streams and farmland. Inside is a time warp, the downstairs parlour and kitchen laid out for a period farmhouse, with creaking floorboards and fresh flowers from the garden on the table.

The End of Broadway

On leaving the farmhouse continue north along Broadway. Cruelly hemmed in by garage premises just beyond 215th Street is the once grand marble gateway of the Seaman Mansion, which stood on the hill behind in the 1850s. Stripped of its

marble and covered in graffiti, the arch nevertheless retains a certain poise in the face of all its indignities.

Continue for another block, and there it is, the BROADWAY BRIDGE. You have now walked the whole of Broadway on Manhattan, 14 miles (22 km) from Bowling Green to the Harlem River.

Return from the bridge, turn right into 218th Street, walk to the end and then on into glorious INWOOD HILL PARK, with its woods, caves and idyllic views across the Harlem River to the mighty cliffs of the Bronx, and out beyond the high Henry Hudson Bridge to the Hudson River. From here you can see that, yes, Manhattan really is an island.

Well, I never knew this
about

UPPER BROADWAY — 110TH
TO THE HARLEM RIVER

GEORGE GERSHWIN wrote *Rhapsody in Blue* while living in the Cathedral Apartments at No. 501 West 110th in 1924.

Between 1988 and 1996 the arches and columns of the main doorway of St John the Divine were decorated with limestone sculptures of Biblical figures, creating what is called a Portal of Paradise. Some of the themes are modern, and one in particular, carved by a local stonemason, Joe Kincannon, is almost prophetic: it shows New York under a mushroom cloud, with the

Twin Towers at the centre, leaning as if about to fall.

The campus of Columbia University is instantly recognisable from numerous films and television programmes, appearing in *Ghostbusters, Spider-Man, House, Gossip Girl, Law and Order* and *The West Wing*, among countless others.

'Who is buried in Grant's Tomb?' is New York's favourite trick question, beloved of the city's schoolchildren almost since the tomb was raised. The answer is 'nobody'. Grant and his wife are not buried but entombed there above ground, in two colossal sarcophagi, each weighing 8½ tons.

A short detour down 125th Street from Broadway will take you to HARLEM'S OLDEST FUNCTIONING THEATRE, THE APOLLO, whose famous *Amateur Night* has been staged since 1934 and quickly established itself as a leading showcase for talented new performers. Amongst the first winners were Pearl Bailey and a 15-year-old Ella Fitzgerald. In 1935 Billie Holiday, Lena Horne and the Count Basie Orchestra made their debuts there. *Amateur Night* winners in the 1940s included Sarah Vaughan and Ruth Brown, in the 1950s Dionne Warwick and James Brown, and in the 1960s Gladys Knight and Jimi Hendrix. From 1987 until 2008 *Amateur Night* was featured on the television programme *Showtime at the Apollo*.

ASTOR ROW on West 130th Street in Harlem is one of New York's most beautiful collections of townhouses. They were built in 1880 by William Blackhouse Astor and are unusual for Manhattan in that they have front gardens and southern-style wooden porches. The houses were neglected and allowed to deteriorate for 60 years between the 1930s and 1990s, until in 1992 Ella Fitzgerald performed a benefit concert at Radio City Music Hall to raise money for their restoration, which has now been completed.

Broadway was the scene on 30 May 1896 of THE FIRST RECORDED AUTOMOBILE ACCIDENT IN AMERICA, when Henry Wells of Springfield, Massachusetts, knocked cyclist Evylyn Thomas off her bicycle on Upper Broadway.

If you walk across Inwood Hill Park to the far north-west corner of Gaelic Field next to the large inlet of the Harlem River you will find the SHORAKKOPOCH ROCK, set within the girth of a long-gone tulip tree and bearing a plaque inscribed with the words: 'According to Legend, on this site of the principal Manhattan village Peter Minuit in 1626 purchased Manhattan Island for trinkets and beads then worth about 60 guilders.

This boulder also marks the spot where a tulip tree grew to a height of 165 feet and a girth of 20 feet. It was until its death in 1938 at the age of 280 years the last living link with the Reckgawawanc Indians who lived here.'

What a perfect place to end our tour of New York.

Gazetteer

Interesting locations and places open to the public.
Please telephone or check websites for opening times
and admission costs which are subject to change.

To call New York from outside the U.S. call:
00 + 1 + Area Code + Tel number
e.g. New York Public Library is 212 930 0800
so the international code is: 00 + 1 + 212 930 0800

To contact the New York Department of Transportation
from within New York call 311

NEW YORK HARBOR

GOVERNORS ISLAND

Trust for Governors Island, 10 South St,
Slip 7, New York, NY 10004
The Governors Island ferry departs
from the Battery Maritime
Building located at 10 South St,
adjacent to the Staten Island Ferry
in Lower Manhattan
Tel: 212 440 2200
www.govisland.com

STATUE OF LIBERTY
& ELLIS ISLAND

Ticket Office, Castle Clinton, Battery
Park, New York, NY 10005
Tel: 212 344 7220
National Park Service, Statue of

Liberty National Monument,
Liberty Island, New York,
NY 10004
www.nps.gov
General information,
tel: 212 363 3200

All visits require the purchase
of a ferry transportation ticket.
Tickets include Liberty Island
and Ellis Island and can be
purchased through Statue Cruises:
www.statuecruises.com
Tel: 1 877 523 9849
or 1 201 604 2800

Or in person at the ferry departure
points: Battery Park, New York or
Liberty State Park, New Jersey

STATEN ISLAND FERRY

The Whitehall Terminal, 4 South St,
New York, NY 10004
www.siferry.com
*www.nyc.gov/html/dot/html/ferrybus/
statfery.shtml*
To contact New York Department
of Transportation by telephone
dial 311

NEW AMSTERDAM &
COLONIAL NEW YORK

NEW AMSTERDAM PAVILION

The Battery Conservancy,
1 New York Plz, Concourse,
New York, NY 10004
Tel: 212 344 3491
www.thebattery.org

NATIONAL MUSEUM OF THE
AMERICAN INDIAN

NMAI in New York, Alexander
Hamilton U.S. Custom House,
One Bowling Green, New York,
NY 10004
Tel: 212 514 3700
www.nmai.si.edu/visit/newyork

FRAUNCES TAVERN

54 Pearl St, New York, NY 10004
Tel: 212 968 1776
www.frauncestavern.com

NEW YORK CITY POLICE MUSEUM

100 Old Slip, New York, NY 10005
Tel: 212 480 3100
www.nycpolicemuseum.org

ELIZABETH ANN SETON SHRINE

7 State St, New York, NY 10004
Tel: 212 269 6865
www.setonshrine.com

CASTLE CLINTON

Battery Park, New York, NY 10004
*Tel: 212 344 7220 or tel 311 for all
Parks & Recreation information;
www.nps.gov/cacl*

LOWER BROADWAY – BOWLING
GREEN TO TRINITY CHURCH

TRINITY CHURCH

74 Trinity Pl, New York, NY 10006
Tel: 212 602 0800
www.trinitywallstreet.org

A WALK DOWN WALL STREET

FEDERAL HALL
NATIONAL MONUMENT

26 Wall St, New York, NY 10005
Tel: 212 825 6990
www.nps.gov/feha

J.P. MORGAN LIBRARY

29 E 36th St, New York,
NY 10016
Tel: 212 685 0008
www.themorgan.org

MUSEUM OF AMERICAN FINANCE

48 Wall St, New York, NY 10005
Tel: 212 908 4110
www.moaf.org

NEW YORK FEDERAL RESERVE BANK

33 Liberty St, New York, NY 10045
Visitors to the bank will be able
to explore the Fed's roles and
responsibilities through a guided
tour and interactive exhibits in the
bank's museum
Tel: 212 720 6130
www.newyorkfed.org

LOWER BROADWAY – TRINITY CHURCH TO ST PAUL'S CHAPEL. THE WORLD TRADE CENTER

ST PAUL'S CHAPEL

209 Broadway, New York, NY 10007
Contact: Trinity Church &
St Paul's Chapel, 74 Trinity Pl,
New York, NY 10006
Tel: 212 233 4164
www.trinitywallstreet.org

NATIONAL SEPTEMBER 11 MEMORIAL AND MUSEUM

1 Liberty Plz, #20, New York,
NY 10006
Tel: 212 312 8800
www.911memorial.org

1 WORLD TRADE CENTER (FREEDOM TOWER)

Vesey St, New York, NY 10006
Tel: 646 524 7885
www.wtc.com

WINTER GARDEN, WORLD FINANCIAL CENTER

220 Vesey St, New York, NY 10281
Tel: 212 417 7000
www.worldfinancialcenter.com

MUSEUM OF JEWISH HERITAGE

36 Battery Pl, New York, NY 10004
Tel: 646 437 4202
www.mjhnyc.org

SKYSCRAPER MUSEUM

9 Battery Pl, New York, NY 10280
Tel: 212 968 1961
www.skyscraper.org

LOWER BROADWAY – VESEY TO CHAMBERS. THE CIVIC CENTER

CITY HALL

City Hall Park, Broadway, New York,
NY 10007
Tel: 212 788 3000
www.nyc.gov

THE TWEED COURTHOUSE

52 Chambers St, New York,
NY 10007
Tours are available on weekdays
and are offered free of charge
Tel: 212 788 2656
*www.nyc.gov/html/artcom/html/
tours/tweed.shtml*

SOUTH STREET SEAPORT MUSEUM

12 Fulton St, New York, NY 10038
Tel: 212 748 8600
www.southstreetseaportmuseum.org

BROADWAY – CHAMBERS TO CANAL. TRIBECA, CHINATOWN & THE LOWER EAST SIDE

AFRICAN BURIAL GROUND

Ted Weiss Federal Building, 290
  Broadway, 1st Fl, New York,
  NY 10007
  Tel: 212 637 2019
  www.nps.gov/afbg

RC CHURCH OF THE TRANSFIGURATION

29 Mott St, Chinatown, New York,
  NY 10038
  Tel: 212 962 5157
  www.transfigurationnyc.org

ST AUGUSTINE'S CHURCH (SLAVE GALLERIES)

290 Henry St, New York, NY 10002
  Tel: 212 673 5300
  www.staugnyc.org

ELDRIDGE STREET SYNAGOGUE

12 Eldridge St, New York, NY 10002
  Tel: 212 219 0888
  www.eldridgestreet.org

TENEMENT MUSEUM

103 Orchard St, New York, NY 10002
  Tel: 212 982 8420
  www.tenement.org

BROADWAY – CANAL TO HOUSTON. SOHO & LITTLE ITALY

NEW YORK CITY FIRE MUSEUM

278 Spring St, New York, NY 10013
  Tel: 212 691 1303
  www.nycfiremuseum.org

EAR INN

326 Spring St, New York, NY 10013
  Tel: 212 226 9060
  earinn.com

ST MICHAEL'S RUSSIAN CATHOLIC CHAPEL

266 Mulberry St, New York, NY 10012
  Tel: 212 226 2644
  stmichaelruscath.org

OLD ST PATRICK'S CATHEDRAL

263 Mulberry St, New York, NY 10012
  Tel: 212 226 8075
  www.oldcathedral.org

LOMBARDI'S

32 Spring St, New York, NY 10012
  Tel: 212 941 7994
  www.firstpizza.com

BROADWAY – HOUSTON TO UNION SQUARE. THE EAST VILLAGE

GRACE CHURCH

802 Broadway, New York, NY 10003
  Tel: 212 254 2000
  www.gracechurchnyc.org

STRAND BOOKSTORE

828 Broadway, New York, NY 10003
Tel: 212 473 1452
www.strandbooks.com

COOPER UNION FOUNDATION BUILDING

41 Cooper Sq, New York, NY 10003
Tel: 212 353 4100
www.cooper.edu/about/history/foun-dation-building-great-hall

MERCHANT'S HOUSE MUSEUM

29 E 4th St, New York, NY 10003
Tel: 212 777 1089
www.merchantshouse.org

MCSORLEY'S OLD ALE HOUSE

15 E 7th St, New York, NY 10003
Tel: 212 473 9148
www.mcsorleysnewyork.com

ST MARK'S IN THE BOWERY

131 E 10th St, New York, NY 10003
Tel: 212 674 6377
www.stmarksbowery.org

GREENWICH VILLAGE

CHURCH OF THE ASCENSION

5th Ave at 10th St, New York, NY 10011
Tel: 212 254 8620
www.ascensionnyc.org

JUDSON MEMORIAL CHURCH

55 Washington Sq South, New York, NY 10012
Tel: 212 477 0351
www.judson.org

ST LUKE IN THE FIELDS

487 Hudson St, New York, NY 10014
Tel: 212 924 0562
www.stlukeinthefields.org

BROADWAY – UNION SQUARE TO TIMES SQUARE

ROOSEVELT BIRTHPLACE MUSEUM

28 E 20th St, New York, NY 10003
Tel: 212 260 1616
www.nps.gov/thrb

CHELSEA

MASONIC HALL

71 W 23rd St, New York, NY 10010
Free tours of Grand Lodge Building and Masonic Hall are available; for tour information or to request a tour, email: TourGuides@nymasons.org
Tel: 212 337 6600
www.nymasons.org

GENERAL THEOLOGICAL SEMINARY

440 W 21st St, New York, NY 10011
Tel: 212 243 5150
www.gts.edu

HIGH LINE

519 W 23rd St, New York, NY 10011
Tel: 212 206 9922
www.thehighline.org

CHELSEA MARKET

75, 9th Ave, New York, NY 10011
Tel: 212 206 8338
chelseamarket.com

HIGHLINER DINER

210, 10th Ave, New York NY 10011
Tel: 212 206 6206
www.thehighlinernyc.com

GRAMERCY & MIDTOWN SOUTH

PETE'S TAVERN

129 E 18th St, New York, NY 10003
Tel: 212 473 7676
www.petestavern.com

NATIONAL ARTS CLUB

15 Gramercy Park South, New York,
NY 10003
Tel: 212 475 3424
www.nationalartsclub.org

THE LITTLE CHURCH AROUND THE CORNER

1 E 29th St, New York, NY 10016
Tel: 212 684 6770
www.littlechurch.org

MARBLE COLLEGIATE CHURCH

1 W 29th St, New York, NY 10001
Tel: 212 686 2770
www.marblechurch.org

EMPIRE STATE BUILDING

350, 5th Ave, New York, NY 10118
Tel: 212 736 3100
www.esbnyc.com

NEW YORK PUBLIC LIBRARY

455, 5th Ave (at 40th St), New York,
NY 10016
Tel: 212 340 0863
www.nypl.org

BROADWAY – TIMES SQUARE TO COLUMBUS CIRCLE

ABC TELEVISION STUDIOS – GOOD MORNING AMERICA

44th St & Broadway, Times Square,
New York, NY 10036
gma.yahoo.com

SARDI'S RESTAURANT

234 W 44th St, New York, NY 10036
Tel: 212 221 8440
www.sardis.com

ED SULLIVAN THEATER

1697 Broadway, New York, NY 10019
For tickets for Late Show with
David Letterman visit
www.cbs.com/shows/late_show
Tel: 212 975 4755

MUSEUM OF ARTS AND DESIGN

2 Columbus Cir, New York,
NY 10019
Tel: 212 299 7777
www.madmuseum.org

CARNEGIE HALL

881, 7th Ave, New York, NY 10019
Tel: 212 247 7800
www.carnegiehall.org

INTREPID SEA AIR SPACE MUSEUM

700 W 46th St, New York, NY 10036
Tel: 212 245 0072
www.intrepidmuseum.org

MIDTOWN & THE UPPER EAST SIDE

GRAND CENTRAL OYSTER BAR

Grand Central Terminal, 89 E 42nd St,
New York, NY 10168
Tel: 212 490 6650
www.oysterbarny.com

CAMPBELL APARTMENT

Grand Central Terminal, 89 E 42nd St,
New York, NY 10168
Tel: 212 953 0409
www.hospitalityholdings.com

UNITED NATIONS

Public enquiries, Visitors Services,
United Nations Headquarters,
Room GA-0305, New York,
NY 10017
Visitor centre, 1st Ave & 46th St
Tel: 212 963 4475
visit.un.org/wcm/content/site/visitors/
lang/en/home/plan

ROOSEVELT ISLAND TRAMWAY

2nd Ave & E 60th St and
Roosevelt Island
Tel: 212 308 6608
www.ny.com/transportation/
ri_tramway

ST PATRICK'S CATHEDRAL

5th Ave 50th–51st St, New York,
NY 10022
Tel: 212 753 2261
www.saintpatrickscathedral.org

ROCKEFELLER CENTER

5th Ave 48th–51st St, New York,
NY 10112
Tel: 212 632 3975
www.rockefellercenter.com

TOP OF THE ROCK

30 Rockefeller Plz, New York,
NY 10112
Tel: 212 698 2000
www.topoftherocknyc.com

ST THOMAS EPISCOPALIAN CHURCH

1 W 53rd St, New York, NY 10019
Tel: 212 757 7013
www.saintthomaschurch.org

MUSEUM OF MODERN ART

11 W 53rd St, New York, NY 10019
Tel: 212 708 9400
www.moma.org

TEMPLE EMANU-EL

1 E 65th St, New York, NY 10065
  Tel: 212 744 1400
  www.emanuelnyc.org

FRICK COLLECTION

1 E 70th St, New York, NY 10021
  Tel: 212 288 0700
  www.frick.org

METROPOLITAN MUSEUM OF ART

1000 5th Ave, New York, NY 10028
  Tel: 212 535 7710
  www.metmuseum.org

NEUE GALERIE NEW YORK

1048 5th Ave, New York, NY 10028
  Tel: 212 628 6200
  www.neuegalerie.org

GUGGENHEIM MUSEUM

1071 5th Ave, New York, NY 10128
  Tel: 212 423 3500
  www.guggenheim.org

COOPER-HEWITT NATIONAL
DESIGN MUSEUM

2 E 91st St, New York, NY 10128
  Tel: 212 849 8400
  www.cooperhewitt.org

ST NICHOLAS RUSSIAN
ORTHODOX CATHEDRAL

15 E 97th St, New York, NY 10029
  Tel: 212 289 1915
  ruschurchusa.org/en/16

GRACIE MANSION

88 East End Ave, New York,
  NY 10028
  Tel: 212 570 4751
  www.nyc.gov/html/om/html/gracie.html

THE UPPER WEST SIDE

LINCOLN CENTER

10 Lincoln Center Plz, New York,
  NY 10023
  Tel: 212 875 5456
  lc.lincolncenter.org

SHEARITH ISRAEL

8 W 70th St, #2, New York,
  NY 10023
  Tel: 212 873 0300
  www.shearith-israel.org

NEW-YORK HISTORICAL SOCIETY

170 Central Park West, New York,
  NY 10024
  Tel: 212 873 3400
  www.nyhistory.org

AMERICAN MUSEUM OF
NATURAL HISTORY

200 Central Park West, New York,
  NY 10024
  Tel: 212 769 5100
  www.amnh.org

CENTRAL PARK

THE CAROUSEL, CENTRAL PARK

66th St, Traverse Rd, Central Park
  West, New York, NY 10023
  Tel: 212 439 6900
  www.centralpark.com/guide/attrac-
  tions/carousel.html

THE DAIRY CENTRAL PARK

www.centralpark.com/guide/attractions/
  dairy.html

WOLLMAN ICE RINK, CENTRAL PARK

Central Park South (59th St) & 6th
  Ave. Wollman Rink is a two-
  minute walk into Central Park
  from this entrance. Follow the
  footpath directly into the park
  Tel: 212 439 6900
  www.wollmanskatingrink.com

VICTORIAN GARDENS
AMUSEMENT PARK

Central Park
  Victorian Gardens is located at
  Wollman Rink in Central Park.
  Enter Central Park from 59th St
  & 6th Av and walk north
  Tel: 212 982 2229
  victoriangardensnyc.com/contact-us.asp

HENRY LUCE NATURAL OBSERVATORY

Belvedere Castle, 79 Mid Park, New
  York, NY 10021
  Tel: 212 772 0210
  www.centralpark.com/guide/attrac-
  tions/nature-observatory.html

DELACORTE THEATER
CENTRAL PARK WEST

New York, NY 10024
  Tel: 212 539 8500
  www.publictheater.org

UPPER BROADWAY – 110TH TO THE HARLEM RIVER

CATHEDRAL OF ST JOHN THE DIVINE

1047 Amsterdam Ave, New York,
  NY 10025
  Tel: 212 316 7540
  www.stjohndivine.org

COLUMBIA UNIVERSITY

116th St & Broadway, New York,
  NY 10027
  Tel: 212 854 1754
  www.columbia.edu

RIVERSIDE CHURCH

490 Riverside Dr, New York,
  NY 10027
  Tel: 212 870 6700
  www.theriversidechurchny.org

GRANT'S TOMB

W 122nd St & Riverside Dr, New
  York, NY 10027
  Tel: 212 666 1640
  www.grantstomb.org/ind-gma.html

HAMILTON GRANGE

St Nicholas Park in Manhattan.
  Located at 414 W 141st St,
  between Convent Ave & St
  Nicholas Ave
  www.nps.gov/hagr/index.htm

TRINITY CHURCH CEMETERY

770 Riverside Dr, New York,
    NY 10032
    Tel: 212 368 1600
    www.trinitywallstreet.org/congrega-
    tion/cemetery

HISPANIC SOCIETY OF AMERICA

Audubon Ter, 613 W 155th St, New
    York, NY 10032
    Tel: 212 926 2234
    www.hispanicsociety.org

ACADEMY OF ARTS AND LETTERS

Audubon Ter, 633 W 155th St, New
    York, NY 10032
    Tel: 212 368 5900
    www.artsandletters.org

MORRIS-JUMEL MANSION

65 Jumel Ter, New York, NY 10032
    Tel: 212 923 8008
    www.morrisjumel.org

LITTLE RED LIGHTHOUSE

Call 311 for all Parks & Recreation
    information; outside of NYC, call
    (212) 344 7220
    www.nycgovparks.org/parks/fortwash-
    ingtonpark/highlights/11044

THE CLOISTERS

99 Margaret Corbin Dr, Fort Tryon
    Park, New York, NY 10040
    Tel: 212 923 3700
    www.metmuseum.org

DYCKMAN FARMHOUSE

4881 Broadway at 204th St,
    New York, NY 10034
    Tel: 212 304 9422
    www.dyckmanfarmhouse.org

APOLLO THEATER

253 W 125th St, New York,
    NY 10027
    Tel: 212 531 5300
    www.apollotheater.org

Index of People

Adams, Abigail 98, 243
Adams, John 22, 98, 126, 243
Adams, John Quincy 243
Adams, Ralph 236
Albee, Edward 97, 128, 129
Alcott, Louisa May 121
Aldrin, Buzz 36
Allen, Woody 193
Amos, Charles Christopher 125
Andersen, Hans Christian 232
Aniston, Jennifer 194
Anne, Queen 41
Armstrong, Edwin Howard 192
Armstrong, Louis 209
Armstrong, Neil 36
Arnold, Aaron 131
Arsdale, John van 35
Arthur, Bea 123
Arthur, Chester 134, 141, 164,
    171
Astaire, Adele 192
Astaire, Fred 136, 176
Astor, John Jacob 98, 101, 104,
    109, 225, 240
Astor II, John Jacob 110
Astor III, John Jacob 42, 166
Astor IV, John Jacob 241
Astor, Brooke 162
Astor, Caroline Schermerhorn
    166, 201, 241
Astor, William Blackhouse 166,
    248
Astor, William Waldorf 42, 166
Audubon, John 105, 240, 241
Axelrod, David 83
Aykroyd, Dan 84

Bacall, Lauren 215
Bacharach, Burt 181
Bailey, Pearl 248
Baker, Josephine 175
Baldwin, Alec 217
Balfour, Arthur 68
Ball, Lucille 165
Bara, Theda 161
Barnard, George Grey 246
Barnes, Djuna 127
Barnett, Charles 57
Barnum, P.T. 32, 95, 106, 137
Barry, Jeff 181
Barrymore, Ethel 161, 179
Barrymore, John 123, 162
Barsotti, Carlo 99
Barthman, William 58
Bartholdi, Auguste 8, 9, 10, 132
Basie, Count 182
Bayes, Nora 142
Beach, Alfred 69
Beatles, The 183
Beckett, Samuel 123
Beekman, Elizabeth 113
Beekman, William 192
Behan, Brendan 112, 154
Bell, Alexander Graham 58, 59,
    107
Bell, Lila 122
Benjamin, Dorothy 165
Bennett Jr, James Gordon 144,
    168, 245
Bennett Sr, James Gordon 144
Benny, Jack 176
Berkeley, Busby 185
Berle, Milton 214

Berlin, Irving 142, 177, 192
Bernhardt, Sarah 179
Bernstein, Leonard 208, 215
Bertholdhi, Madame 142
Bitter, Karl 136, 148
Blass, Ben 107
Blass, Bill 157
Bliss, Henry 218
Block, Captain Adriaen 4, 5, 39
Blondin, Charles 95
Bloomingdale, Lyman and
    Joseph 194
Bogardus, Everardus 21, 41
Bogardus, James 21
Bogart, Humphrey 162, 163,
    192, 211, 218
Bogart, John B. 91
Bono 216
Booth, Edwin 115, 134, 163, 164,
    177
Booth, John Wilkes 104, 115, 125
Booth, Julius 115
Bosio, Angiolina 95
Boyer, Isabella 10
Bradford, Barbara Taylor 192
Bradford, William 25, 43
Bradley, Omar 206
Brady, Mathew 104, 105
Brevoort, Henry 105, 106, 118
Brill Brothers 180
Broadhurst, George Howells 177
Broderick, Matthew 123
Brodhead, John Romeyn 18
Brooks Brothers 88
Brooks, Garth 234
Brown, James 99, 248

Brown, Ruth 248
Brown, William 84
Brush, John T. 242
Bryant, William Cullen 170, 202, 225
Buchalter, Louis Lepke 214
Bullock, Private First Class, Dan 27
Bunche, Ralph 191
Burnett, Frances Hodgson 231
Burnham, Daniel 133
Burns, Robert 224
Burr, Aaron 53, 54, 98, 243
Burroughs, William 154
Bush, George H. W. 54
Bush, George W. 60, 195
Bushnell, David 14

Cabrini, St Francesca Xavier 196
Cadman, S. Parkes 68
Cage, Nicolas 45
Cagney, James 83, 162, 178
Cahn, Sammy 88
Calder, Alexander Stirling 179
Campbell, John 188
Campbell, Mrs Patrick 161
Cantor, B. Gerald 202
Cantor, Eddie 175
Capone, Al 26
Capote, Truman 162, 200
Carey, Hugh 201
Carnegie, Andrew 185
Carradine, John 162
Carrey, Jim 233
Carroll, Nancy 211
Carter, Jimmy 54
Cartier, Louis 199
Cartier, Pierre 199
Cartwright, Andrew 147
Caruso, Enrico 147, 165, 211
Castellano, Big Paul 102
Castro, Fidel 225
Cert, Josep 198
Chanin, Irwin 212
Chaplin, Charlie 136
Charles II, King 21
Charlotte, Queen 21
Chase, William Merritt 118
Christy, Howard Chandler 213
Chrysler, Walter 51, 188, 189
Churcher, Richard 44
Churchill, Lord Randolph 137
Churchill, Sir Winston 118, 122, 137
Clark, Edward 215
Clarke, Arthur C. 154
Clarke, Gilmore D. 230
Clarke, Thomas 149

Cleveland, Grover 9, 60, 137
Clinton, Bill 201, 229
Clinton, DeWitt 30, 72, 73
Clinton, George 20, 60
Clinton, Sir Henry 37
Clooney, Rosemary 215
Cohen, Leonard 155
Colbert, Claudette 176
Colden, Cadwalader 34
Collins, Joan 139
Collins, Michael 36
Coltrane, John 182
Columbus, Christopher 184
Comaneci, Nadia 157
Compson, Betty 127
Conkling, Roscoe 140
Connick, Charles 196
Constable, James 131
Coogan, James 242
Cooke, Alistair 162
Cooper, Gary 176, 182
Cooper, James Fenimore 101
Cooper, Peter 109, 110, 111, 112, 115, 116, 164
Coppola, Sophia 123
Corbett, Gentleman Jim 142
Corlear, Jacobus van 91
Cornbury, Lord 5, 44, 216
Cosby, Bill 122
Cosby, William 6, 54
Costello, Frank 214
Coutan, Jules-Felix 188
Coward, Noel 198, 213
Crawford, Joan 114
Creeft, Jose de 232
Crosby, Bing 176
Crosland, Alan 213
Crystal, Billy 90, 129
cummings, e.e. 112, 127
Curtis, Tony 88, 123
Curtiss, Glenn 7
Cushman, Don Alonzo 150

Daley, Sandy 155
Dam, Rip Van 54
Damon, Matt 190
Davis Jr, Sammy 182, 209
Davis, Bette 121, 153
Davis, John W. 138
Davis, Miles 182
Delacorte, George 223, 232
Delancey, James 87, 89
Delancey, Stephen 21
Delmonico, John 24
Delmonico, Peter 24
Delmonico's 102
Deluise, Dom 114
Dempsey, Jack 211

DeSapio, Carmine 118
DeWitt, Simeon 73
Di Modica, Arturo 36
Diamond, Neil 181
Dickens, Alfred Tennyson 241
Dickens, Charles 85, 94, 110, 160
Dietrich, Marlene 182
DiMaggio, Joe 194, 200
Dimmick, Mary 199
Di Suvero, Mark 56
Doherty, Henry 52
Dorsey, Tommy 176
Douglas, Michael 216
Downing, Sir George 122
Doyer, Hendrik 86
Doyle, Alexander 144
Drifters, The 44
Duane, James 159
Dubin, Al 44
Duchovny, David 115
Duckworth, Isaac F. 96
Duffy, Father Francis P. 180
Duffy, George 30
Dunaway, Faye 217
Duncan, Isadora 118, 213
Dyck, Hendrick van 40
Dyckman, William 246
Dylan, Bob 121, 122, 154, 162

Edison, Thomas 70
Edward VII, King 134, 160
Edward VIII, King 189
Eiffel, Gustave 10
Eikerenkoetter, Frederick 244
Eisenhower, Dwight D. 54
Eisenhower, Julie 165
Elizabeth II, Queen 25, 45, 194
Ellington, Duke 198, 241
Ellis, Samuel 9
Ellison, Ralph Waldo 241
Eno, Amos 134
Escobar, Marisol 29

Farley, James A. 156
Farragut, Admiral David 140
Farrow, Mia 218
Fayed, Dodi 216
Feigenbaum, Harriet 136
Ferber, Edna 214
Fey, Tina 198
Field, Cyrus W. 37
Fields, W. C. 175
Fish, Elizabeth 112
Fish, Hamilton 112
Fish, Nicholas 112, 113
Fish, Stuyvesant 162
Fisher, Avery 208

Fisk, Diamond Jim 134
Fitzgerald, Ella 248
Fitzgerald, F. Scott 122, 124, 198, 199
Fitzmaurice, George 213
Flack, Roberta 215
Flagg, Ernest 57
Fleischmann, Louis 106
Foley, Thomas F. 76
Fonda, Henry 80, 137
Fonda, Jane 128
Ford, Gerald 201
Ford, Harrison 123
Forrest, Edwin 108
Fox, Michael J. 152, 217
Franklin, Benjamin 60, 70
Fraunces, Samuel 21, 22
Frazier, Joe 157
French, Daniel Chester 20, 136, 162, 237
Frick, Henry Clay 201
Fuller, George 133
Fulton, Robert 13, 43, 123

Gaga, Lady 209
Gallatin, Albert 43
Gandhi, Mohandas 132
Garbo, Greta 178, 192
Gardiner, Julia 110, 118
Gardner, Ava 182
Garfield, James 164, 171
Garibaldi, Giuseppe 120
Garland, Judy 215
Geer, Seth 110
Gehry, Frank 79
Gest, David 165
George II, King 41
George III, King 34, 35, 45
German, Jacob 171
Gershwin, George 142, 177, 247
Gershwin, Ira 89, 177
Getchell, Margaret 145
Getty, Estelle 88
Gibbons, Thomas 13
Gifford, Walter S. 59
Gigante, Vincent 'The Chin' 214
Gilbert, Bradford 39, 40
Gilbert, Cass 20, 67, 137
Gillespie, Dizzy 182
Ginsberg, Allen 124, 125, 154
Gish, Lillian 161, 215
Gleason, Jackie 183
Goddard, Paulette 211
Goffin, Gerry 181
Goldberg, Whoopi 150
Gomez, Estevan 14
Goodman, Benny 176
Gorbachev, Mikhail 8

Gotti, John 102
Gould, Jay 134
Gracie, Archibald 204
Grant, Cary 123, 167, 183
Grant, Ulysses S. 72, 134, 238, 247
Grateful Dead 114
Greeley, Horace 70, 143, 144
Green, Andrew Haswell 230
Greenfield, Howie 181
Greenwich, Ellie 181
Griffiths, Albert 57
Grossman, Edwin Booth 164
Guastavino, Rafael 80
Guggenheim, Benjamin 44
Guggenheim, Solomon R. 203

Haas, Richard 97, 169
Haigh, J. Lloyd 107
Hale, Nathan 71
Haley, Bill 209
Halleck, Fitz Greene 225
Hamilton, Alexander 43, 47, 51, 52, 53, 112, 231, 237, 240, 243
Hamilton, John C. 231
Hamilton, Margaret 162
Hammerstein, Arthur 182, 183
Hammerstein, Oscar 142, 173, 175
Hammerstein II, Oscar 185
Hanks, Tom 167, 190
Hardenbergh, Henry J. 198
Harding, Warren G. 54, 209
Hargrove, Roy 125
Harper, James 162
Harrigan, Ned 93
Harris, Charles K. 142
Harrison, Benjamin 60, 162, 199
Harrison, William Henry 118
Harrison, William K. 190
Hart, Lorenz 142
Hart, Tony 93
Hassam, Childe 118
Hatkoff, Craig 91
Haughwout, E. V. 92, 93
Hawke, Ethan 155, 163
Hayes, Helen 161, 178
Hayes, Rutherford B. 163, 225
Hayworth, Rita 216
Healy, Thomas 211
Hearst, William Randolph 164
Heins and LaFarge 79, 236
Helleu, Paul 187
Hellman, Richard 218, 219
Helmsley, Leona 189
Hemingway, Ernest 122, 200
Henderson, John 205
Hendricks, Harmon 123

Hendrix, Jimi 114, 122, 248
Hepburn, Audrey 200
Herbert, Victor 143, 177
Herman, Jerry 128
Hester, Kate 124
Heth, Joice 95
Hitchcock, Alfred 200
Hoffman, Dustin 177, 216
Holiday, Billie 209, 248
Holland, George 164
Holland, George & Andrew 141
Holliday, Judy 215
Holly, Buddy 118, 181, 209
Holmes, Oliver Wendell 143
Hone, Philip 113
Hooper, John 241
Hoover, Herbert 59, 87, 167, 185
Hoover, J. Edgar 214
Hopper, Edward 119
Horne, Lena 248
Houghton, Rev. George 164
Howe, Julie Ward 104
Hudson, Henry 3, 4
Hughes, John 196
Hunt, Richard Morris 9, 42, 119, 128
Huntington, Anna 218, 241
Huntington, Archer 241
Hyde, William 124

Irving, Washington 108, 110, 160, 161, 171
Ivet, Robert 4

Jackson, Andrew 74, 105
Jackson, Michael 200
Jacobs, Marc 214
Jagiello, King 231
James, Henry 119
Javits, Jacob 162
Jay, John 6, 52, 237
Jefferson, Joseph 164
Jefferson, Thomas 66, 127, 243
Jencks, Penelope 217
Jerome, Jennie 137
Jerome, Leonard 136, 137
Joan of Arc 218
John, Elton 157
Johnson Jr, J. Seward 57
Johnson, Andrew 140
Johnson, Daniel Larue 191
Johnston, John Taylor 202
Jolson, Al 181, 182
Jones, James Earl 227
Joplin, Janis 155
Judge, Father Mychal 79
Judson, Adoniram 121

Jumel, Eliza 243
Jumel, Stephen 243

Karan, Donna 157, 213
Karloff, Boris 215
Katz Brothers 90
Kean, Charles 95
Keaton, Buster 191
Keene, Laura 104
Kelly, Grace 195
Kemeys, Edward 232
Kennedy, Archibald 36, 37
Kennedy, Jackie 162
Kennedy, John F. 121, 162, 183
Kennedy, Joseph 162
Kennedy, Robert 39
Kennedy, Robert F. 197
Kern, Jerome 142, 185
Kerouac, Jack 125, 154
Kerr, Deborah 166, 167
Keys, Alicia 242
Khan, Prince Aly 192
Khrushchev, Nikita 190
Kidman, Nicole 112, 205
Kimlau, Lt. Benjamin 86
Kincannon, Joe 247
King Jr, Martin Luther 225
King, Carole 181
Kinigstein, Joseph 194
Kirshner, Don 181
Kissinger, Henry 192
Klein, Calvin 155, 157, 194, 213
Klinghoffer, Leon 115
Knight, Gladys 248
Koch, David H. 208
Koch, Mayor Ed 27, 80, 215
Kool and the Gang 122
Kubrick, Stanley 155

L'Enfant, Pierre 48
La Guardia, Fiorello 169
Laboulaye, Edouard de 8
LaFarge, John 118, 121
Lafayette, Marshall 110, 132
Lamb, Thomas W. 209
Langdon, Charles 94
Langtry, Lillie 58, 155
Lansbury, Angela 163, 233
Lansky, Meyer 214
Lauren, Ralph 157
Lauria, Fat Tony 126
Lawrence, Captain James 43
Lazarus, Emma 10, 128
Lee, Gypsy Rose 175
Lee, Sergeant Ezra 14
Leeson, James 42
Lefcourt, Abraham 180, 181
Lefcourt, Alan E. 180, 181

Leiber, Jerry 181
Leighton, Barbara 125
Lennon, John 157, 215, 222, 225
Leoni, Téa 115
LeRoy, Jennifer 222
LeRoy, Warner 222
Letterman, David 183
Levy, Asser 31, 32
Lewis, Francis 43
Lewis, Jerry 176, 177
Lincoln, Abraham 72, 104, 109, 111, 112, 125, 132, 140, 185
Lincoln, Mary Todd 93
Lind, Jenny 32134
Lindbergh, Charles 118
Liu, Lucy 83
Livingston, Robert 'the Chancellor' 13, 48, 53, 150, 237
Lombardi, Gennaro 100
Lombardo, Guy 176
Lord & Taylor 168
Lovelace, Francis 23
Lowry, Malcolm 125
Loy, Myrna 114
Luciano, Lucky 214

MacArthur, Douglas 206
MacMonnies, Frederick 71
Macready, William 108
Macy, Rowland H. 145, 147, 148
Madison, James 134
Madonna 155
Mahler, Gustav 214
Mailer, Norman 124, 125
Makemie, Francis 44
Mangin, Joseph 72, 100
Manship, Paul 198
Maples, Marla 165
Mapplethorpe, Robert 155
Marbury, Bessie 161, 193
Marlborough, Duchess of 201
Marlborough, Duke of 137, 199
Marsh, Reginald 20
Martin, Dean 176
Martin, Steve 216
Marx Brothers 204
Mason, Marsha 213
Matthau, Walter 88
McComb Jr, John 30, 72, 83, 113
McComb, Alexander 38
McCoy, Charles 'Kid' 143
McDougall, Alexander 121
McKim, Mead & White 157
McKinley, William 147, 209, 238
McPherson, Craig 66

McSorley, John 112
Melville, Herman 20, 21, 108
Menken, Helen 162
Mey, Cornelius 5
Millay, Edna St Vincent 118, 123, 124
Miller, Arthur 154
Miller, Barry 3
Miller, Glenn 157, 176
Miller, Israel 179
Miller, Marilyn 179
Milne, A. A. 170
Milne, Christopher 170
Milton, John 163
Minnelli, Liza 163, 165
Minsky, Bill 175
Minuit, Peter 17, 18, 19, 248
Mitchel, James Purroy 229
Moby 217
Monk, Thelonious 83, 182, 208
Monroe, Marilyn 182, 194, 200
Montgomery, General Richard 66
Mooney, Edward 86
Moore, Annie 9
Moore, Clement Clarke 124, 149, 151, 158, 241
Moore, Demi 216
Moore, Dr Benjamin 149
Morgan, Anne 191, 193
Morgan, J. P. 51, 58, 191, 216, 225
Morris, Dick 83
Morris, Gouverneur 73, 237
Morris, Roger 242
Morse, Samuel 7
Mortier, Major Abraham 97
Morton, Gary 165
Moses, Robert 122, 190, 208, 217, 221
Mostel, Zero 88, 214
Mould, Jacob Wrey 71
Murray, Bill 84
Murray, Sir Evelyn P. 59

Namath, Joe 216
Nast, Thomas 75
Naumburg, Elkan 225
Nesbit, Evelyn 138, 139, 146
Niblo, William 94, 95
Nieporent, Drew 84
Nin, Anaïs 125
Niro, Robert De 84, 91
Nixon, Richard 165, 201
Noguchi, Isamu 56
Novak, Kim 147
Noworth, Jack 142
Nureyev, Rudolph 215

O'Brien, Conan 214
O'Neill, James 176
O'Neill, Eugene 118, 121, 124, 125, 155, 176
Ochs, Adolph S. 173
Oliver, Betty Lou 167
Olmsted, Frederick Law 217, 220, 245
Onassis, Jackie Kennedy 229
Ono, Yoko 215, 222
Orbach, Jerry 241
Orteig, Raymond 118
Osgood, Samuel 168
Otis, Elisha 93, 110
Otway, Howard 114

Pacino, Al 102, 210
Paine, Thomas 125, 126
Palance, Jack 215
Papp, Joseph 110, 227
Parker, Charlie 125, 182
Parker, Dorothy 192
Parker, Sarah Jessica 233
Patti, Adelina 95
Peale, Dr Norman Vincent 165
Peck, Gregory 163
Pelli, Cesar 63
Pemberton, Brock 178
Penn, Sean 205
Penn, William 74
Perkins, Frances 120
Perry, Antoinette 178
Pershing, General 195
Peter, Paul & Mary 122
Peterssen, Arne 11
Phelps, Anson Greene 211
Piaf, Edith 150, 155
Piccard, Jean 158
Piccard, Rev. Jeannette 158
Pickford, Mary 179
Pierce, Henry L. 84
Pills, Jacques 150
Pinchot, Gifford 162
Pitney, Gene 181
Pitt, William 86
Platt, Thomas Collier 134
Poe, Edgar Allan 126, 127, 136, 217
Poitier, Sidney 163
Pollock, George 239
Pollock, St Claire 239
Pons, Lily 211
Ponselle, Rosa 179
Pont, Pierre du 166, 167
Pope John Paul II 196
Pope John Paul VI 29
Pope Paul VI 196
Porter, Cole 142, 195

Pound, Ezra 122
Powell, Alexander 84
Presley, Elvis 164, 183
Presley, Lisa Marie 200
Provost, Samuel 42
Pryor, Richard 122
Pulitzer, Joseph 7, 9, 70, 201
Putnam, General 176

Rainier, Prince 195
Ramis, Harold 84
Randel Jr, John 73
Raskob, John Jakob 166, 167
Rathbone, Justus H. 209
Reagan, Ronald 8, 201
Redford, Robert 163
Reed, John 127
Reiner, Estelle 90
Reiner, Rob 90
Renwick Jr, James 106, 107, 196
Revere, Paul 22, 123
Richardson, Natasha 201
Riis, Jacob 85
Ringling, Alfred 162
Rivera, Diego 198
Robards, Jason 215
Robbins, Tim 83
Roberts, Julia 128, 162
Robeson, Paul 121, 242
Robinson, Rev. Gene 158
Rockefeller, John D. 38, 190, 238, 245, 246
Rockefeller Jr, John D. 197
Rockefeller III, John D. 192, 208
Rockwell, Norman 213
Roddenberry, Gene 158
Rodgers, Richard 142
Rodrigues, Jan 14
Roebling, John A. 78
Roebling, Washington 78
Rogers, Ginger 213
Rogers, Will 175
Rogosh, Fr. Andrew 100
Roosevelt, Eleanor 217
Roosevelt, Franklin D. 47, 75, 120, 137, 195, 209
Roosevelt, Isaac 47
Roosevelt, Theodore 68, 112, 131, 133, 147, 163, 201, 208
Rosenberg, Julius and Ethel 123
Rosenfeld, Monroe 142
Rosenthal, Jane 91
Rosenthal, Tony 108
Ross, Diana 227
Rothschild, Evelyn de 192
Rotolo, Suze 122
Rowson, Susanna 42

Rubinstein, Anton 160
Ruckstuhl, Frederick 136
Ruggles, Samuel 159
Rushdie, Salman 201
Russell, Rosalind 211
Russo, Gaetano 184
Ruth, Babe 162, 197, 211
Rutherford, John 73
Ryan, Meg 90, 129, 167
Ryder, Winona 123

Saint-Gaudens, Augustus 116
Salinger, J. D. 222, 233
Sandow, Eugen 142
Santiago, Maria Elena 181
Santos-Dumont, Alberto 199
Sardi, Vincent and Eugenia 178
Schein, Françoise 96
Schenck, Joseph 191
Schermerhorn, Abraham 113
Schermerhorn, Peter 77
Schieffelin, Eugene 224
Schott, Walter 230
Schumacher, Joel 155
Schovz, Carl 204
Scorsese, Martin 163
Scott, George C. 227
Scott, Sir Walter 224
Seabury, Gertrude 111
Sedaka, Neil 181
Sedgwick, Edie 154
Seton, Elizabeth Ann 28, 29, 79, 196
Seton, William 29
Seward, William 140
Shakespeare, William 163
Sharansky, Anatoly 191
Shaw, George Bernard 161
Sheldon, Edward 162
Sheridan, General Philip 126
Sherman, General William Tecumseh 201, 210
Shreve, Lamb and Harmon 166
Shubert, S. 177
Simon & Garfunkel 205, 227
Simpson, Mrs 189
Sinatra, Frank 177, 182
Singer, Isaac 10, 57
Smith, Alfred E. 87, 137, 166, 167, 185, 196
Smith, Edward 51
Smith, John 4
Smith, Rev. Matthew Hale 106
Somerindyck, Jacob 149
Sonnenberg, Benjamin 162
Spacey, Kevin 163
Spector, Phil 181
Spelling, Aaron 216

Spielberg, Steven 216
Springsteen, Bruce 122
Sprout, Betty 230
Spungen, Nancy 155
St Laurent, Yves 194
Stanlaws, Penrhyn 213
Stanley, Charlotte 43
Stanley, Henry 160
Stearns, John Noble 39, 40
Stebbins, Emma 226
Steell, Sir John 225
Steinweg, Heinrich Engelhard 101
Stewart, A.T. 81, 82, 95, 105, 113, 131, 168
Stewart, Jimmy 137, 147
Stiller, Jerry 88
Stokes, William 210
Stoughton, Charles & Arthur 217
Straus, Isidor & Ida 44, 146, 212
Stravinsky 211
Streep, Meryl 176
Strong, George Templeton 43, 162
Stuyvesant, Peter 21, 40, 46, 107, 112, 116, 162
Stuyvesant, Petrus 112
Sullivan, Ed 183
Sullivan, John L. 138, 143
Sutherland, Samuel 29
Sutton, Effingham B. 191
Swanson, Gloria 114
Swift, Hildegarde 244

Talmadge, Natalie 191
Talmadge, Norma 191
Tamamend 74
Tekakwitha, Kateri 196
Thaw, Harry K. 139
Thomas, Dylan 122, 125, 154
Thomas, Evylyn 248
Thompson, Kay 200
Thomson, Virgil 154
Thumb, General Tom 106
Thurman, Uma 155, 163
Tiffany, Charles Lewis 68
Tiffany, Louis 118
Tilden, Samuel J. 163
Tobin, Steve 61
Tommy James & the Shondells 184
Tompkins, Daniel 12, 113

Toscanini, Arturo 197, 211
Travolta, John 3
Tredwell, Seabury 111
Truman, Harry 195
Trumbull, Edward 189
Trump, Donald 165
Tryon, Sir William 246
Tschirky, Oscar 171
Tucker, Sophie 175
Twain, Mark 94, 95, 128, 134, 155, 168
Tweed, William 'Boss' 74, 75, 112, 134
Tyler, John 118

Upjohn, Richard 42, 106, 118

Valentino, Rudolph 213
Vanderbilt, Alfred Gwynne 198
Vanderbilt, Anne 191, 192
Vanderbilt, Consuelo 199
Vanderbilt, Cornelius 12, 13, 110, 134, 187
Vanderbilt, George 199
Vanderbilt, Gloria 192
Vanderbilt, William 137
Vanderbilt, William K. 191
Vanderbilt III, Mrs Cornelius 202
Vaughan, Sarah 248
Vaux, Calvert 162, 217, 220, 222
Verdi, Giuseppe 210
Verhulst, Willem 5
Verrazano, Giovanni da 2
Vesey, William 66
Vicious, Sid 155
Vidal, Gore 134
Voight, Jon 177

Walker, Jimmy 122, 127, 137
Wallace, DeWitt 122, 169
Walton, William 47
Wanamaker, John 105
Ward, John Quincy Adams 48, 224
Ward, Samuel 104
Warhol, Andy 114, 147, 154
Warner Brothers 182
Warner, Jack 193
Warner, Sam 182
Warren, Harry 44
Warren, Lavinia 106
Warwick, Dionne 248

Washington, George 22, 23, 35, 37, 38, 39, 47, 48, 54, 60, 71, 80, 97, 98, 99, 120, 132, 164, 167, 176, 242
Watson, James D. 28
Weaver, Sigourney 213
Webster, Daniel 105, 226
Weil, Cynthia 181
Weisberger, Lauren 176
West, Mae 176, 193
Wharton, Edith 148
White, Stanford 71, 118, 121, 138, 144, 146, 162, 201
Whitney, Cornelius, Vanderbilt 192
Whitney, Gertrude Vanderbilt 119, 231
Whitney, Mary 118, 121
Wilde, Oscar 161
Wilder, Billy 194
William III, King 41
William IV, King 32, 60
Williams, Captain Alexander 'Clubber' 145
Williams, Tennessee 155
Wilson, Woodrow 163
Winchell, Walter 33, 214
Windsor, Duke & Duchess of 195
Winnie the Pooh 170
Winston, Harry 200
Wintour, Anna 176
Wolfe, Elsie de 161, 191
Wolfe, Tom 162
Wollman, Kate 223
Woods, Tiger 216
Woolworth, F. W. 67, 68
Worth, General William Jenkins 139
Wray, Fay 168
Wright, Frank Lloyd 200, 203
Wright, Wilbur 7

Yale, Frankie 26
Young, Teddy 68

Zaslav, David 214
Zeckendorf, William 190
Zelnickova, Ivana 165
Zenger, John Peter 5, 6, 48
Zeta-Jones, Catherine 216
Zexu, Lin 87
Ziegfeld 211
Zukor, Adolph 156

Index of Places

125th Street Subway Station 239

ABC TV Studios 177
Academy of Music 136, 160
African Burial Ground 82, 83
Albany 33, 73
Alphabet City 73, 113
American Academy of Arts &
    Letters 241
American Express Tower 66
American Geographical Society
    241
American International Building
    52
American Numismatic Society 241
Andrew Haswell Green
    Memorial Bench 230
Angel of the Waters 226
Ansonia, The 210, 211
Appellate Division of the
    Supreme Court of New York
    135, 136
Armory, 69th Regiment 164
Armory, Squadron A 203, 204
Arthur's Tavern 125
Asch Building 120
Astor Building 101
Astor Place 108
Astor Place Cube 108
Astor Place Opera House 108
Astor Plaza 178, 179
Astor Row 248
AT&T Building (Former) 195
    Broadway 58, 59
Audubon Terrace 241
Avery Fisher Hall 208

Baltimore 29
Bank of Manhattan Trust Building
    50, 51, 52, 54, 65, 68
Bank of New York Mellon
    Corporation 47
Barthman Clock 58
Baruch College 164
Battery 16, 36
Battery Maritime Building 8, 27
Battery Park 1, 15, 19, 29, 30, 37
Battery Park City 31, 62
Battery Place 37, 63
Beaver Street 38
Bedford Street 123, 124
Beekman Place 192
Belvedere Castle 227
Bennett Park 245
Bethesda Terrace 225
Birdland Jazz Club 182
Bloody Angle 86
Bloomingdale's 194
Boston, Massachusetts 43
Bow Bridge 226
Bowling Green 34, 35, 36, 44,
    45, 71, 103, 132, 247
Bowling Green Control Station
    31
Brevoort Apartments 118
Bridge Café 80
Brill Building 180, 181
Broad Financial Center 21
Broad Street 46
Broadway Bridge 247
Broadway, No 1 36, 37
Bronx 40, 76
Brooklyn 1, 27, 77, 78

Brooklyn Bridge 26, 70, 77, 78,
    80
Brooklyn Heights 77
Brooklyn–Battery Tunnel 7
Bryant Park 170
Butler Library 237
Buttermilk Channel 14

Cable Building 103, 104, 138
Café des Artistes 213
Café Reggio 121
Café Wha? 121, 122
Canyon of Heroes 36
Carl Schurz Park 204
Carnegie Hall 160, 185, 186
Cartier 199
Castle Clinton 30, 31
Catskill Mountains 77
Central Park 73, 110, 115, 198,
    215, 220–234
Central Park Blockhouse 229
Central Park Carousel 222
Central Park Dairy 222, 223
Central Park Mall 224
Central Park Obelisk 231
Central Park West 212–217, 218
Central Park Zoo 146, 190, 233
Central Park, Great Lawn 77
Century Apartments 212
Charles A. Dana Discovery
    Center 229
Charlton-King-Vandam Historic
    District 97, 98
Chatham Square 86
Chelsea 149–158
Chelsea Market 152

Chelsea Piers 152
Chelsea Studios 156
Cherry Lane Theater 123
Cherry Street 39, 75
Chinatown 84–87
Chrysler Building 51, 52, 56, 65, 115, 164, 167, 180, 188, 189, 190, 205
Chumley's 123, 124
Church of Our Lady of the Rosary 28
Church of the Ascension 118
Church of the Most Precious Blood 101
Church of the Transfiguration 85
City College of New York 239, 240
City Hall 30, 35, 69, 71, 72, 79, 80, 85, 131
City Hall Park 36, 70, 71, 77, 81, 93, 144
Civic Center 76
Cloisters, The 246
Collect Pond 76, 95
Colonnade Row 110
Columbia University 41, 70, 197, 237, 240, 247
Columbia University, St Paul's Chapel 237
Columbus Circle 184, 186, 221
Columbus Park 85
Con Edison Building 160
Condé Nast Building 175, 176
Conservatory Garden 230, 231
Conservatory Water 232, 233
Coogan's Bluff 242
Cooper Square 109
Cooper Union Academic Building 111
Cooper Union Foundation Building 109, 110, 116
Corlear's Hook 91
Corner House 104
Croton Aqueduct 77, 100, 226, 228
Croton Aqueduct Distributing Reservoir 168
Croton Fountain 71
Croton River 76
Cunard Building 38
Cushman Row 150
Custom House (Alexander Hamilton U.S.) 17–20, 31

Daily News Building 189
Dakota Building 198, 214, 215, 218

Dance Theater Workshop 150
Delacorte Clock 224, 227
Delmonico's 24
Dorilton, The 210
Downing Street 122
Doyers Street 86
Duffy Square 179, 180
Dyckman Farmhouse 246, 247

Ear Inn 98, 99, 102
East River 7, 21, 26, 27, 28, 77, 78, 87, 115, 193, 201
East Village 73
Edward Mooney House 86
Eldorado Apartments 217
Eldridge Street Synagogue 88, 89
Elevated Acre 26
Elizabeth Ann Seton Shrine 28
Ellis Island 1, 9, 11, 12, 15, 29, 31
Empire State Building 51, 52, 56, 65, 159, 165–168, 180, 188, 198
Engine Ladder Company 10 66
Equitable Building 55, 56, 66
Equitable Life Assurance Building 56
Erie Canal 47, 73
Eternal Light Memorial Flagpole 141

Fashion Avenue 157
Fashion Institute of Technology 155
Fashion Walk of Fame 157
Federal Hall 24, 47, 48, 53, 54
Federal Reserve 48, 52
Fifth Avenue 134, 168, 171, 195, 198
First Shearith Israel Cemetery 87
Five Points 76, 84, 85, 99
Flatiron Building 130, 133, 147
Foley Square 75, 76, 85
Fort Amsterdam 19, 34
Fort Tryon Park 245
Fort Washington Park 244
Fraunces Tavern 21, 22, 23, 39, 52, 80
Freedom Tower 62
Frick Collection 201
Friends Building 124
Fulton Fish Market 77

General Electric Building 195
General Post Office 156
General Theological Seminary 149, 150, 151, 158

George Hecht Viewing Gardens 112
George Washington Bridge 244
Ghostbusters Building 213
Golden Swan Park 121
Governors Island 1, 5–8, 15, 26, 27
Governors Island, Castle Williams 1, 6
Governors Island, Fort Jay 6
Governors Island, Governor's House 5
Governors Island, Liggett's Hall 7
Grace Church 105, 106, 107, 115, 196
Gracie Mansion 204, 205
Gramercy Park 159, 161, 162, 163
Grand Army Plaza 201
Grand Central Oyster Bar 188
Grand Central Terminal 157, 187, 205
Grand Central, Campbell Apartment 188
Grant's Tomb 7, 238, 239, 247, 248
Great Hill 229
Great Lawn 227, 228
Great White Way 139, 140, 141
Greeley Square 143, 144
Greene Street 96, 97, 101
Greenwich Village 29, 117–129, 154
Grove Court 124
Gucci 200
Guggenheim Band Shell 208

Hamilton Fish House 112
Hamilton Grange 240
Hamilton Place 239
Hamilton Terrace 240
Hanover Square 24, 25, 26, 32
Harlem 73, 79, 196, 235, 240
Harlem Meer 229
Harlem River 76, 247
Harrison Street Houses 83
Haughwout Building 92, 93
Henderson Place 205
Henry Hudson Bridge 247
Henry Luce Natural Observatory 227
Herald Square 144, 145, 146
High Bridge 243
High Bridge Aqueduct 76
High Bridge Park 243
High Bridge Water Tower 243
High Line 151, 152
Highliner Diner 153

Hispanic Society of America 241
Hoboken 40
Holland Tunnel 102
Holocaust Memorial 136
Holy Trinity Lutheran Church 212
Hook and Ladder 8 84
Hotel des Artistes 213
Hotel, Beekman Tower 191
Hotel, Brevoort 118
Hotel, Broadway Plaza 141
Hotel, Chelsea 125, 149, 153–155
Hotel, Claridge 177
Hotel, Fifth Avenue 134, 135
Hotel, Gilsey 142, 143
Hotel, Gramercy Park 162
Hotel, Madison Square 137
Hotel, New York Helmsley 189
Hotel, Peninsula 199
Hotel, Pennsylvania 157
Hotel, Plaza 148, 198, 200, 201, 233
Hotel, St Denis 107
Hotel, St Nicholas 93, 94
Hotel, St Regis 199
Hotel, Waldorf-Astoria 166, 171, 195, 206
Hudson Heights 245
Hudson River 4, 6, 15, 43, 62, 73, 76, 83, 151, 176, 207, 238, 246, 247

India House 25
Inwood Hill Park 248
Irish American Historical Society 201
Irish Hunger Memorial 62, 63
Iron Palace 105
Irving House 162
Irving Place 160, 161, 171
Isaacs-Hendricks House 123
Israel Miller Building 179

James Watson House 28
Jacqueline Kennedy Onassis Reservoir 228, 229
Jefferson Market Courthouse 127, 128
Jeffrey's Hook 244
Jerome Mansion 136, 137
Jones Street, Greenwich Village 122
Judson Memorial Church 120, 121, 138

Kalustyan's Indian Grocery Store 164
Katz's Delicatessen 90

Kimlau Memorial Arch 86
Klein Deutschland 107, 108
Knickerbocker Club 201

Ladies Mile 130, 131, 150
Ladies Pavilion 227
Lasker Rink and Pool 229
Laura Keene's Varieties Theater 104
Lexington Avenue 73, 79, 164, 171, 189, 194, 195
Liberty Island, Fort Wood 9
Lincoln Center 147, 207, 208, 209
Lincoln Highway 185
Little Church Around the Corner 164, 165
Little Italy 99–101
Little Red Lighthouse 244, 245
Little Singer Building 94
Loeb Boathouse 232
Lombardi's Pizzeria 100
Lord & Taylor 168
Low Library 237

Macy's 145, 146, 148, 150
Madison Avenue 73, 195, 204
Madison Square 9, 128, 133, 134–141, 147, 148, 173
Madison Square Garden 57, 143, 157, 163
Maiden Lane 66
Maine Memorial 221
Majestic Apartments 214
Manhattan Bridge 88
Manhattan Club 137
Manhattan Life Insurance Building 40, 64, 167, 168
Marble Collegiate Church 165
Marie's Crisis Café 125
Masonic Hall 150
McComb Mansion 38, 39, 80
McSorley's Old Ale House 111, 112
Merchandise Mart Building 136
Metropolitan Club 201
Metropolitan Life Tower 65, 68, 135
Metropolitan Opera House 146, 147, 148, 160, 173, 190, 208
Mill Lane 21, 24, 31
Minetta Brook 117
Minetta Lane 122
Minetta Tavern 122
Morgan Library 49
Morgan's Bank 49, 50
Morningside Heights 235, 236
Morris-Jumel Mansion 242, 243

Mortier House 97, 98
Morton Street, Greenwich Village 122, 123
Mount Tom 217
Mulberry Bend 85
Mulberry Street 99
Municipal Building 74, 75, 77
Museum Mile 201, 202
Museum of American Finance 51
Museum of Arts and Design 184
Museum of Jewish Heritage 63
Museum of Modern Art 199
Museum of the American Indian 241
Museum of the City of New York 206
Museum, American Natural History 216, 224
Museum, Cooper Hewitt National Design 203
Museum, Guggenheim 44, 203
Museum, Intrepid Sea Air Space 186
Museum, Jewish 206
Museum, Merchant's House 111
Museum, Metropolitan Museum of Art 201, 202
Museum, New York City Fire 98
Museum, New York City Police 26
Museum, New-York Historical Society 216
Museum, Skyscraper 63, 64, 65
Museum, South Street Seaport 77
Museum, Tenement 89, 90

Narrows 20
National Arts Club 162, 163
Naumburg Bandshell 225
Netherlands Memorial 17
Neue Galerie New York 202
New Amsterdam 5, 14, 16–19
New Amsterdam Plein and Pavilion 17
New Jersey 1, 10, 17, 176
New York by Gehry 79
New York City Aquarium 31
New York County Courthouse 76, 80
New York Life Insurance Company Building 137
New York Public Library 77, 110, 168–171
New York Stock Exchange 15, 36, 46, 50
New York Times Building 52, 70
New York University 43, 115

New York World Building 64, 70

Niblo's Garden 94, 95, 101

Nom Wah Tea Parlor 86

Northern Dispensary 126, 127

Old Biscuit Factory 152

Old Police Headquarters 101

Old Slip 26

Old St Patrick's Cathedral 100, 102, 196

Old Standard Oil Building 38

One Liberty Plaza 57

Osgood House 80

Palisades 4, 14, 245

Paramount Building 176, 177, 185

Paramount Plaza 181

Park Avenue 195

Park Row 69, 70

Park Row Building 64, 67, 69

Patchin Place 127, 128

Peace Park 191

Pear Tree Corner 116

Pearl Street 21, 24, 46, 47

Pennsylvania 24

Pennsylvania Station 156, 157

Pete's Tavern 162

Peter McManus's Café 150

Peter Minuit Plaza 17, 28

Philadelphia 9

Pier 17 77

Pier 54 152

Pier 62 152, 153

Players Club 163

Polo Grounds 242

Pomander Walk 211

Powell Building 70, 84

Printing House Square 70, 77, 79

Provincetown Playhouse 121

Public Theater 110, 111

Puck Building 100

Pythian, The 209

Queen Elizabeth II September 11th Garden 25

Queensboro Bridge 193, 205

Quong Yuen Shing & Company General Store 85

Radio City Music Hall 197

Rainbow Room 198

River House 192

Riverside Church 238, 246

Riverside Drive 237, 238, 239

Riverside Park 217

Riverview Terrace 193

Robert Moses Playground 190

Rockefeller Center 38, 57, 197, 198, 228

Roosevelt Island Tramway 205

Salmagundi Club 118

San Juan Hill 207, 208

San Remo Apartments 207, 216

Sardi's Restaurant 178

Schermerhorn Row 77

Schreyers Hook 28

Seneca 233

Septuagesimo Uno Park 218

Seward Park 88

Seward Park High School 88

Shakespeare Garden 224

Shanley's Restaurant 143

Shearith Israel Synagogue 32, 213, 218

Sheep Meadow 221

Shepard Hall 240

Shubert Alley 177

Singer Building 57, 58, 65, 69

Smithsonian National Museum of The American Indian 20

SoHo 95–99

SoHo Playhouse 97

Soldiers' and Sailors' Monument 217

South Cove 63

St Augustine's Church 88, 91

St Bartholomew's Church 195

St James's Church 87

St John the Divine Cathedral 79, 236

St Luke in the Field 124

St Luke's Place 122

St Mark's Evangelical Lutheran Church 114

St Mark's in the Bowery 85, 112, 113

St Michael's Russian Catholic Chapel 100

St Nicholas Russian Orthodox Cathedral 203

St Patrick's Cathedral 187, 196, 197, 236

St Paul's Chapel 59, 60, 61, 66, 85

St Peter's Church 78, 79, 87

St Thomas Episcopalian Church 199

St Vincent de Paul Church 150

St Vincent's Hospital 125

Stadt Huys 16, 23, 48

State Street 29

Staten Island 1, 2, 13, 17, 40

Staten Island Ferry 12

Staten Island, Tompkinsville 12

Statue of Liberty 1, 8–10, 12, 20, 29, 31, 36, 63, 119, 132

Steinway Hall 160

Stewart House 115

Stone Street 21, 23, 24, 31

Stonewall Inn 126

Strand Bookstore 107

Straus Park 212

Strawberry Fields 215, 226

Stuyvesant Fish House 162

Stuyvesant High School 83

Stuyvesant Street 112

Sugar Hill 241

Summit Rock 227

Sun Building 82, 91

Surrogates Court and Hall of Records 74

Sutton 191

Sutton Place 192, 193

Sylvan Terrace 243

Tavern on the Green 221, 222, 233

Temple Emanu-El 201

Tenth Street Studio Building 128

Theater 80 114

Theater District 173

Theater New Amsterdam 174, 175

Theater, Apollo 248

Theater, Booth 177

Theater, Broadhurst 177

Theater, Broadway 182

Theater, Claire Tow 209

Theater, David H. Koch 208

Theater, Ed Sullivan 182, 183

Theater, Helen Hayes 178

Theater, Lyceum 179

Theater, Majestic 178

Theater, New Victory 175

Theater, Olympia 173

Theater, Shubert 177

Theater, St James's 178

Theater, Vivian Beaumont 209

Theater, Warner's 181

Theater, Winter Garden 181

Tiffany's 68, 69, 200

Time Warner Center 184, 185

Times Square 79, 141, 172–177, 185, 221

Times Tower 173, 174, 175, 179, 185

Tin Pan Alley 142, 143, 174

Titanic Memorial Lighthouse 77

Tom's Restaurant 235, 236

Tompkins Square 113

Tontine's Coffee House 50, 51

Top of the Rock 198

Tower Building 39, 40

Triangle Shirtwaist Factory 120
TriBeCa 83, 84
TriBeCa Grill 84
Trinity Cemetery 104
Trinity Church 29, 40–45, 47, 53, 70, 106, 124, 174
Trinity Church Cemetery 240, 241
Trinity Churchyard 42, 43, 44
Trump Tower 50, 200
Tudor City 189, 190, 191
Turtle Pond 228, 231
Tweed Courthouse 74, 75, 76, 80

Union Square 33, 130, 131, 132, 139, 140, 147, 160, 173
United Church Science of Living Institute 244
United Nations 190, 191, 205
United States Courthouse 76
University Club 199
Upper New York Bay 1

Vanderbilt Gate 231
Verdi Square 210
Verrazano Narrows Bridge 2, 3, 29, 190
Versace 199
Vesey Street 66
Victorian Gardens Amusement Park 223
Vietnam Veterans Plaza 27
Vista Rock 228

Walk of Fame, St Mark's Place 114
Wall Street 36, 46–51, 54
Washington Irving High School 160
Washington Market Park 83
Washington Mews 119
Washington Place 13
Washington Square Arch 119, 120, 129, 138
Washington Square North 119
Washington Square Park 119, 128

Weehawken, New Jersey 53
West 10th Street 128, 129
West End Collegiate Dutch Reform Protestant Church 24, 218
White Horse Tavern 125, 154
White Wood House 164
Whitehall Street 20, 27
Whitehall Terminal 17
William Hyde House 124
Winter Garden Atrium, World Financial Center 63
Wo Kee Store 84
Wollman Ice Rink 223
Woolworth Building 47, 51, 65, 67, 68, 79, 135
World Financial Center 31, 63
World Trade Center 20, 25, 61, 62, 66, 167
World Trade Center 1 65
Worth Monument 139
Worth Square 139

Zuccotti Park 56

Acknowledgements

My warm thanks to Cormac O'Malley for his generous hospitality and for introducing us to so many fascinating aspects of New York. His enthusiasm, wide-ranging knowledge and fascination for all things New York were infectious and invaluable.

A special thanks to Carey Smith whose support, advice and wisdom is always greatly appreciated and whose encouragement and belief in this series, and this book in particular, has been stalwart and unwavering.

Many thanks also to Roxanne Mackey for all her hard work and dedication. Her brilliance and thoroughness shine through on the page and her ability to create order out of chaos is priceless.

Thanks also to Steve Dobell for his excellent editing work – and if this book has encouraged him to visit New York, then our work is done!

I would like to give particular thanks to my agent Kevin who looks after us so well and inspires us all onward and upward. We are safe in his hands.

And finally my eternal thanks to Mai. She is my motivation, my inspiration, my companion and the love of my life. It is her talent and grace that make all things possible.